Organising Poor Women

Published by
ACADEMIC FOUNDATION
in association with

CENTRE FOR ECONOMIC AND SOCIAL STUDIES,
(CESS), HYDERABAD

Organising Poor Women

The Andhra Pradesh Experience

Editors

S. Mahendra Dev
Ravi Kanbur
S. Galab
G. Alivelu

ACADEMIC FOUNDATION
NEW DELHI

www.academicfoundation.com

First published in 2012
by

ACADEMIC FOUNDATION
4772-73 / 23 Bharat Ram Road, (23 Ansari Road),
Darya Ganj, New Delhi - 110 002 (India).
Phones : 23245001 / 02 / 03 / 04.
Fax : +91-11-23245005.
E-mail : books@academicfoundation.com
www.academicfoundation.com

In association with

Centre for Economic and Social Studies (CESS), Hyderabad

Cataloging in Publication Data--DK
Courtesy: D.K. Agencies (P) Ltd. <docinfo@dkagencies.com>

Organising poor women : the Andhra Pradesh experience /
edited by S. Mahendra Dev ... [et al.].
p. cm.
ISBN 13: 9788171889389
ISBN 10: 8171889387

1. Poor women--Services for--India--Andhra Pradesh--Congresses. 2. Poor women--India--Andhra Pradesh--Societies, etc.--Congresses. 3. Self-help groups--India–Andhra Pradesh--Congresses. 4. Women in rural development--Government policy--India--Andhra Pradesh--Congresses. 5. Poverty--Government policy--India--Andhra Pradesh--Congresses. 6. Indira Kranthi Patham (Scheme)--Congresses. I. Mahendra Dev, S.

DDC 305.42095484 23

Typeset by Italics India, New Delhi.
Printed and bound in India.

Contents

Section III

Organisational Assessment and Improvement

List of Tables and Figures

Tables

Figures

About the Editors/ Contributors

Editors:

S. Mahendra Dev is currently Director (Vice-Chancellor), Indira Gandhi Institute of Development Research (IGIDR), Mumbai. He received his PhD from the Delhi School of Economics and his Post-doctoral research at the Economic Growth Centre, Yale University. He has written extensively on agricultural development, poverty and public policy, food security, employment guarantee schemes, social security, farm and non-farm employment. He has more than 100 research publications in national and international journals. His recently published book is *Inclusive Growth in India: Agriculture, Poverty and Human Development* (2011). He has been a consultant and adviser to many international organisations, such as UNDP, World Bank, IFPRI, ILO, FAO and ESCAP. He has been a member of several government committees including the Prime Minister's Task Force on Employment and Rangarajan Commission on Financial Inclusion. He was member of several working groups for Ninth, Tenth and Eleventh Five Year Plans.

Ravi Kanbur is T.H. Lee Professor of World Affairs, International Professor of Applied Economics and Management, and Professor of Economics at Cornell University. He holds a bachelor's degree from Cambridge and a doctorate from Oxford. He has taught at Oxford, Cambridge, Princeton and Columbia. He has published in the leading economics journals such as *American Economic Review, Journal of Political Economy, Review of Economic Studies, Journal of Economic Theory,* and *Economic Journal.* Prof. Kanbur has served on the senior staff of the World

Bank, including as Principal Adviser to the Chief Economist of the World Bank, and as Director of the World Bank's World Development Report.

S. Galab (PhD from Andhra University) is currently Professor, Centre for Economic and Social Studies (CESS), Hyderabad, India. He has written extensively on agricultural development, poverty, women empowerment, child well-being, agrarian relations, safety networks and self-help groups. He has more than 30 research publications in national and international journals. He has been a project director for Andhra Pradesh District Poverty Initiatives Programme, Andhra Pradesh Rural Poverty Reduction Programme (World Bank Projects) and Young Lives an international project and various other projects like NREGS, Wage Employment Programmes etc. He has been a member in the Commission on Farmers' Welfare in Andhra Pradesh, Departmental Committee of Centre for Regional Studies, Working Group on Poverty Elimination Programs and associated with Expert Group on Agricultural Indebtedness.

G. Alivelu is currently Assistant Professor, Centre for Economic and Social Studies, Hyderabad, India. She received her PhD from B.R. Ambedkar Open University in 2007. Her research interests include areas of industry and services. She has published research articles in both national and international journals. Her recently published book is on Indian Zonal Railways. She has contributed papers on industry for Human Development Report of Andhra Pradesh. She is a member of working group for the Twelfth Five Year Plan for the Government of Andhra Pradesh. She also conducted collaborative projects with Department for International Development (DFID), Bill & Melinda Gates Foundation, IRC International Water and Sanitation Centre, the Netherlands on issues like state business relations and also on water and sanitation costs and service levels.

Contributors:

K.S. Babu, Associate Professor, Centre for Economic and Social Studies, Hyderabad, Andhra Pradesh, India.

Nicola Jones, Research Fellow, Overseas Development Institute in London and previously worked as the Policy Research Manager, Young Lives project, Save the Children, London, UK.

Rama Kandarpa, Vice-President, BASIX, Hyderabad, Andhra Pradesh, India.

T. Vijay Kumar, Chief Executive Officer, Society for Elimination of Rural Poverty (SERP), Government of Andhra Pradesh, India.

G.K. Mitra, Professor, Centre for Economic and Social Studies, Hyderabad, Andhra Pradesh, India.

Madhuri Mukherjee, Previously National Coordinator, Young Lives Policy Coordination Office, Hyderabad, Andhra Pradesh, India.

D. Sree Rama Raju, Assistant Professor, Acharya N.G. Ranga Agricultural University, Hyderabad, Andhra Pradesh, India.

K. Raju, IAS, Secretariat, Andhra Pradesh, India.

S. Ramalakshmi, Andhra Pradesh Mahila Abhivruddhi Society, Hyderabad, Andhra Pradesh, India.

Nandita Ray, Chairperson (Outreach), Vice-Chairperson (APMAS), Hyderabad, Andhra Pradesh, India.

C. Ravi, Associate Professor, Centre for Economic and Social Studies, Hyderabad, Andhra Pradesh, India.

C.P. Nagi Reddy, State Project Manager (Monitoring and Learning), Society for Elimination of Rural Poverty (SERP), Government of Andhra Pradesh, India.

C.S. Reddy, CEO, Andhra Pradesh Mahila Abhivruddhi Society, Hyderabad, Andhra Pradesh, India.

K.S. Reddy, Associate Professor, Centre for Economic and Social Studies, Hyderabad, Andhra Pradesh, India.

M. Gopinath Reddy, Professor, Centre for Economic and Social Studies, Hyderabad, Andhra Pradesh, India.

P. Prudhvikar Reddy, Associate Professor, Centre for Economic and Social Studies, Hyderabad, Andhra Pradesh, India.

P.V. Satheesh, Director, Deccan Development Society, Hyderabad, Andhra Pradesh, India.

N. Tirupathaiah, Andhra Pradesh Mahila Abhivruddhi Society, Hyderabad, Andhra Pradesh, India.

Preface

Organisations of the poor are central to inclusive growth. Andhra Pradesh has been in the forefront of promoting these organisations, especially for poor women. This experience was assessed and analysed at a conference held at the Centre for Economic and Social Studies (CESS), Hyderabad, in 2007. A selection of the papers presented at the conference, revised and updated, are presented in this volume. We believe that they will be useful to researchers and policymakers alike since they chart a specific and concrete experience enhancing organisations of poor women.

The editors would like to thank the Society for Elimination of Rural Poverty (SERP), Government of Andhra Pradesh, CESS (Hyderabad), the Broad Reach Foundation (Ontario), Women in Informal Employment, Globalizing and Organizing (WIEGO), UK and Cornell University for funding support. They would also like to thank the contributors, chairpersons and discussants of the conference sessions, and Sue Snyder of Cornell University for administrative support.

— S. Mahendra Dev, Ravi Kanbur,
S. Galab and G. Alivelu

Section I

Overview

1

Organisation, Poverty and Women

Andhra Pradesh in Global Perspective

S. Mahendra Dev, Ravi Kanbur, S. Galab and G. Alivelu

Introduction

The World Bank's 2000/01 World Development Report, *Attacking Poverty*, identified three categories of actions for addressing poverty: empowerment, security and opportunity. Opportunity refers to the conventional dimensions of income, education and health that have now become well accepted in the human development paradigm. Security refers to the risks and vulnerabilities that the poor face in their everyday lives, negative shocks that can set off a downward spiral, or can set back the long slow haul out of poverty. These risks have become better understood, and better integrated into analysis and policy over the past decade. Empowerment is perhaps the least conventional of the three. It refers to the fact that all the policies and interventions, and their implementation, takes place in a real world where power is central.

Why does poverty, particularly poverty among women, persist? One reason might be that we do not have the appropriate knowledge pedestal on which to base policies and interventions. Of course, knowledge can always be improved, and there are significant debates and controversies between different schools of thought in economics and other social sciences. But even if there was technical consensus, the real issue is whether the power structures in society will allow interventions that reduce the advantages of the wealthy.[1] Without power, the poor in general, and poor women in

1. See Kanbur (2009).

particular, will not be able to argue for and to force the introduction of policies and interventions that improve their well-being. Hence the need for empowerment.

Empowerment is not easy to define in a technical sense, nor is it easy to delineate causal chains on the correlates of empowerment. However, there is a broad consensus that organisation is a key factor. An individual woman may be powerless in the face of traditional authority and power structures. An 'organisation of women' is a different matter; it can bring its collective strength to bear in making its voice heard, and in holding policy-makers and implementers to account. Organisations of organisations, federations and other structures, provide further collective strength. It is not surprising, perhaps, that *Organising Poor Women* has taken on a prominent position in the current policy debate. This volume brings together a number of studies on the organising of poor women, its consequences and the determinants of its success, in the Indian state of Andhra Pradesh, where policymakers have been highly supportive of the strategy of empowering poor women through organising. In this introduction to the volume we set the global scene on organisations of the poor, and then provide an overview of the papers in the volume.

Organisations of the Poor in Global Perspective[2]

Organisation is important for empowerment and for lifting the poor out of poverty. But what sort of organisation? Of particular interest, globally and in Andhra Pradesh, are membership based organisations of the poor (MBOP)—organisations whose governance structures respond to the needs and aspirations of the poor because they are accountable to their members. These are to be distinguished for many standard non-governmental organisations (NGOs) which, although they do good work and benefit the poor, operate as entities outside of the poor themselves. MBOPs, on the other hand, are organisations of the poor, by the poor and for the poor. In MBOPs, members elect their leaders, and these leaders are held accountable through democratic principles.

Crowley *et al.* (2007) suggest the following criteria for identifying MBOPs: (i) the majority of members are poor, (ii) they have joined on a

2. This section draws heavily on Chen *et al.* (2007).

voluntary basis, (iii) they have developed, agreed upon, and engage in their own decision-making structures and (iv) they provided contribution, financial or in kind, as a condition of membership. Chen *et al.* (2007) identify a wide range of MBOPs globally, including: trade unions, cooperatives, worker committees, savings and credit groups/self-help groups (SHGs), community based finance associations, funeral associations, informal insurance institutions, producer groups, village or slum associations, community based organisations representing traditional social groupings based on kinship or caste, and clubs such as for youth or recreation. In addition to these primary groups, there are sometimes federations which link them to each other and to the broader institutional system. From this very broad range of structures that might qualify as MBOPs, of particular interest are those that organise themselves around the identity of poor members as workers or around work or livelihood related issues.

Chen *et al.* (2007) provide an overview of a volume devoted to global experience with MBOPs including informal workers' committees in China; committees formed to manage specific projects in Brazil; trade unions in India and South Africa; cooperatives in South America, India and Cambodia; small SHGs in Africa and India; street vendor organisations in Peru; and community based organisations in Pakistan, Bangladesh and South Africa. Based on these experiences, they synthesise factors explaining success and failure, and draw policy implications. As a backdrop to the specific experience of Andhra Pradesh, we first review the main lessons from this global experience.

What is 'success' for an organisation of the poor? Crowley *et al.* (2007) define success in terms of four criteria: (i) achieving the objectives agreed upon by members, (ii) retention or expansion of membership, (iii) progress towards financial and managerial self-reliance and (iv) improvement of self-esteem, economic and social well-being of members. Roever (2007) distinguishes between 'internal' and 'external' dimensions of success. The internal dimensions of success include building individual capacity, fostering expression and debate, and carrying out concrete projects. External dimensions include gaining access to policy discussions, achieving favourable policy, and representing voices of the excluded.

With these dimensions of success, what are the explanatory factors? Chen *et al.* (2007), summarise the global experience as follows. The factors internal to MBOPs are: (i) democratic governance structures, (ii) significant role of membership dues, in cash and kind, (iii) sufficiently homogeneous membership along key dimensions (poverty, occupation, gender, etc.), (iv) capacity to manage the organisation, (v) the use of federated governance structures as the organisation expands and (vi) a strongly internalised 'code of moral conduct' that guides actions. The external factors, on the other hand, are: (i) supportive community power structures, (ii) a broadly enabling legal, political and policy environment, (iii) sympathetic individuals in government and bureaucracy, (iv) external funding and support that do not subvert democracy within the organisations and (v) diversified sources of external finance.

The above lessons are drawn from 17 case studies of organisations of the poor from around the world. These case studies include some from India, but none of these are from Andhra Pradesh. This volume, on the other hand, is devoted entirely to the Andhra Pradesh experience, which can then be compared with lessons from the global arena.

Overview of the Volume

The volume is divided into three sections. The two chapters in Section I are followed by five chapters in Section II on 'organisations and outcomes'. Section III has five chapters on 'organisational assessment and improvement'. We now provide an overview of the chapters in the volume that follow this introduction.

Chapter 2, 'Organisation of Poor Women in Andhra Pradesh', begins with the local perspective to complement the global perspective discussed in the Section II of this volume. It sets out how the Government of Andhra Pradesh has actively promoted a policy to develop SHGs for poverty alleviation and the empowerment of women. The programmes in this vein include: Development of Women and Children in Rural Areas (DWCRA); Andhra Pradesh District Poverty Initiatives Project (APDPIP); Andhra Pradesh Rural Poverty Reduction Project (APRPRP); Cooperative Development Foundation (CDF) and many others. S. Galab *et al.* provide an account of each of these interventions, and a brief assessment of their poverty and empowerment impact (more details are provided in subsequent chapters in this volume). The assessment framework suggested for empowerment is one of 'power to' (control their own lives), 'power with' (other women in collectivity), and 'power within' (themselves to challenge gender norms in their own personal lives).

To take a specific example, consider APDPIP, popularly known as *Velugu* ('light'). This project combines empowerment of women with enhancing assets and ability to cope with shocks. In a sense, therefore, it builds on the same three pillars as the World Bank's 2000/2001 World Development Report, *Attacking Poverty*, namely empowerment, security and opportunity. Among the documented results are better educational outcomes, resulting in part from the demand for better quality services by women. Joint decision-making in households between husband and wife has increased, as has the budget allocated in favour of women and children. There are improvements needed, of course, and there are variations in results across districts, but it is clear that APDPIP is a good start and provides lessons for others to learn from.

The authors also provide an account of the many NGOs in Andhra Pradesh who have helped in promoting the women's SHGs. The NGOs discussed specifically include BASIX, Andhra Pradesh Mahila Abhivruddhi Society (APMAS), Spandana, Swayam Krishi Sangam (SKS), SHARE Micro Fin Limited. The chapter highlights and commends the complementary roles these organisations have played; even though they are not themselves membership based organisations. Some of these organisations are discussed further in the rest of the volume.

In Chapter 3, in Section II, M. Gopinath Reddy and D. Sree Rama Raju focus on 'Self-Help Groups and Political Empowerment in Andhra Pradesh'. The chapter starts with Naila Kabeer's definition of empowerment: 'it is the process of acquiring the ability to make strategic life choices in a context where this ability has previously been denied. The core elements of empowerment have been defined as agency (the ability to define one's goals and act upon them), awareness of gendered power structure, self-esteem and self-confidence.' It also uses as its base the findings of earlier studies that even though SHGs are formed around issues of savings or microcredit, their formation sets in train political processes as women are enabled to speak out and question traditional family status. The authors present their own analysis using two data sets: from the mid-term assessment of DPIP, with a survey of 2,640 households from the three districts of Srikakulam, Adilabad and Anantapur; and a data set on the final round of DPIP, where all the *mandals* covered in the selected districts are analysed.

The authors' conclusions are striking. Participation of women in village assemblies (*gram sabhas*) is higher in project areas than in non-project areas. Moreover, in programme areas more men and women felt the village assemblies were useful compared to control villages. In the second data set, collected at the end of DPIP, although overall awareness of constitutional provisions for local government was low, the situation was better among SHG participants than among non-participants. Of course these cannot be conclusive comparisons until the nature of the controls is further investigated, but the authors argue that they are suggestive. They conclude with a plea for more systematic incorporation of empowerment considerations into SHG programmes focussed on savings and microcredit.

Chapter 4, 'Ripple Effects or Deliberate Intentions? Assessing Linkages between Women's Empowerment and Childhood Poverty', wherein Nicola Jones *et al.* describe well their programme of work. The database is from four *mandals* (three rural; one urban): Amrabad *mandal* in Mahabubnagar district, Atlur *mandal* in Cuddapah district, Seethampeta *mandal* in Srikakulam district and Anantapur *mandal* in Anantapur district. The research methodology was primarily qualitative, with 29 focus group discussions (FGDs) and 113 semi-structured interviews with SHG members and non-members, SHG leaders, service provider, local government officials and elected representatives.

A wide range of empowerment issues are discussed and highlighted by the authors. Their findings on intra-household decision-making are worth quoting in full: 'Both women and men we interviewed noted that there had been a shift in the intra-household balance of power following women's participation in self-help groups. As a result of greater economic independence, they had been able to assert some decision-making power over issues such as their children's and especially their daughters' education, household consumption, access to health services and their children's marriage partners. Although husbands are still reported to have the final say on most matters and in some cases forced their wives to reverse their decisions in cases where they had taken these without consulting their spouse, participation in decision-making in and of itself is viewed as a significant change and should therefore not be underestimated.'

Another finding, consistent with findings of other chapters in this volume, is that of empowerment through knowledge. Women involved in *Velugu* and DWCRA-SHGs also had greater likelihood of having knowledge about different aspects of child rearing. However, the authors point out that since SHG members were more likely to be women with older children, information on early child care might not be available.

While broadly commending the empowerment and child well-being consequences of SHG programmes, the authors do raise a number of issues and questions, including the following: (i) the impact on fundamental power relations at the village level has been not very strong, (ii) the benefits are unevenly distributed across sites, groups and individual women and (iii) the balance between expanding SHG coverage and consolidating gains needs to be examined.

We have referred several times to the *Velugu* project. This project was continued by a new state government under the name of Indira Kranti Patham (IKP). Chapter 5, 'Women Empowerment and Functioning of Formal and Informal Institutions: The Case of the Indira Kranti Patham of Andhra Pradesh', provides a detailed account and assessment of this project. Among the objectives of the project, as stated by S. Galab *et al.*, are: (i) building self-managed grassroot organisations of the poor at village, *mandal* and district levels, (ii) aiding local institutions to address problems of the poor and (iii) enhancing the role of women in the household and the community. Focussing on women's empowerment, the authors consider the impact of IKP on its different dimensions.

An interesting and important issue taken up by some women's groups is the issue of untouchability. The authors highlight IKP's impact in the district of Mahabubnagar on the practice of *Jogini* (the dedication of girls from lower castes to deities and effectively institutionalising prostitution). According to the authors, DPIP formed a 'District *Jogini* Vyathireka Porata Committee' together with local NGOs. Sensitisation campaigns were conducted and the action 'was able to prevent at least 80 probable cases of young girls being inducted into the system.' Further, the project was also involved in helping to form SHGs among *joginis*.

The above discussion is a backdrop to a quantitative analysis of the impact of women's village organisations (VOs) on better functioning of formal institutions and overcoming the unequal structures of informal institutions. A mass of information is available on participant and non-participant households based on a survey conducted for the purpose of assessment. By and large, the authors argue that there is a positive effect of VOs on the delivery of a range of services, including water and sanitation. Moreover, a VO is more likely to initiate such successful actions the older it is, the greater the number of constituent SHGs there are in the VO, and if it meets more than once a month.

Of late, there is a growing concern regarding the mobility of the households in regard to their poverty status overtime. This concern has emerged due to two significant dynamics of poverty *viz*., chronic poverty (remaining in poverty for long time); and the drivers and the barriers contributing to remaining in poverty, moving out of poverty, and falling into poverty differ. In Chapter 6, 'Indira Kranthi Patham and Poverty Reduction in Andhra Pradesh', S. Mahendra Dev *et al.* analyse the contribution of IKP to these dimensions of poverty. The data shows that poverty reduction is much faster for the backward castes (BCs) compared to other castes (OCs). Scheduled tribes (STs) and OC groups did not gain much in this regard. The correlates of mobility in poverty unfolds that caste affiliation of the household did not have relationship with mobility in poverty. The households with larger family size remained to be poor and those with smaller family size could move out of poverty and continued to be non-poor. Similarly, the households with higher proportion of workers could move out of poverty and continue to be non-poor and those with lower proportion of workers remained poor. Further, the probit results indicate that SC and ST households have higher probability of being poor, while non-poor SC, ST and BC households have higher probability of falling into poverty.

In Chapter 7, 'DPIP Outcomes: Assets, Livelihoods and Security', S. Galab *et al.* continues with the theme of outcomes from efforts to strengthen organisation, using data on the performance of DPIP in three districts of Andhra Pradesh, focussing on livelihoods. It presents a wealth of information on DPIP in these districts at two points in time (Follow up Surveys I and II). For example the data show that landholdings increased a little among participants but fell drastically among non-participants. Once again, caution is in order in interpreting this too strongly in causal fashion, since participation is itself endogeneous and has not been controlled for. In other words, it could just be that the sort of households whose landholdings were going to increase in any case are the households likely to participate in DPIP. Thus it cannot easily be inferred that participation in DPIP is responsible for the good outcome, even if the correlation might be suggestive.

Section III of the volume contains five chapters on the theme of 'organisational assessment and improvement'. Here in Chapter 8, 'Emerging Self-Help Groups: Federations and Challenges', C.S. Reddy *et al.* start by recognising that each SHG is small—around 10 to 20 members. In their set up, they need help from self-help promotion institutions (SHPIs). These include NGOs, banks, microfinance institutions, government agencies, cooperatives, etc., which provide training and supportive services including help with the formation of the SHG itself. But a particular type of support organisation which grows out of the SHGs themselves is the SHG federation. In the authors' definition: 'a SHG federation is a democratic body formed with certain number of SHGs functioning in a specific geographical area with the objective of uniting such SHGs for common cause and for achieving those causes which an individual SHG would not be able to do. In short, the SHG Federation has to be necessarily "Of SHGs, by SHGs and for SHGs."'

The chapter gives a detailed account of the features and activities of SHG federations, which were pioneered by two NGOs, PRADAN and MYRADA. The arguments in favour of SHG federations include: (i) scaling up of activities, (ii) taking up community level action programmes, (iii) lobbying at institutional and governmental level and (iv) supervisory services to strengthen SHGs. But the authors also point to several dangers and notes of caution: (i) since individual SHGs do have a bank linkage, the link at the SHG level might be redundant in some cases, (ii) the creation of 'federations of federations' to create financial institutions may be adding to an already crowded field (commercial and regional banks, primary agricultural credit societies, district central cooperative banks, etc.) and (iii) capture of benefits of federations by the better-off among the poor, including the attractiveness of large federations to political capture.

What has been the performance of SHG federations? The authors use the assessments conducted by the Andhra Pradesh Mahila Abhivruddhi Society (APMAS) to provide an answer. This assessment system focusses on the following key areas: governance and strategy, resources, asset quality, design of systems and implementation, efficiency and profitability and services to SHGs. These criteria are applied using qualitative assessment but also quantitative performance benchmarks, including: regularity of meetings, attendance in board and general body meetings, available funds, idle funds to total assets ratio, repayment rates, etc. The analysis is conducted on 83 SHG Federations rated by APMAS in 2003-2005. The summary of the results is as follows: 'The SHG federations' overall performance is moderate that converted into a letter grade "B-".'

On the basis of the detailed assessment, the authors develop a list of specific recommendations which will be useful to policymakers. These include: (i) federations must be member-driven and chief executives must be accountable to elected Boards, (ii) moving beyond the current focus on financial services only, to broader set of support services to SHGs and (iii) all federations must comply with their legal obligations, including ensuring annual audit of accounts, preparing annual reports, conducting an annual general body meeting with at least 50 per cent participation by members.

In Chapter 9, 'Self-Help Group: An Institutional Model—A BASIX Experience', Rama Kandarpa provides an interesting account of the BASIX organisation, which promotes livelihoods. In doing so it 'works with the entire cross-section of the rural economy, that comprises of small enterprises, commercial farmers, small farmers, subsistence workers and marginal farmers, who are in turn inter linked.' There is a strong dimension of working with SHGs. But their methodology of engagement is interesting.

BASIX promotes SHGs through microfinance agents (MFAs) who are paid on performance. The programme was run in the experimental phase by Indian Grameen Services, and then taken over by Bhartiya Samruddhi Finance Ltd. According to the author, 'This experiment demonstrated that

SHG promotion can be a business proposition for promoting institution and the MFAs. It has been a good method of developing a channel to lend to the landless and poor and that too in a forested tribal area where credit discipline is acknowledged to be weak. The portfolio quality has been very high, even better than SHGs promoted by NGOs. This is because there has been intensive monitoring of the groups by BASIX and MFAs.' The BASIX model of SHG support is surely worth exploring further as we consider the best way of helping empowerment among poor women.

In Chapter 10, 'Microfinance Organisations for Women: The Cooperative Model', Nandita Ray starts by recognising that there are four basic models of microfinance institutions (MFIs): (i) NGO promoted MFI, (ii) government promoted MFI, (iii) corporate MFI and (iv) the savings and credit cooperative. Her focus is on the last of these, which are registered under the Andhra Pradesh Mutually Aided Cooperative Societies Act, which was enacted in 1995 'with the specific idea of making it easier for cooperative institutions to function as autonomous bodies as the existing laws had, over the years, resulted in severe erosion of cooperative independence.'

The author begins by looking closely at cooperatives promoted by the Cooperative Development Foundation (CDF). In keeping with cooperative principles, these organisations do not access external funds for on-lending. In general there is no explicit targeting the poor or the women, but this is changing with the recent promotion of dairy cooperatives for women only. These have met with considerable success. Membership is based on the principles of the cooperative movement—anyone in need of its services can become a member of a cooperative. Moreover, while these CDF promoted cooperatives do not restrict dual membership, to include membership of government supported groups in the DWCRA programmes, for example, they do not alter or change their rules or regulations in any way as a response to other schemes. Despite the success of the CDF promoted cooperatives, Ray notes that, 'the cooperative model has been taken up by few organisations outside the influence of CDF. It is possible that this is because of the emphasis that the latter places on autonomy both financial and otherwise.'

While much of the assessment is based on quantitative indicators from a sample survey, it also has qualitative information based on case studies, which provide the human element to the dry statistics: 'Laxmi is a resident of Ratnagiri...She and her husband Sappaiah live with a married son who owns just one acre of dry land. The family also has a fruit and vegetable vending business in which the whole family is engaged...[I]n 1999-00...the family...tried to grow cotton on 2 acres of land with a loan from moneylenders, from which venture they incurred a loss of Rs. 20,000...While the above household does not appear to have been very successful, Laxmi's membership in fact saved the family from starvation, as they were at least able to continue their fruit and vegetable vending business with help of loans from the cooperative.'

In Chapter 11, 'What have the Women and the Poor Taught us?', P.V. Sateesh presents a very different perspective on the themes discussed in this volume by questioning the very notions of self-help groups and empowerment, and illustrates the discomfort he has with these terms through the work of the Deccan Development Society (DDS).

He contrasts the word *sangham* with SHG. *Sangham* has spiritual meaning, and also denotes strength and bonding, which is more than self-help. SHG, on the other hand, 'is extremely limited and limiting', and 'suggests a sense of mundane practicality.' Moreover, 'In recent times led by microfinance operators and government programmes—[i]t is so much dependent on outside support and dictation that it has lost much of its identity.' Sateesh also takes to task the word empowerment: 'It connotes that some people have the power to *empower* others and therefore smacks of a quiet arrogance...What is currently happening in the name of empowerment is a mime of empowerment defined by a culture of monetisation of women's concerns that it makes it all the more disempowering and degrading.'

The DDS works in 70 villages in the Zaheerabad region of Medak District in Andhra Pradesh, with each village having a *sangham*. Membership is about 5,000 women from low income families, primarily from the Dalit castes. The author gives a fascinating account of how in the early days of DDS the theoretical framework combined 'the Gandhian vision of community self-sufficiency with Maoist strategy of creation of barefoot cadres. Though these were noble intentions, they were clouded by a thinking that outsider solutions could work for the poor.' Based on a critique of earlier approaches, three principles now guide the work of DDS—gender justice, environmental soundness and people's knowledge. Of these, the author considers people's knowledge to be the most critical, forcing DDS 'to move away from a *Think Tank* approach to using intense Participatory Processes with the communities.' The governance of DDS reflects this philosophy, with the activities being overseen by a policy group of women from the *sanghams* who are Dalits, rural and non-literate.

A detailed and rich account is given of the workings of DDS and their recent initiatives. Sateesh concludes with some lessons which include: (i) listening and learning from rural women, (ii) build people's confidence in their own knowledge and (iii) autonomy is the key to development.

Chaper 12, 'Poverty Reduction through Community Based Organisations: A Case Study of Indira Kranthi Patham', is the final paper by K. Raju *et al.* in this volume. The authors are senior civil servants who have been committed to the cause of poverty reduction, and have been deeply involved in designing and implementing government policies and interventions in Andhra Pradesh. They give a detailed and informative account of the genesis of the projects culminating in the current Indira Kranthi Patham (IKP): 'The IKP focuses on rural families in all the 1097 Rural Mandals in 22 rural districts of the State. The IKP evolved in two phases as two projects. The first phase and first project was Andhra Pradesh District Poverty Initiatives Project (APDPIP). The second phase project is Andhra Pradesh Rural Poverty Reduction Project (APRPRP). Presently it is the extension of APRPRP to all rural Mandals in 22 districts that is IKP. Both are partly externally aided projects, with financial support from the World Bank.'

After a detailed assessment of IKP, the authors draw a number of lessons for the future for building women's SHGs and federations of SHGs into community based organisations, which can also be relevant for other projects in the parts of India and elsewhere in the world. These lessons include: (i) the need for continuous nurturing and handholding over a period of 6 to 8 years, (ii) a minimum investment of Rs. 1,00,000 per family in terms of loans over this period, and integration with financial institutions such as commercial and regional rural banks and (iv) convergence between and with the key line departments of government is central. Looking ahead, the authors project outcomes forward to 2014, among them: (i) more than 1 crore women in SHGs, (ii) support for all ultra-poor families and (iii) low cost sustainable agricultural development in over 50 lakh acres. They conclude, 'the institutions of poor are well geared up to play a crucial role in enabling the state of Andhra Pradesh to plan to achieve the Millennium Development Goals (MDGs) relating to hunger and poverty eradication, women empowerment and gender equality, maternal health and reduction of child mortality by 2015.'

Conclusion

This volume surveys the terrain of organisations of poor women, and organisations that in turn support such organisations, in Andhra Pradesh. It is clear that the state has a rich and verdant ecology of such organisations, with plenty of experience to share with the rest of the world. It should also be clear from the discussion so far that the lessons of the Andhra Pradesh experience are remarkably consistent with global experience and lessons.

There are of course many ways in which the operation of organisations of poor women can be improved, and these are discussed in great detail in the chapters in this volume. Perhaps the two most important, interlinked, lessons are: (i) support for the formation and operation of organisations of the poor, from governments and NGOs, but (ii) this support to be given in a way that does not undermine democracy of membership based organisations of poor women, but instead enhances the voice and the confidence of poor women. There are good (and bad) examples of these lessons in the Andhra Pradesh experience, and in a general sense they match the lessons of global experience.

But the major conclusion of the Andhra Pradesh and the global experience has to be that organisations of poor women and of the poor generally, are indeed central to poverty reduction. They can act as a vital bridge between the poor and policymakers—holding policymakers accountable for sound implementation of programmes intended to benefit the poor, and ensuring that the voices of the poor are heard and represented in policymaking arena.

References

Chen, Martha, Renana Jhabvala, Ravi Kanbur and Carol Richards (2007). "Membership Based Orgnisations of the Poor: Concepts, Experience and Policy", in Martha Chen, Renana Jhabvala, Ravi Kanbur and Carol Richards (Eds.), *Membership Based Organisations of the Poor.* London and New York: Routledge. *http://www.arts.cornell.edu/poverty/kanbur/MBOPVolumeOverview.pdf*

Crowley, Eve *et al.* (2007). "Organisations of the Poor: Conditions for Success", in Martha Chen, Renana Jhabvala, Ravi Kanbur and Carol Richards (eds.), *Membership Based Organisations of the Poor*. London and New York: Routledge.

Roever, Sally (2007). "Informal Governance and Organisational Success: The Effects of Non-compliance Among Lima's Street Vending Organisations", in Martha Chen, Renana Jhabvala, Ravi Kanbur and Carol Richards (Eds.), *Membership Based Organisations of the Poor*. London and New York: Routledge.

Kanbur, Ravi (2009). "What Determines Poverty Reduction?", *http://www.kanbur.aem.cornell.edu/papers/WhatDeterminesPovertyReduction.pdf*

2 Organisation of Poor Women in Andhra Pradesh

S. Galab, K.S. Babu, K.S. Reddy and
P. Prudhvikar Reddy

Introduction

Speeding up economic growth and creating an environment for making sure 'spread effect of growth' have been emphasised, especially during 90s, for poverty alleviation. This macro-strategy contributes to the materialisation of production indivisibilities (Rao, 1994). Poor should be able to respond to the incentive for poverty alleviation (Vyas and Bhargava, 1995). But the poor can internalise the production indivisibilities in groups only. Moreover, the partaking of the poor in planning and implementation of anti-poverty programmes is required to reduce the string of intermediaries between the government and the actual beneficiaries to improve their bargaining power (Rao, 1994). Further, the institutions—joint family system, patron-client relationships and traditional occupation based institutions that provide social security to the poor are breaking down at the grassroot level. Thus, there is an institutional void at the grassroot level to uphold the interests of the poor (Galab, 1999). In this context, there is substantial evidence that organising women around thrift and credit services is one of the most effective methods, not only for alleviating poverty but also for empowering women (World Bank, 1995; 2000/2001). Thus, the macro- and micro-anxieties are giving rise to the demand for women based collectives centred on thrift and credit services. Subsequently, the issue is how the Government of Andhra Pradesh (AP) has responded in this regard.

The state government granted larger space to women self-help groups (SHGs) in its approach for poverty alleviation and women empowerment. The promotion of women groups under Development of Women and

Children in Rural Areas (DWCRA) programme and adoption of the model of South Asia Poverty Alleviation Programme (SAPAP) with suitable improvements to develop and implement Andhra Pradesh District Poverty Initiatives Project (APDPIP) and the Andhra Pradesh Rural Poverty Reduction Project (APRPRP) stand as a demonstration to this. On the other hand, the model promoted by Cooperative Development Foundation (CDF), which is purely a microfinance model, helps to measure the contribution of DWCRA beyond microfinance induced forces.

Against this background, this chapter aims at looking into the various models of women empowerment and their impact on poverty in the state of Andhra Pradesh.

Model of the Cooperative Development Foundation (CDF)

The CDF model is implemented in two districts (Warangal and Karimnagar), and also in and around the Mulkanoor Cooperative (a well-functioning diversified cooperative) area to take advantage of the acceptability of the cooperatives by the people—both poor as well as the non-poor. The Mutually Aided Cooperative Societies Act, 1995 (MACS Act, 1995) of Andhra Pradesh has given impetus to the growth of the cooperatives of CDF. Women's Thrift Cooperatives (WTC) is the basic entity promoted under this model. These are federated into Association of Women's Thrift Cooperatives (AWTC) to facilitate better functioning of WTCs, to perform higher order functions and inter-flow of loanable funds among WTCs. As the CDF model depends only on internal funds and contemplates no linkages of WTCs/AWTCs with any other organisations, it is considered as a model of untargeted microfinance institution (MFI) (Biswas and Mahajan, 1997).

Any adult woman, irrespective of her economic status, can become member of the WTCs. This indicates that women from all socioeconomic spectrums, except the very privileged participate in groups. Members save Rs 20 per month and earn a monthly interest of one per cent, while, monthly interest of 2 per cent is charged on the loan. The loanable funds are generated from member's savings only. Small groups with group leaders monitor loan repayment, savings collection and disbursement of loans. Members themselves take responsibility to ensure that others repay loans regularly and occasionally make the thrift contribution on behalf of other members who may be away (Ray and Vasundhara, 1996).

CDF Model: Impact on Poverty

As a result of their participation in the WTCs, creditworthiness of women with other financial institutions and money providers had improved, thus giving them access to more funds. The relatively low amount of both share capital per member (Rs 10 or 20) as well as monthly-required thrift (typically Rs 20) allows women from across spectrum of the village to participate and accumulate their savings. For some women, their ability to save is considered as a sign of security. Few others noted the improvement of their financial situation and having 'money at hand' as their reasons for feeling secure. Yet another impact of this model is that the interest rate outside the WTCs dropped from 36 per cent to 30 per cent per annum (Ray and Vasundhara, 1996).

Women are able to obtain loans that can be repaid in easier instalments without collateral in timely manner whenever necessary at a reasonable interest rate from the WTCs of CDF. The pattern of utilisation of loans taken from WTCs provides indications for assessing the income improvements of the member households of WTCs. It is interesting to note that 50 per cent of the loans have been utilised for immediate generation of income and the rest 50 per cent of the loans have been utilised for creation of productive assets. Access to loans enabled the women to involve in economic activities significantly. In addition, the access to credit at lower interest rates and patterns of utilisation of credit indicate that there is improvement in the incomes of the households. This is substantiated by the husbands of WTC members who reported that their wives are adding additional income to the households' income (Ray and Vasundhara, 1996). All these indicate that the CDF model helped in the reduction of income poverty of the member households of WTCs.

Women after becoming members of WTCs started non-traditional tasks and enterprises *vis-à-vis* the activities they were already doing. The solidarity in the cooperatives has given scope to share their problems and seek help. The cooperatives have become a shelter for widows and single women who face particular pressures in the society. Thus, freedom to interact and make friends outside the four walls of the family has improved. WTCs have expanded avenue for women to assume leadership positions. Role of women in decision-making in the family has improved and have become more independent after joining the WTCs (Ray and Vasundhara, 1996; Ghosh, 1998).

Development of Women and Children in Rural Areas (DWCRA)

The Development of Women and Children in Rural Areas (DWCRA) programme started in 1982-83 in the state with UNICEF cooperation to provide opportunities of self-employment on a sustained basis for the rural poor women. Women living in neighbourhood with similar socio-economic background form groups consisting of 10-15 members. These SHGs of DWCRA are federated into Mahila Banks under Andhra Pradesh Mutually Aided Cooperative Societies Act, 1995. Training in leadership, attitudinal changes, skill for income generation is the mandate of the DWCRA model. Lump sum grant of Rs 25,000 is provided to the group for undertaking economic activities. This is a common fund, which is recouped and revolved periodically. Apart from this, the Integrated Rural Development Programme (IRDP) subsidy and bank loans over and above the grant can be accessed. In addition to these funds, groups mobilise monthly savings for interlending to meet the consumption needs of the members. This programme also aims to improve women's access to basic services like health, education, child care, nutrition, water and sanitation and other rural development programmes of the government. Further, DWCRA 'bazaars' and linkage with corporate sector are the initiatives undertaken by the government to capture non-local markets for the DWCRA group products (GoAP, 1999).

Women from all caste groups are covered under this programme—backward castes, scheduled castes and scheduled tribes put together constitute significant proportion of the beneficiaries covered. Selection of leaders is democratic in 87 per cent of the groups. It was found that savings per month equal the average daily wage and some groups discontinue savings once the revolving fund is availed by the group. Equal distribution of funds dominates the pattern of lending and internal lending activities have not developed fully in the districts. However, 78 per cent of internal funds are in rotation (ORG-MARG, 2000).

DWCRA: Impact on Poverty

Because of access to credit under this programme, women undertake economic activities that are dominantly production oriented rather than service and largely continuous activities rather than seasonal. Most of the enterprises (activities), which are facilitated through DWCRA groups helped to utilise the existing skills by making use of the credit assistance provided. The diversification of occupation to non-agriculture activities enhanced the quality of income of the households since the dependency on risk based agriculture has come down to some extent. The additional income accrued to the beneficiary women led to considerable improvement in the incomes of the poorest of the poor that enables the near poor to cross the poverty line. A part of the income gained was spent, by some of the women member households, on nutritious food for family especially children (YFA, 1996; Kanchanya, 1998). Further, women are able to improve their access to health care and educational institutions to some extent. They are also able to handle some of the issues relating to their lives independently.

Model of South Asia Poverty Alleviation Programme (SAPAP)

Next, we look at the model of the South Asia Poverty Alleviation Programme (SAPAP) assisted by United Nations Development Programme (UNDP), which was a response to Dhaka declaration of the SAARC Summit held in 1993 on eradication of poverty by 2002 in all SAARC countries. This programme was initiated in 1995 in Andhra Pradesh. The programme was implemented in the three poverty-stricken—drought prone-districts, *viz.*, Anantapur, Kurnool and Mahabubnagar. The empowerment model of SAPAP consists of three components—social mobilisation, capital formation and capacity building of the poor which help to remove the obstacles that perpetuate poverty and enable them to overcome their vulnerable conditions (UNDP, 1998). The SAPAP was implemented in collaboration with local NGOs and the state government.

The SHGs of SAPAP are federated into village organisations (VOs) at the village level and Mandal Mahila Samakhya (MMS) at the *mandal* level (UNDP, 2000). These interact with the state, market and civil society to achieve the objectives of alleviating poverty and empowering women, besides making the state accountable and transparent to poor and transforming the civil society to more pro-poor and markets (labour, financial and commodity markets) to become more perfect. Homogeneous as well as heterogeneous groups of women with caste dimensions are formed and the principles underlying the group formation are physical proximity, homogeneity and affinity. Community coordinators, community volunteers and village specialists (para-professionals) were trained.

SAPAP: Impact on Poverty

As a consequence of SAPAP, the financial and saving status improved due to improvement in access to formal credit institutions. Further, dependency on moneylenders had declined (Outreach, 2001; Ranjani *et al.*, 2002; Mahendra Dev *et al.*, 2002). The credit enabled the poor to make more effective use of skills they already possessed rather than skill development induced demand for credit. The strengthening of skill base of members in a limited way through providing training in tailoring, embroidery, knitting and word processing helped women to diversify their occupations to some extent. Women have undertaken microenterprises relating to petty business activities. There was a slight improvement in the quality of employment i.e., shift from casual/bonded employment to self-employment. Dependency on migration as a livelihood strategy has declined. Demand for higher and equal wages, releasing women members or members of her family from bondage, and also establishing 'Ammavadis' (baby care centres) to facilitate poor women with young children to work without pulling their elder daughters out of school have improved the labour market conditions in favour of poor.

The levels of income of households increased in all the categories of participants of the SHGs of SAPAP. The reduction in poverty was less pronounced among Dalits and women-headed households compared to non-Dalits and male-headed households. Interestingly, gender poverty is lower among the Dalits compared to other communities despite relatively higher levels of poverty among the Dalits (Ranjani *et al.*, 2002). However, there is a decline in the living conditions of some of the women households due to the failure of economic activities undertaken by them after joining the groups. The gender poverty measured in terms of gender bias with respect to norms of eating, male preference in distribution of food and access to clothing has not declined significantly. Food security has improved after participation in groups, also cutting down consumption as a coping strategy when households faced with food shortage has come down. However, women and girl children mostly bear the brunt of food shortage. There is an improvement both in school enrollment and regularity in attending school by children. Gender disparities were much lower among the member households with respect to nutrition, child/adult premature death and ability of women to sign. Gender differences in children education and infant mortality have declined moderately and young children using government child care services have increased. Drainage and toilet facilities and access to *pucca* houses, electricity and gas have improved. The improvements in access to productive assets, improved livelihoods and control over all aspects of life of women have contributed to the decline of disparities (Ranjani *et al.*, 2002).

Highest achievements are made with respect to women's mobility, dissolution of gender division of productive labour, access to their own savings, access to friendship outside their family and access to leadership positions in *gram panchayat*; moderate achievements are made with respect to reproductive rights and body rights (freedom from violence); and lower achievements are made with respect to extent of access of women to husband's labour (productive and reproductive), rights of women to land and house, their ability to control male alcohol consumption and their ability to influence setting of wages. Women have intervened collectively in several institutions, *viz*., family, community, markets (labour, commodity and financial), and State including local self-government institutions. Within the family, higher collective achievement has been with respect to girl child education followed by release of bonded labour. At the community level, women groups at various levels are changing attitudes on girl child education and caste based discrimination. Linkages with government departments are stronger with those departments that deal with women's reproductive tasks or women managed productive activities and weaker with those activities which are controlled by men. This has resulted in accessing the government services and resources (Mahendra Dev *et al.*, 2002). Lesser degree of son preference shown by women members and breaking of caste norms within the group indicate that women pursue gender specific concerns.

Andhra Pradesh District Poverty Initiatives Project (APDPIP)

The SAPAP programme has been replicated with suitable modification in the most backward *mandals* of AP in the form of Andhra Pradesh District Poverty Initiatives Project (APDPIP) and Andhra Pradesh Rural Poverty Reduction Project (APRPRP). The successful institution-building model of SAPAP is being emulated in the APDPIP.

The APDPIP, popularly known as *Velugu* (meaning light) is a Rs 600 crore World Bank supported five-year poverty elimination project. In keeping with the development commitment, and as boldly envisaged in the vision 2020 document, the Government of Andhra Pradesh (GoAP) has initiated the 'Rural Poverty Elimination Programme' under the project *Velugu*. An independent, autonomous society under the Societies Act was created to implement the project named the 'Society for Elimination of Rural Poverty' (SERP). The project is being implemented in the six most backward districts of the state since June 2000. The main aim of the project is to facilitate the poor to play a decisive role in shaping their own destinies. APDPIP brings together the lessons learnt from earlier experiences and experiments of both the governmental and non-governmental initiatives. It builds on the strengths of a number of projects, particularly the UNDP assisted SAPAP which have shown that the poor have a tremendous potential to help themselves and that this potential can be harnessed by organising them. The poor have demonstrated that when adequate skills and inputs in community organisation, management and action are provided they can shape their destinies. Further, the project planning and implementation takes into consideration the opportunity, empowerment and security framework for poverty alleviation of the World Bank.

This project aims at enhancing assets, capabilities and the ability of the poor to deal with shocks and risks. It recognises that the livelihood strategies and income levels of the poor are inadequate not only due to lack of financial capital but also due to low/lack of physical and human capabilities. It assumes that empowerment of poor women should come prior to the access to financial capital for the better utilisation of existing resources and expanding the resource base. This project is implemented in three districts of Srikakulam, Anantapur and Adilabad.

APDPIP: Impact on Poverty

Proportion of households possessing own land has increased for the participant households of APDPIP across all the districts. The composition of livestock shows an improvement in draught animals and milch animals for participants. The composition of income has undergone change, i.e., income from self-employed activities against wage employment has increased considerably for participant households. This led to the improvement in the quality of income of the poor. The improved educational services due to the programme have resulted in better educational outcomes apart from improvement in the demand for better quality services by the empowered women. Improved safe motherhood and childhood practices are being practiced by a large proportion of participant households and this has resulted in improved health seeking behaviour and awareness. The share of households where both wife and husband, jointly taking decisions, has increased significantly. Household budget has been reallocated in favour of women. Women spending time with their children and spending time on family chores has shown substantial improvement indicating that women are now spending quality time on household activities. The collective action of the women federations contributed in lessening the social evils like child marriages, child labour etc. Interventions by the project (direct and indirect) helped the most vulnerable sections of the poor to cope up by adopting different strategies (resorting to more borrowing and use of savings rather than mortgage/selling the assets) that made them withstand the distress events compared to non-participants. However, access to market needs to be strengthened. Moreover, there is scope for improving the functioning of the public health institutions to cater to the needs of the poorest of the poor and the poor. Fieldwork has shown that there are variations in regard to the realisation of the benefits from different interventions in the project across the districts

(Mahendra Dev *et al.*, 2007). This means that the best practices that are enabling the poor to realise the potential benefits from interventions need to be replicated through out the project area. The pilot interventions made should be replicated universally so that there is profound impact on the functioning of the public and private institutions affecting the livelihoods of the poor.

The Role of NGOs and SHGs

Having looked at the various government programmes that promote SHGs, we will now look into the role of NGOs in promoting the women self-help groups. NGOs have surfaced as an essential part of the institutional structure for addressing poverty as well as rural development, gender equality, environmental conservation, disaster management, human rights and other social issues. The NGOs, in order to support social and economic empowerment of the poor, have immensely enlarged their activities to include group formation, microcredit, formal and non-formal education, training, health and nutrition, family planning and welfare, agriculture and related activities, water supply and sanitation, human rights and advocacy, legal aid and other areas. These organisations mostly follow the target-group strategy under which the poor with similar socioeconomic interests are organised into groups to achieve their objectives. The following are some of the models that have carved a niche for themselves in promoting SHGs thus leading to reduction in poverty.

BASIX

BASIX, a new generation rural livelihood promotion institution, was set up in 1996. The mission of BASIX is to promote a large number of sustainable livelihoods for the rural poor and women, by providing financial services and technical assistance in an integrated manner. Through provision of financial services, BASIX will strive to yield a competitive rate of return to its investors to enable them to access mainstream capital and human resources on a continuous basis. It comprises a group of companies, of which one is a holding company and others are its subsidiaries. The holding company is called Bhartiya Samruddhi Investments and Consulting Services Ltd. (BASICS). The financial arm of the group comprises a non-banking financial company, Bhartiya Samruddhi Finance Ltd. (Samruddhi or BSFL) and a bank, Krishna Bhima Samruddhi Local Area Bank Ltd. (KBSLAB). Apart from these, Indian Grameen Services is a non-profit subsidiary company, which provides technical assistance and support services to the entire clientele of the BASIX group. BASIX's strategy is to provide a comprehensive set of livelihood promotion services to rural poor households under one umbrella known as Livelihood Triad. This Triad includes livelihood financial services, agriculture/livestock/business development services and institutional development services. The rationale behind the Livelihood Triad strategy is as follows: microcredit by itself is helpful for the more enterprising poor people in economically dynamic areas. Less enterprising poor households need to start with savings and insurance before they can benefit from microcredit, because they need to cope with risk. However, in backward regions, poor people, in addition to microfinance, need a whole range of agricultural/business development services (productivity enhancement, risk mitigation, local value addition and market linkages, etc.). To offer these services in a cost-effective manner, it is not possible to work with poor households individually and they need to be organised into groups, informal associations and sometimes cooperatives or producer companies. The formation of such groups and making them function effectively, requires institutional development services (Basix India).

BASIX had extended credit to the women members of SHGs of SAPAP project; it also worked closely with the UNDP-SAPAP staff to improve the capacity of SHGs and their federations in accounting, financial management and adoption of new livelihood ideas. Similar efforts were also on with the federations and groups supported by CARE in Chevella, Rangareddy district of Andhra Pradesh. Thus, in the first 3 to 4 years of setting up its operations, BASIX's engagement with SHGs and/or their federations (used interchangeably with village organisations) was more in the nature of promotion, capacity building towards creditworthiness, assessment and lending. This work was highly acclaimed as it was setting the norms of quality and successful objective assessment based lending, and was the cornerstone for all future institutional development efforts of BASIX. From 2000 onwards, while continuing with the work with SHGs and federations, BASIX's area of operations, there was demand from other

NGOs/microfinancial institutions (MFI) to help with their own microfinance programmes, a very significant part of which was SHG based. Similarly, there was an increasing demand from various government and apex agencies to provide direction to and support their own SHG programmes. BASIX actively involved itself in this sector, working upon its own experiences while building the capabilities of the human resources of those organisations and providing specific inputs on vision building, systems, legal and capital structures, among others. BASIX, therefore, has been dealing with the development of SHGs as institutions, in the context of its social mission of sustainable livelihoods promotion (Rama, 2007).

Andhra Pradesh Mahila Abhivruddhi Society (APMAS)

APMAS is a national level technical and managerial support institution with a vision, 'sustainable self-help movement in India'. It works for women's empowerment and poverty alleviation through capacity building, quality assessment, livelihood promotion, communication and research & advocacy on a fee-for-service basis. APMAS funded by United Kingdom's Department for International Development (DFID) through CARE India, Ford Foundation, Aga Khan Foundation, became fully operational in July 2001 and today it has a functional team of highly experienced professionals providing services to diverse stakeholders across the state and in a limited way to other states. A variety of tools and content have been developed by APMAS to take up quality assessment (rating) and capacity building services towards wider dissemination of best practices and for impacting the quality of community based institutions. To facilitate an independent third party assessment of the quality of the SHG federations, APMAS has established a strong professional team within the organisation. The rating of SHG federations would aid the promoters to understand the performance of the federations. The rating could also facilitate financial flows to the federations from banks and other financial institutions.

APMAS as a resource organisation is deeply committed to support the sustainability of the SHG federations. It emerged from the felt need to have a resource organisation that provides high quality technical and managerial support for strengthening the SHG movement in India, more specifically in Andhra Pradesh. One of the mandates of APMAS is to establish standards for the SHG federations based on practice. To enable the promoters of SHG federations in adopting the standards, it provides capacity building through a series of training of trainers' programmes. The SHG federation model has achieved significant scale and considerable acceptance among all the major stakeholders. There is great potential for the SHG federation model to address issues of poverty. In many ways, the model is unique—the women are the owners, managers, users and beneficiaries. Within the SHG federation model there are several variations driven by local considerations and strategy of the promoting organisation (Reddy *et al.*, 2007).

Spandana

Spandana envisions itself as a financially self-sustainable MFI with a diversified ownership. It is mainly committed to strengthening the socio-economic status of poor women in rural and urban areas by providing technical and financial services on a sustained basis for establishing their identity and self-image. There are two important challenges ahead. Spandana at present is a non-profit making society and has started the process of transformation into a regulated company. Spandana has outperformed the most performing organisations by setting up trends with high level of efficiency, productivity and thereby profitability levels. Thus, the biggest challenge lies in retaining these levels in the pace of increasing competition.

Swayam Krishi Sangam (SKS)

Swayam Krishi Sangam (self-cultivation society) is an initiative in rural India to empower the poorest of the poor to become self-reliant. In June 1998, SKS began operating its main activity, microfinance, which follows the Grameen Bank model by seeking to eradicate poverty through the provision of small loans for income generating activities in the form of collective peer lending. SKS established its first women's banking *sangams* (centres) in the Narayankhed region. SKS Microfinance operates in six districts of Telangana and serves over 100,000 clients. SKS also began its education activities by implementing a pre-school (*balwadi*) programme in February 2001 in one of the poorest parts of India—the Narayankhed region of Medak district in Andhra Pradesh.

SHARE Microfinance Limited

Share Microfinance Limited (SML) started operations in 1989 as a not-for-profit society. It was the first MFI in India to obtain a non-banking financial company (non-deposit accepting) licence and also the first Indian MFI to carry out a microfinance securitisation transaction. SML adopted a not-for-profit approach to create social returns by channelling funds from development institutions and commercial banks as collateral-free loans to joint liability groups (JLGs). JLGs are the central element of the *grameen* lending methodology adopted by SML. The vision includes improving the quality of life of the poor by providing access to financial and support services and to be a viable financial institution developing sustainable communities.

Conclusions

The above discussion clearly brings out the fact that both the government and non-government organisations play a major role in organising women around thrift and credit services not only to alleviate poverty but also to empower them. Participation in SHGs improved the access of women to credit helping them in reducing their dependence on moneylenders. As a consequence of access to credit, women are in a position to meet their production and consumption demands. The women have invested the credit obtained from SHGs in strengthening old activities or in new economic activities. This led to the occupational diversification at the household level. The non-agricultural activities undertaken by women helped the households to procure money through low risk activities. This resulted in an increase in the quality of income of the households. There is also an improvement in the quality of employment, indicated by as shift from wage to self-employment. Here, it can be concluded that the incomes of the poor have increased, as a consequence of which the intensity of poverty has declined.

The interventions of the DPIP programme have contributed to the betterment of the livelihoods in terms of improvements in the asset base, levels and quality of income and consumption. Further, it has also contributed to the better functioning of the public institutions relating to education, health and other institutions implementing social safety net programmes. The improved social and political empowerment at household and community level of women has contributed to these changes. Further, the programme indicates that empowerment has gone up significantly at the household and community level. There was also an increase in the quantity and quality of credit. Women's share in savings and borrowing capacity registered an increase resulting in the formal credit institutions becoming inclusive of poor. Risks are managed well by resorting to savings and borrowings. Ultimately there is an improvement in well-being. These are all the pointers towards decline in the poverty. But, the bottom line is the sustainability of contributions flowing from the interventions. The project cannot be sustained unless we have vibrant, sustainable SHGs and their federations. The sustainability of these institutions depends upon the functioning of the trained book-keepers, community activists and community resource persons. Conducting meetings regularly is one of the important indicators to assess the performance of SHGs.

Thus, the various programmes initiated by the government of AP, enabled women to form into groups resulting in thrift and credit activities.

References

APMAS (2002). "Evaluation of Self-Help Groups in Adilabad, Cuddapah, and Visakapatnam Districts", Draft Report Prepared for the Government of Andhra Pradesh, Hyderabad.

BASIX, CARE–AP and Vikasdharshini (1999). "Women's Savings and Credit Movement in Andhra Pradesh and A Proposal for a New Institution APMAT", A Report Prepared for DFID (UK) India Office and Commissionarate of Rural Development, Government of Andhra Pradesh, July.

Biswas, Arun and Vijay Mahajan (1997). *Sustainable Banking with the Poor: A Case Study on Women Thrift Cooperative System in Warangal and Karimnagar Districts of Andhra Pradesh.* Hyderabad: Cooperative Development Foundation. July.

Centre for Economic and Social Studies (2001). *Report on Baseline Survey for Andhra Pradesh District Poverty Initiatives Project.* Prepared for the Society for Elimination of Rural Poverty. Hyderabad, November.

CDF (1999). *Member Participation in New Generation Thrift Cooperatives around Warangal Town in AP: 1997.* Hyderabad: Cooperative Development Foundation.

———. (2001). *Annual Report.* Hyderabad: Cooperative Development Foundation.

DWCRA Schemes in Adilabad District, Report Submitted to the Government of Andhra Pradesh. Institute of Cooperative Management, Hyderabad.

Ghosh, Jayati (1998). *Cooperatives under the Andhra Pradesh Mutually Aided Cooperatives Societies Act, 1995.* Centre for Economic Studies and Planning, School of Social Sciences. New Delhi: Jawaharlal Nehru University. December.

Galab, S. (1999). "Some Micro-Level Arrangements of Social Security in Andhra Pradesh", *The Indian Journal of Labour Economics* 42(3). July-September.

GoAP (1999). *DWCRA and Women's Empowerment: A Success Story of Self Help Movement in Andhra Pradesh*. Panchayat Raj and Rural Development Department, Andhra Pradesh, Hyderabad.

———. (2002). *Achievements under Women Action Plan 2002-2003*. Rural Development Department, Government of Andhra Pradesh, Hyderabad.

———. (2002). *Economic Survey 2001-2002*. Department of Planning, Government of Andhra Pradesh, Hyderabad.

Kanchanya, K. (1998). "Women and Development: A Case Study of DWCRA Programme in West Godavari District of A.P". Unpublished Dissertation Submitted to Dr. B.R. Ambedkar Open University, Hyderabad.

Mahendra Dev, S. and P. Padmanabha Rao (2002). "Poverty Alleviation Programmes in Andhra Pradesh: An Assessment", Report of the Study Sponsored by Planning Commission, Government of India.

Mahendra Dev, S., S. Galab, M. Gopinath Reddy, K.S. Reddy, C. Ravi, K.S. Babu and G.K. Mitra (2002). *Baseline Survey Report in Sustainable Livelihood Framework*. Prepared for the Society for Elimination of Rural Poverty, Centre for Economic and Social Studies, Hyderabad.

Mahendra Dev, S., S. Galab, P. Prudhvikar Reddy, D. Sreerama Raju, C. Ravi, K.S. Babu, K.S. Reddy, M. Gopinath Reddy, G.K. Mitra and G. Alivelu (2007). "End Term Appraisal of Andhra Pradesh District Poverty Initiatives Project", Prepared for the Society for Elimination of Rural Poverty, Centre for Economic and Social Studies, Hyderabad.

Outreach (2001). "South Asia Poverty Alleviation Programme: Policy Lessons Emerging in Andhra Pradesh in India", Report of the Study Commissioned by UNDP, India, Hyderabad.

ORG-MARG Research Limited (2000). "Consultancy on Strengthening of Self Help Groups in Andhra Pradesh: SWOT Analysis of the Groups Surveyed in AP", Report of the Study Sponsored by Department of Rural Development, Government of Andhra Pradesh, Hyderabad.

Rama Kandarpa (2007). "SHG—An Institutional Model A BASIX Experience", Paper presented on the occasion of the International Conference on *Andhra Pradesh Experience with Membership Based Organisation of the Poor*. CESS, Hyderabad. June.

Ranjani, K.M., K. Raju and Amitha Kamath (2002). "Towards Women's Empowerment and Poverty Reduction: Lessons from the Participatory Impact Assessment of South Asian Poverty Alleviation Programme in Andhra Pradesh, India", Report of the Study Commissioned by United Nations Development Programme.

Rao, C.H.H. (1994). *Agricultural Growth, Rural Poverty and Environmental Degradation in India*. New Delhi: Oxford University Press.

Ray, Nandita and D.P. Vasundhara (1996). "Like my Mother's House: Women's Thrift and Credit Cooperatives in South India", in M. Carr, M. Chen and R. Jhabvala (eds.), *Speaking Out-Women's Economic Empowerment in South Asia*. New Delhi: Vistaar Publications.

Reddy, C.S., N. Tirupathaiah and C.S. Ramalakshmi (2007). "Emerging SHG Federations and Challenges", Paper presented on the occasion of the International Conference on *Andhra Pradesh Experience with Membership Based Organisation of the Poor*, CESS, Hyderabad June 5th- 6th.

UNDP (1998). "South Asia Poverty Alleviation Programme: Progress Report, 1996-1998", *UNDP,RAS/96/600.* India, Hyderabad.

———. (2000). *South Asia Poverty Alleviation Programmes: Regional Progress Report*. India, Hyderabad.

Vyas, V.S. and Pradeep Bhargava (1995). "Public Intervention for Poverty Alleviation: An Overview", *Economic and Political Weekly* XXX(41 and 42), October 14-21.

World Bank (1995). *World Bank Participation Handbook*. IBRD Social Policy and Resettlement Division, Washington D.C.

———. (2000/2001). *World Development Report 2000/2001: Attacking Poverty*. New York: Oxford University Press.

Youth for Action (1996). *Evaluation Report on DWCRA in Mahaboobnagar District of Andhra Pradesh*. Study Commissioned by UNICEF.

Section II

Organisations and Outcomes

3

Self-Help Groups and Political Empowerment in Andhra Pradesh

M. Gopinath Reddy and
D. Sree Rama Raju

Conceptual Framework

The concept of empowerment has been the subject of much intellectual discourse and analysis. United Nations conceptualise the empowerment as 'the processes by which women take control and ownership of their lives through expansion of their choice.' Kabeer's famous definition of empowerment is that 'it is the process of acquiring the ability to make strategic life choices in a context where this ability has been previously denied. The core elements of empowerment have been defined as agency—the ability to define ones goals and act upon them, awareness of gendered power structures, self-esteem and self-confidence' (Kabeer, 2001).

From the above conceptualisation of empowerment, a clear shift can be discerned from women in development (WID) approach to gender and development (GAD) approach which brings power relations between men and women within the focus of attention. GAD approach stresses on power, conflict and gender relations in understanding women's subordination. It regards women as agents of change, rather than as passive recipients of development assistance (Mooij, 2002). According to Batliwala, (1994), 'empowerment is the process of challenging existing power relations and of gaining greater control over the resources of power. It is manifested as a redistribution of power'.

Studies conducted on the impact of self-help groups (SHGs) reveal that women's groups' formation, new knowledge and groups' mobilisation are capable of creating an alternative to women's traditional status in the family. Group mobilisation also enables women to speak out in the village meetings (Vijayanthi, 2002). While SHGs are formed round an economic issue of micro-credit and savings, the formation of groups is a political process. This process picks up momentum with the SHGs being federated and also establishing links with local self-governing bodies (Ranadive, 2004).

It is argued that even through 'micro-credit' through SHGs does not lead to virtuous spiral of economic, social and political empowerment of women (Mayoux, 1999) it does lead to empowering some women. In economic terms, it also reduces the vulnerability at the time of natural calamity, so to that extent, the power relation at the family level changes. It is also noticed that if men are involved in the programme, women's 'practical needs' are met (Leach and Sitaram, 2002). In addition, the programme helps in creating the 'social capital' in a community, since it encourages collective action. The social mobilisation created by SHGs gets reinforced by another factor namely, women's participation in the political process through campaigns, addressing the meetings and casting their votes (Mohanty, 2007). Political space can be perceived at two levels—private and public. While private political space is concerned about power dynamics within the domestic unit, public political space is related to women's access and control of public spaces. Political activity as widely understood takes place within the public domain and is connected with the administration and governance of society/institutions locally as well as in larger context (Ranadive, 2003).

Context

In the past decade, there have been two significant interventions affected by the Central government to usher and strengthen the women's empowerment. The 73rd and 74th Constitutional Amendments are one such intervention which provides mandatory one-third of seats to women candidates in local bodies while the other intervention is mobilisation of women into SHGs. Both these interventions have so far proved enriching experience in advancing women's empowerment in varying intensity in different parts of the country. In Andhra Pradesh (AP), for example, the SHG movement in empowering rural poor women is a big success while in some other states like Kerala and Karnataka, Panchayati Raj Institutions

(PRIs) provided poor women a platform to claim leadership roles and assert themselves in local self-government.

The major impetus in the constitutional amendments for women's political empowerment is the provision of reservation of one-third seats for women in local bodies. The provision of reservations in the system of local self-governance in India has been hailed as an empowering process for women since it has not only brought women out of their houses and into public place but also given them a voice and platform to express themselves.

The state of AP has been using development of SHGs as a primary tool of poverty alleviation and empowerment. The SHGs largely are the conduit through which microcredit is routed to the poor in the belief that it will serve as a catalyst in helping them to pull out of poverty (Ranadive, 2004). It is also pointed out that women of neighbourhood committees act as 'watchdogs' in compelling the elected women to deliver at least some public goods.

There are about 6.35 lakh women SHGs in AP covering nearly 80.21 lakh poor women, out of which there are 21.18 lakh scheduled caste (SC) SHG members, 9 lakh scheduled tribe (ST) members and the rest 49.34 lakh belong to other categories. AP alone has about half of SHGs organised in the country (Rama, 2003; Reddy, 2007). The formation of groups, participation in them, the responsibility of running the groups, holding positions of leadership have all contributed towards involving women members in political processes. Women from SHGs have also been elected to public office, their participation in such groups serving as an incubator for community leadership. However, these instances are still incipient and not wide spread and they remain largely islands of activity (Ranadive, 2004).

These SHGs interface with large number of government and elected institutions at the grassroot level, particularly PRIs. The efficiency of these SHGs would be considerably enhanced if a symbiosis could be worked out between the SHGs and PRIs by statutorily making SHG members as the members of the standing committees of the PRIs at all the key levels (Bandhyopadhyay *et al.*, 2002).

Self-Help Groups and Political Empowerment in Andhra Pradesh

The case study on AP discusses where state initiative has extensively used the SHGs as a tool of empowerment, in general and economic and political empowerment in particular. The AP Government's initiative of District Poverty Initiative Programme (DPIP) forms the background for our analysis.

This chapter basically looks at how SHG movement helped its members to become articulate politically by becoming members of constitutional mandated bodies like *gram panchayats, mandal panchayats* and *zilla panchayats*. It is further hypothesised that members from SHG movement occupying the positions of power in constitutional bodies bring in qualitative difference in terms of better governance unlike women members directly getting into local bodies without SHG background. Although the presence of SHG members in local institutions is inadequate at the present juncture, it is assumed that SHG members may actively mediate in the political process in the form of attending meetings of *gram sabha* and other related institutions and raising issues concerning the poor thus bringing service providers to account. It is these processes which are equally important to make local governance accountable to the poor and disadvantaged.

The critical questions examined are:

i) Has the involvement of women members in the DPIP project increased awareness among women about political participation?

ii) Has the involvement of women members in the project increased the participation of SHG (DPIP) members in local politics?

iii) Has the participation increased initiation of collective actions of women?

Objectives of the Study

i) To analyse the extent of SHG members' participation in the political institutions like *panchayats*.

ii) To analyse the extent of SHG participants' mediation in the political process.

Methodology

Two sets of primary data pertaining to DPIP have been used. The first set of data relate to the Mid-Term Appraisal (MTA) of DPIP where 2,640 households data from three districts of AP, (Srikakulam, Adilabad and Anantapur) has been analysed. In the first set of data, the variation in political participation of the members is analysed in programme and control villages. The second set of data relates to final round of DPIP. It needs to be mentioned that by the final round of impact assessment, all the *mandals* in the selected districts are covered under the programme hence we analysed the data pertaining to participants (62.14 per cent) and non-participants (37.86 per cent) in the programme by adopting panel method instead of programme and control villages comparison.

Results and Discussion

The number of women entering into the arena of political institutions is a good indicator to gauge whether there is equal participation of men and women in the political process. As already mentioned, reservation of seats for women in the local bodies through Constitutional Amendment Act has provided multiple channels of awareness for women into these bodies. In the recent elections held both to the rural and urban local bodies, women have contested and won in more than one-third of the seats reserved for them. For our discussion it is important to see the extent to which SHG women entering into local bodies.

The numerical status of the SHG members entering into various levels of PRIs is analysed in Table 3.1.

The per cent of SHG members among the total number of *gram panchayat* (GP) ward members constitutes less than 5 per cent (10,000 members out of total 208,291 ward members). The situation is not better at Mandal Parishad Territorial Committee (MPTC) level less than 1 per cent (95 SHG members out of 14,617 MPTC members). But the situation is much better at Zilla Parishad Territorial Committee (ZPTC) level which stands at 8 per cent (88 SHG members out of 1,095 total ZPTC members). Viewed from the above data, it reveals that SHG members' representation among the positions reserved for women at GP ward level is nearly 5 per cent, but at MPTC level it is still low around 2 per cent (see Figure 3.1).

Table 3.1

Numerical Strength of Various Positions in PRIs and SHG Members Participation in PRIs

	Total Members in PRIs and Reservation for Women and Participation of SHG Members in PRIs
Gram Panchayat (GP) Sarpanches	21,807
Positions reserved for women	7,269
Number of SHG members as *sarpanches*	NA
Gram Panchayat members	208,291
Positions reserved for women	68,736
Number of SHG members in *Gram Panchayats*	10,000
Number of Mandal Praja Parishad presidents (MPP)	1,096
Positions reserved for women	361
Number of SHG members as MPP presidents	NA*
Number of MPTC members	14,617
Positions reserved for women	4,919
Number of SHG members as MPTC members	95
Number of ZPTC members	1,095
Positions reserved for women	364
Number of SHG members as ZPTC members	88

Note: * NA – Not available.

Source: Society for Elimination of Rural Poverty (SERP) Office, Hyderabad.

Figure 3.1

Percentage of SHG Members in PRI Institutions

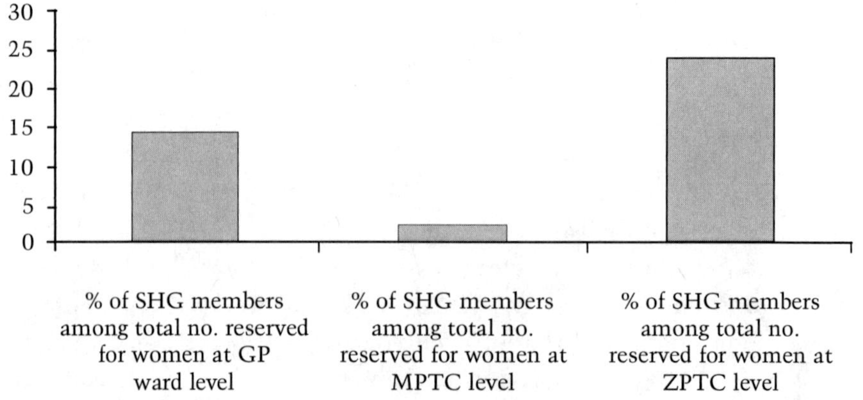

However, at ZPTC level, SHG members' participation is high which is around 25 per cent. The analysis is constrained by the fact that *sarpanches'* level data is not available. It is the office of the *sarpanch* which is an important position for SHG member operating at village level that can influence resource allocation and distribution of benefits to the poor. (Table 3.1 and Figure 3.1).

Results from Mid-Term Assessment (MTA) of DPIP Report[1]

Empowerment at Community Level

Participation by women in the grassroot level institutions and collective actions of the community is considered for assessing the empowerment of women in the domain of the community. Data on women's participation in village assemblies (*gram sabhas*) and raising issues in these forums support the hypothesis that the greater empowerment of women within the household enables them to participate more effectively in community level decisions and provides an opportunity gradually to close the gap with economically and socially more advanced regions. Even though the share of women who participated regularly in *gram sabhas* is only between one-third and half of what is found outside the project area, the significantly larger rate of change in such participation in project as compared to non-project areas suggests that this gap is slowly being narrowed. In fact, the overall share of women (not only among participants) who report that they have raised issues in such meetings is significantly higher and has increased at a faster rate in project as compared to non-project areas and among members of SHGs as compared to non-members. The mere participation of members in meetings does not signify anything unless the members feel that it is worthwhile attending such meetings. In other words, the perception of members on the utility of meetings becomes critical for the success of such meetings. Responses by

1. District Poverty Initiatives Project (DPIP) popularly known as 'Velugu' Project was launched in Andhra Pradesh with the World Bank Support by Andhra Pradesh Government. In the first phase (2000-2005) six districts were covered namely, Vizianagaram and Srikakulam in Coastal Andhra, Mahabubnagar and Adilabad in Telangana and Anantapur and Chittoor in Rayalaseema regions. Centre for Economic and Social Studies (CESS) has undertaken both baseline and Impact study of DPIP. The data used for this paper was largely drawn from the study report.

women and men on the utility of attending *panchayat gram sabha* and 'Janmabhoomi'[2] *gram sabha* show that a very small percentage (14 per cent in case of *panchayat gram sabhas* and 20 per cent in the case of Janmabhoomi *gram sabhas*) felt that attending such meetings was of some use. However, the position is better in programme villages as compared to control villages. More men respondents as compared to women felt that the meetings were useful. Here again the situation is better in programme villages than in control villages. It is possible that a wider level of participation in programme villages in *panchayat gram sabhas* and 'Janmabhoomi' *gram sabhas* would have resulted in the better functioning of the institutions which might be the reason why more persons felt that attending such meetings had been to achieve some purpose. Comparing the present position with the situation three years ago, there is a perceptible increase in the number of persons who felt that participating in grassroot institutions was fruitful, which is clearly shown by the data. Thus, the nature of participation in programme areas is qualitatively different from non-project areas.

The participation of women in collective community actions against the practice of child labour is much more pronounced among women who participated in SHGs than those who did not. They are also participating in community collective actions for accessing credit from formal institutions as well as the poverty alleviation programmes of the government.

Civic Participation in Local Governance

Civic participation or civic engagement refers to the participation of citizens in governance. Local governance has linkages with poverty reduction and growth. Civic participation in governance requires political capability for citizens, who refer to the capacity to represent oneself or others, access information, form associations, and participate in the political life of a community or country. In a society of deep inequalities, people belonging to SCs and STs have been generally excluded from

2. 'Janmabhoomi' was a state sponsored programme during Telugu Desam Party (TDP) regime (1999–2004) under which various developmental initiatives were launched for the welfare of the rural poor. The biggest criticism levelled against 'Janmabhoomi' programme was that it was manned by nodal officers rather than elected representatives.

participation in state institutions that make the decisions and administer the resources that affect their lives. Similarly, in the cultural context of the prevalence of patriarchic value systems in Andhra Pradesh as elsewhere in India, women have also been excluded from the participation in these institutions.

Hence, rules and laws have been framed to ensure inclusion and participation of the excluded or marginalised groups in local governance. In local governance, providing quotas for the SCs and STs and the recent amendments to extend quotas to other backward castes (OBCs) and women through 73rd Constitutional Amendment are a case in point. These reforms in local governance focussed primarily on the supply side of the formal system and not on strengthening the demand-side actions that enable citizens effectively to utilise the space created through new rules and regulations. Social inequalities, cultural norms, lack of a support system and training still constrain vulnerable social groups and women's roles. In order to assess political capability, two parameters, *viz.*, participation in local governance structures and the voice of citizens in local governance are considered. Participation in governance structures is measured in terms of contesting for and getting elected as *sarpanch*, vice-*sarpanch* and ward members of *gram panchayat*. Participation in *gram sabhas*, representation of grievances to the peoples' representatives, and inspecting 'Janmabhoomi' records are used to assess the voices of citizens in local governance. Functioning of governance institutions is also assessed through three issues *viz.*, conduct of *gram sabhas*; visits of peoples' representatives to the villages; and maintenance of 'Janmabhoomi' records.

Participation in Local Governance Structures

For every 10 positions of *sarpanch* of *gram panchayats*, 19 candidates have contested in programme villages and 22 in control villages. Among the social groups, 70 from SCs; 20 from STs; 80 from backward castes (BCs) and 30 from other castes (OCs) have contested for every 100 positions in the programme villages. The corresponding figures are 40, 10, 100 and 60 in the control villages. Between men and women, 130 men in both the programmes and control villages, and 80 and 100 women in programme and control villages respectively have contested for every 100 positions. In general, the number of contestants is lower in the programme villages for all social classes, except for STs. However, BCs are able to contest in greater numbers even in the absence of reservation. This provides substantial evidence to the argument that reservations for SCs, STs and women in local governance structures are a must to ensure adequate space for them. The same scenario prevails in programme and control villages across social groups and women in respect of elected *sarpanches* of *gram panchayats*.

The social and gender composition of contestants for ward members of *gram panchayat* are similar to those of *sarpanch* of *gram panchayat*. However, in contrast to the *sarpanches* elected, the elected ward members from OCs and women are found to be higher in programme villages compared to control villages. Elected vice-*sarpanches* from SCs, BCs and OCs are relatively less in programme villages compared to control villages. Interestingly, they are more or less the same for men and women in programme and control villages. A comparison of the persons elected for *sarpanch* and vice-*sarpanch* shows that more SCs and STs are elected as *sarpanch* than as vice-*sarpanch* in programme as well as control villages. This again reinforces the inference that the number of persons elected from the social groups—SCs and STs would be low in the absence of reservations (there is no reservation for vice-*sarpanch* positions as he is elected by the ward members). The extent and pattern of participation of people in general, social and gender groups in particular for the positions of *sarpanch*, vice-*sarpanch* and ward members of *gram panchayat* are more or less the same between programme and control villages across the districts.

Access to Information

Schemes relating to poverty eradication, natural resource management and functioning of schools are discussed in meetings conducted by institutions such as *panchayat gram sabhas*, 'Janmabhoomi' *gram sabhas*, Water Users Associations (WUAs) and Village Education Committees (VECs). Information about when and where such meetings are organised becomes critical for the people to be able to access the benefits from these institutions (Table 3.2).

Table 3.2

Female Participation in Village Meetings and Awareness of Elections to the Committees

Know when and where this meeting is organised		
	Programme	*Control*
Participation in		
Panchayat gram sabha	1199	280
Per cent	57.81	51.47
participation in		
'Janmaboomi' *gram sabha*	1657	371
Per cent	79.89	68.2
elections to		
Water Users Association	186	71
Per cent	8.98	13.08
elections to		
Vidya Committee	997	148
Per cent	48.12	27.31

Source: Field Survey.

A higher proportion of women have access to the information in the programme villages than in the control villages. This is particularly so in the case of 'Janmabhoomi' *gram sabhas* as compared to *panchayat gram sabhas*. This supports the assumption that the programme would make a significant contribution to raising awareness among women. However, access to information regarding WUAs is found to be very low among women, and the programme has not led to any improvement in this area. This may be because this activity primarily lies in the male domain. The contribution of the programme in case of access to information with regard to VECs is slightly better which augurs well for the functioning of schools. Gender inequalities in accessing information have come down due to the programme.

Data on levels of information on reservation for women in *panchayats* shows that less than a third of the women respondents, both in programme (33 per cent) and control (31 per cent) villages are aware of these provisions. Of these, a negligible percentage have been able to state the exact provision made for women in *gram panchayats*, which highlights the very poor and inadequate understanding among women respondents on the position of women in the grassroot political institution. However, the programme has brought a noticeable improvement in this regard among women who are members of DPIP-SHGs compared to non-members. The awareness levels among women respondents about the reservation provisions for SC/STs in the *panchayats* are also very low. However, in the programme villages, the awareness level is better (32 per cent) than in control villages (29 per cent). Of the respondents who knew about SC/ST reservation in *panchayats*, none knew the exact percentage of reservations under these categories in either the programme or the control villages. The programme has not made any significant improvement in this regard. This may be because members in these institutions do not focus in the DPIP programme on increasing awareness levels about political institutions, and the need for participation in these institutions. (Table 3.3)

Table 3.3

Awareness on Panchayati Raj Institutions and Modes of Acquisition of Knowledge in Mid-Term Assessment (MTA)

	MTA DPIP	
	Programme Area	*Control Area*
Awareness of reservation for GP seats for women	692	169
Per cent	33.4	30.9
Awareness of 33% reservation for women	45	14
Per cent	2.41	2.61
Awareness of reservation for SC/ST seats	669	160
Per cent	32.41	29.25

Source: Field Survey.

Results from End-Term DPIP

Awareness and Acquisition of Knowledge

Awareness of the constitutional provision for the elected bodies is a first step if people wanted to take advantage of such provisions to contest the elections. It is all the more important for the poorer categories belonging to scheduled castes/scheduled tribes and women. The extent of awareness of such provisions among SHG participants and non-participants is discussed below.

Among participant members there is higher awareness found (33.30 per cent) as compared to non-participants (24.57 per cent) in case of the provision of reservation for *gram panchayat* seats for women. However, very less per cent of participants (only 1.6 per cent) and more than 2 per cent of non-participants could tell exact per cent of seats allotted to women, here again SHG participants score better (31.9 per cent) than non-participants (23.1 per cent). Even though one-third of the participants and one-fifth of the non-participants were aware of reservation position for SC/STs, but none of them could tell exact per cent of seats reserved for them (Table 3.4).

Table 3.4

Awareness of the Provision of the Reservation to SC/ST and Women in Panchayats

Level of Awareness	*Participants*	*Non-Participants*
Awareness of reservation for GP seats for women	496	243
Per cent	33.29	24.57
Awareness of 33% reservation for women	24	23
Per cent	1.61	2.28
Awareness of reservation for SC/ST seats	475	228
Per cent	31.9	23.1

Source: Field Survey.

Participation in Political Process

Besides awareness of the provision of the seats reserved for women, SC/ST, certain political activities such as attending rallies/speeches, campaigning/motivating, attending party meetings etc., indicate political maturity on the part of citizens. This dimension was also analysed among participant and non-participants. Although overall participation in these activities is found low, SHG participants' political maturity is higher than non-participants. This may be attributed to the intense capacity building, built up in the programme not only around issues such as savings and credit but also larger socio-political issues (Figure 3.2).

Participation in Village Meetings and Raising/ Speaking up Issues

Apart from contesting the elections and participation in village meetings that affect resource allocation and speaking up in such meetings would make leaders vigilant and responsive to the needs of the poor people. It is evident from the data that in the three important institutions namely

Figure 3.2

Participation in Political Process

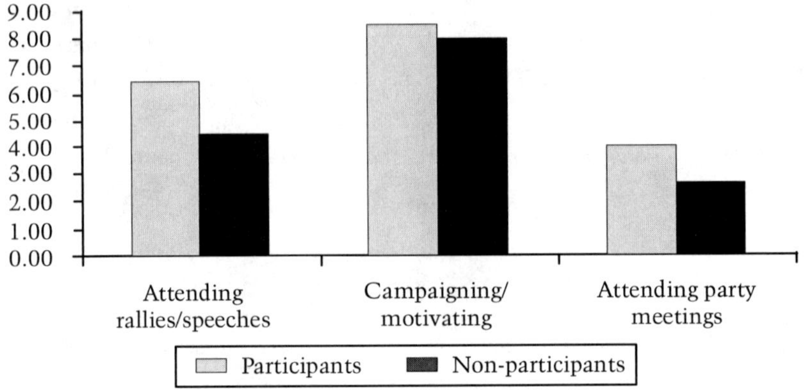

panchayat gram sabha, 'prajapatham'[3] and 'Rajeev pallebata'.[4] SHG participants' attendance is higher (25 per cent, 24 per cent and 22 per cent) than non-participants (20 per cent, 20 per cent and 21 per cent) in such meetings (Table 3.5a and Table 3.5b).

Table 3.5a

Participation in Panchayat GS and Other Institutions

	Participation in Village Meetings					
	Non-Participants			*Participants*		
	Yes	*Rarely*	*Never*	*Yes*	*Rarely*	*Never*
Panchayat gram sabha	150	151	461	291	225	653
Per cent	19.69	19.82	60.50	24.89	19.25	55.86
'Prajapatham'	47	48	140	78	59	190
Per cent	20.00	20.43	59.57	23.85	18.04	58.10
Rajeev Pallebata	46	48	128	61	61	159
Per cent	20.72	21.62	57.66	21.71	21.71	56.58
Water Users Association	6	1	18	1	3	28
Per cent	24.00	4.00	72.00	3.13	9.38	87.50
Vidya Committee	8	3	29	6	9	50
Per cent	20.00	7.50	72.50	9.23	13.85	76.92

Source: Field Survey.

3. 'Prajapatham' was launched by the present congress government after it got elected to the power in 2004. This was basically addressed to understand peoples' grievances periodically and trying to solve them.
4. 'Rajeev Pallebata' was yet other scheme (similar to that 'Janmabhoomi') launched by the new Chief Minister who conducted periodical visits to the villages to understand their needs and trying to solve them through government machinery.

Table 3.5b

Participants Speaking up Issues during Meetings

Did the participants speak up/raise issues during the following?	*Non-Participants*		*Participants*	
	Yes	*No*	*Yes*	*No*
Panchayat gram sabha	87	217	154	364
Per cent	28.62	71.38	29.73	70.27
'Janambhoomi' *gram sabha*	23	102	57	189
Per cent	18.40	81.60	23.17	76.83
'Prajapatham'	14	81	42	94
Per cent	14.74	85.26	30.88	69.12
Rajeev Pallebata	19	75	28	93
Per cent	20.21	79.79	23.14	76.86
Water Users Association	4	4	1	2
Per cent	50.00	50.00	33.33	66.67
Vidya Committee	3	6	5	11
Per cent	33.33	66.67	31.25	68.75

Source: Field Survey.

Confidence in Elected Representatives in Discharge of Service Delivery

People's confidence in elected representatives is critical factor for the efficient and equitable service delivery at the cutting-edge level. Efficient and honest elected representatives make significant difference to the deliverance of the programme benefits to the poor, otherwise large scale leakages in the programme benefits would occur. In the following analysis we looked at the way participants/non-participants rank the qualities that elected representatives should possess for them to get elected. Ranking the confidence in elected representatives is measured in terms of high, medium and low scores. The results are discussed below (Figure 3.3).

It is evident from the data that SHG participants look for better qualities in the elected representatives like honesty and fairness, ability to solve community and village problems, ability to represent village problems to government in case of ward member, *sarpanch*, vice-*sarpanch*, MPP president, MPTC member and accord higher values to these qualities than non-participants. This augurs well for the responsive administration. However for the *zilla parishad* (ZP) chairperson and ZP vice-chairperson non-participants seemed to have accorded higher values to the above

Figure 3.3

Confidence in Elected Representative in Better Service Delivery

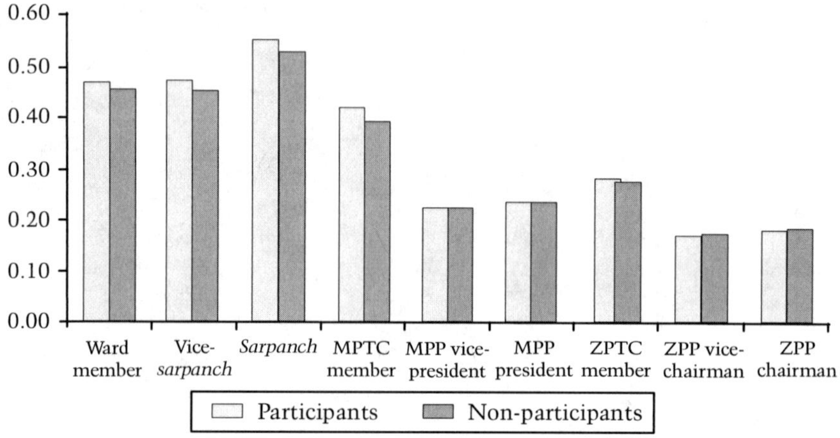

qualities than participants. It can be inferred that SHG participants who are basically poor and do not have wider networks have looked for better qualities in the representatives who are available in their vicinity/locality like ward member, *sarpanch*, MPTC member, ZPTC member whereas non-participants who are not poor exclusively and have better networks because of their endowments have looked for good qualities mentioned above for the higher level of elected representatives like ZP chairman and vice-chairman. As the poor in the SHG groups (participants) do emphasise on these qualities in the leaders because of adequate capacities built up for the members as a part of social mobilisation process. This result in better accountability of the elected representatives to the poor and the vulnerable and service delivery can be efficient and equitable.

Concluding Observations and Way Forward

Notwithstanding the fact that SHG members' participation in the political institutions at present juncture is in incipient and nascent state, the paper shows that there is some good potential at the level mediating the political process by SHG members. This was evident from the analysis of SHG participants' attending village level institutions (both *panchayats* and community based organisations (CBOs) as well as articulating and speaking up issues that affect them. In addition to this, SHG members showed maturity in according higher values to the attributes such as honesty/fairness, ability to represent community problems and ability to represent problems to government bureaucracy etc., that village elected representatives should possess, particularly for leaders available in close proximity, which augurs well for responsive and transparent local government and administration. On all these parameters very clear differences were shown in the DPIP programme and control village as well as DPIP participant and non-participant members.

In order to take SHG movement in Andhra Pradesh forward and make it strong and sustainable, there is need for moving ahead on the lines of the Kerala State's model of 'Kudumbashree Experience' which works on three-tier structure—neighbourhood groups (NHGs) at group level and area development society (ADS) at ward level and community development society (CDS) at local body/*panchayat* level.

The important lesson to be learnt here that micro plans prepared by NHGs integrated at CDS level becomes anti-poverty sub plan of village *panchayat* and municipality. And also NHGs act as 'watchdogs' on the functioning of the local bodies.[5] It is to be mentioned that NHGs and its activities could facilitate women to enter into public life and more than 100 functionaries of the CDS became the potential executives of the urban local bodies (Jos, n.d.; Radha and Chowdhury, 2002). Even from a state like Bihar, there is clear evidence that from 394 *panchayats* covered by 36 Poorest Areas Civil Society (PACS) programme partners on Panchayat Abhiyan which shows that 1,009 candidates supported by CBOs won unopposed in these areas while 400 other candidates won a seat after contest (Report of the Empower Poor, n.d.).

These experiences from diverse states clearly show that there is a need in Andhra Pradesh also to mobilise SHG women into political process much vigorously. There is need for APSHG movement to start focussing on issues beyond savings and credit and social issues but also on political

5. Under Kudumbashree programme, 3,000 women from the Kudumbashree CBOs contested local body elections under the banners of various political fronts and also as independents, 1,408 women were elected from various constituencies covering 449 local self-government Institutions (LSGIs). Among them 14 were elected to corporations, 92 to municipalities, 1,212 to *gram panchayats*, 83 to block *panchayats* and 7 to district *panchayats*. It is also observed that a good number of them have been elected as presidents/chairpersons of the LSGs.

questions like entering into the local bodies in a big way. Once SHG members in large measure become part of local bodies there is every possibility that ills of decentralisation like elite capture, inequitable distribution of resources, corruption etc., can be squarely addressed by these conscious women members. Only then, it is hoped that SHG members bring in pressure and demand for effective decentralisation of powers, functions and functionaries in a more concerted way. This will result not only in deepening democracy at grassroot level but also equitable distribution of benefits to the poor and needy. For this to happen, there is an urgent need to work for mechanisms/systems that will allow SHGs and PRIs to work in tandem and establish a system of reinforcing each other's work.

References

Bandhyopadhyay, D., B.N. Yugandhar and Amitava Mukherjee (2002). "Convergence of Programmes by Empowering SHGs and PRIs", *Economic Political Weekly*, June 29.

Batliwala, Srilatha (1994). "The Meaning of Women's Empowerment: New Concepts from Action", in Gita Sen, Adrienne Germain and Lincoln C. Chen (eds.), *Population Policies Reconsidered, Health, Empowerment and Rights*. Boston: Harvard University Press.

Empower Poor. *http://www.empowerpoor.org/programmereport.asp?report=328)*

Jos, Chathukulam (n.d.). "Survival through Social Capital formation: The Case of Women's Self Help Groups in Kerala", *Kerala Research Programme on Local Level Development*. Thiruvanthapuram: Centre for Development Studies.

Jos, Mooij (2002). "Welfare Policies and Politics: A Study of Three Government Interventions in Andhra Pradesh, India", *Working Paper* No.181. London: Overseas Development Institute, UK.

Kabeer, N. (2001). "Resources, Agency, Achievements: Reflections on the Measurement of Women's Empowerment", in *Discussing Women's Empowerment—Theory and Practice*, SIDA Studies No.3.

Leach, Fiona and Shashikala Sitaram (2002). "Microfinance and Women's Empowerment: A Lesson from India", *Development Practice* 12 (5): 575-88.

Mayoux, Linda (1999). "Questioning Virtuous Spirals: Micro-finance and Women's Empowerment in Africa", *Journal of International Development* 11: 957-984.

Mohanty, Bidyut (2007). "Women and Local Power in India and China: Revisiting the Ghosts of Manu and Confucius", in Manoranjan Mohanty *et al.* (eds.), *Grass-roots Democracy in India and China: The Right to Participate*. New Delhi: Sage Publication.

———. (n.d.). "Women and Panchayats in India: Creating a New Space for Leadership in Asia", New Delhi: Institute of Social Sciences.

Radha, S. and B.R. Chowdhury (2002). "Women in Local Bodies", *Discussion Paper* No. 40, Kerala Research Programme on Local Level Development, Thiruvanthapuram: Centre for Development Studies.

Rama, Lakshmi C.S. (2003). "Women Empowerment through Self-Help Groups", *Economic Political Weekly* 38 (12 and 13), March 22-28/April 29.

Ranadive, Joy Deshmukh (2003). "Women in Self Help Groups and Panchayat Raj Institutions: Suggesting Synergistic Linkages", *Occasional Paper*. New Delhi: Centre for Women's Development Studies. *http://www.cwds.org/OCPaper/Women SelHelpGroups.pdf)*

———. (2004). "Women's Self-Help Groups in Andhra Pradesh—Participatory Poverty Alleviation in Action", *Scaling up Poverty Reduction: A Global Learning Process and Conference Shanghai*, May 25-27.

Reddy, B. Chandra (2007). *Sthanika Samsthala Praja Pratinidula Sangham*. Hyderabad: MB Bhavan.

United Nations Development Programme (1997). "Sustaining Livelihoods: Promoting Informal Sector Growth in Pacific Island Countries", Unpublished paper.

Vijayanthi, K.N. (2002). "Women's Empowerment through Self-Help Groups: A Participatory Approach", *Indian Journal of Gender Studies* 9 (2).

Paper presented at the International Conference on *Andhra Pradesh Experience with Membership Based Organisations of the Poor* held at CESS in collaboration with Cornell University, USA on 5th and 6th of June 2007. Hyderabad, India.

4 Ripple Effects or Deliberate Intentions?

Assessing Linkages between Women Empowerment and Childhood Poverty

Nicola Jones, Madhuri Mukherjee, and S. Galab

Introduction

Women empowerment is increasingly conceptualised as an important component of broader poverty reduction programme. The World Bank made this link explicit in its 2001/02 *World Development Report* and gender has been included as a cross-cutting issue in many least developed countries' *Poverty Reduction Strategy Papers* (Whitehead and Lockwood, 1999). Empowering women, it is argued will improve household well-being, lead to better outcomes for children and promote social capital development and community involvement in social development and poverty alleviation initiatives (Kabeer, 2003). One of the most common approaches to promoting women's empowerment has been through microfinance programmes, and perhaps nowhere this method been adopted more enthusiastically than in the state of Andhra Pradesh (AP). Mooij (2002) argues that with over five million women organised into half a million groups, AP accounts for approximately 40 per cent of women's self-help groups (SHGs) internationally.[1] Established by the Department of Women Development & Child Welfare with support from UNICEF in the 1980s, groups have proliferated since 1990s. They include the US $530 million World Bank funded *Velugu* (Telugu for 'light')[2] or District Poverty

---

1. It is important however to contextualise these numbers within the overall population size of a country—Andhra Pradesh is India's fifth most populous state with over 75 million inhabitants.
2. Velugu's name was changed to Indira Kranthi Patham (IKP) in 2005.

Initiatives Programme (DPIP), which has now been scaled up to cover all districts in the state, as well as a number of independent non-governmental organisation (NGO) led programmes (Batliwala and Dhanraj, 2004).

These initiatives have generated widespread attention and debate about the nature of linkages between micro-level transformations in gender relations at the household and community level on the one hand, and macro-level economic development on the other (Kabeer, 2001; Mayoux, 2002). However, only limited systematic attention has been paid to the international impacts of these poverty reduction efforts. In what ways, is childhood poverty affected by shifting power relations among men and women and changes in the resources at their disposal? Although governments and donors typically group women and children well-being together, empirical literature suggests that a reduction in aggregate poverty levels does not automatically translate into diminished poverty for children (Marshall, 2003) and that the relationship between women and children rights is complex (Durrant and Sathar, 2000; Glick, 2002). It is important to evaluate more carefully how women empowerment through microcredit programmes affects children's welfare.[3] What are the transmission mechanisms? Are they automatic, or the result of deliberate complementary policy strategies? Does an improvement in women's status lead to changes in some dimensions of children's poverty but not others? Are there circumstances in which women and children rights come into conflict? For example, does women empowerment lead to a reconfiguration of their social opportunities and caring responsibilities? If so, how can poverty reduction strategies best mitigate these?

Linking Women Empowerment and Child Well-Being: Conceptualising Empowerment

Conceptualising power as a relational concept that operates at the personal, intra-household, community, national and international levels, feminist theorists have identified four aspects of power: 'power from

3. We wish to emphasise that the intention of this paper is not to call into question the value of initiatives to empower women as an end goal. The authors are fully supportive of efforts to address gender inequalities. The objective of the paper is analytically distinct—we wish to evaluate in what ways different dimensions of women's empowerment affect childhood poverty.

within', 'power to', 'power with' and 'power over' (Wong, 2003). 'Power within' refers to personal psychological power, and empowerment is the process whereby someone develops a sense of self-confidence and self-respect that was previously lacking. It is critical in terms of overcoming internalised oppressions, which often underpin more tangible and structural forms of power. 'Power to' is the capacity to make decisions and take action to change one's life's circumstances. This is typically linked to notions of human capital development stemming from access to economic resources, information, education and other services. 'Power with' focusses on collective action, and the ability to solve problems and claim citizenship rights through cooperation and networks. 'Power over', however, can be viewed as both negative and positive. It can be negative in the sense that it entails forcing others to do something against their will, but such power may be necessary to overcome unequal power structures and bring about more fundamental social, political and economic transformation (Kabeer, 2001; Mosedale, 2005).

Ideally this fourfold framework should be seen as inter-connected and dynamic, and about both process and outcomes (Kabeer, 1998). However, real world efforts to promote women empowerment have tended to be less holistic, with many initiatives in the 1980s and 1990s focussing predominantly on women's financial self-reliance and human capital development (primarily education). Wong (2003) argues that the emphasis on individual 'power to' was framed within an instrumentalist approach whereby the underlying objective was to improve market efficiency by creating linkages with the poor. The proliferation of microcredit and income-generating programmes for women during this period is emblematic of this trend.

The late 1990s and 2000s saw a broadening of the conceptualisation of empowerment to include a power with dimension, as scholars of social capital recognised that social networks and relationships could complement or even compensate for limited material (financial, human, natural) assets/capital (Grootaert, 1998; Ellis, 2000). Thus the design of women self-help group programmes started to incorporate not only capacity-building in economic management, but also a new paradigm involving citizenship rights and the important role of civil society acting together to ensure that service providers and authorities meet their service delivery responsibilities

(Robinson, 2007). Batliwala and Dhanraj (2004) argue that the successful expansion of programmes focussing on women's economic empowerment came at the expense of women's time and the space and energy to challenge broader political structures.

This is clearly at odds with Mosedale's (2005) conceptual work on empowerment which highlights that empowerment is a multidimensional process, 'whereby women redefine gender roles in ways which extend their possibilities for being and doing'. Similarly, Wong (2003) contends that because the World Bank-led model of empowerment and poverty reduction has ignored the 'power over' dimension of power, it has been limited to working within the confines of and even reinforcing 'prevailing power distribution and inequalities' rather than tackling patterns of social exclusion and the gendered division of labour. Lastly, Kabeer's (2001) work on microfinance models and their impact on different dimensions of women empowerment highlights the dangers of a 'one-size-fits-all' approach to empowerment. Thus, empowerment to enjoy individual freedoms may take on different connotations in different socioeconomic and cultural contexts. For example, if restricted physical mobility is associated with higher-class/status, as lower-class women gain greater economic empowerment, they may opt to self-restrict their movement in public spaces in order to avoid the stigma of poverty (Durrant and Sathar, 2000).

Women Empowerment and Impacts on Child Poverty

Linkages between women and children's status or welfare are theoretically and empirically complex. Given women's traditional responsibility for the care economy, it is often assumed that advances in women's status will have a positive spillover impact on child's well-being through access to greater power and resources in the private and public spheres. However, the mechanisms through which these effects are transmitted remain imperfectly understood. The following discussion looks at a number of hypothesised channels and the weight of relevant evidence in each case.

First, a considerable body of literature demonstrates that maternal education—a critical dimension of women empowerment—is positively associated with better child education, health and nutrition outcomes (Barrera, 1990; Glewwe, 1999). However, there is less consensus as to how this relationship works (Durrant and Sathar, 2000). Some studies suggest that maternal education is likely to result in better caring practices that lead to children's improved human development and greater uptake of public services (Barrera, 1990; Mehrotra, 2004). In case of child health and nutrition in particular, other analysts argue that it is not women's educational levels *per se* but rather specific knowledge or information about health and nutritional care that is critical (Thomas *et al.*, 1991). Some scholars have found that individual women's education levels are less important than the overall level of female education at the community level (Escobal *et al.*, 2004). Yet other researchers contend that rather than education *per se* being responsible for greater child well-being, maternal education levels may serve as a proxy for greater intra-household bargaining and decision-making power, and income levels (Desai and Alva, 1998).

A second potential transmission mechanism relates to women's economic empowerment. The argument made here is that when women have access to greater financial resources not only can it improve women's position within the household but they are also more likely to invest on their children compared to men (Smith *et al.*, 2003; UNICEF, 2007). However, depending on whether the source of women's income is home-based or located outside the home, improved finances may come at the cost of reduced quantity and quality of caring time for children and/or a greater work burden, especially for older (female) children (Leslie, 1989). Although women may be responsible for managing a triple work burden, empirical evidence suggests that in the absence of accessible and affordable child care, children typically share this burden too (Schroeder, 2000). This is particularly the case given that too rarely are women's empowerment initiatives complemented by awareness-raising programmes among the rest of the community about the need to view child welfare as a joint household and community responsibility (World Bank, 2006).

Increased intra-household decision-making power is a third important channel of influence. It is hypothesised that, as a result of greater economic resources, psychological confidence and/or knowledge, women empowerment may translate into better outcomes for children because mothers are more likely to advocate for their children's interests in contexts of intra-household bargaining and to be taken seriously by their male partners. This may take the form of negotiating for greater material investments on sons and daughters (Haddad *et al.*, 1997). However, women's positive role is certainly not universal, and in some contexts has been found to be negligible or more conservative than that of their male counterparts (Hobcraft, 1993; Mayoux, 2002). Indian District Poverty Initiatives Programme (DPIP) mid-term assessment (World Bank, 2006) indicates that there has been a considerable reduction in child labour among the children of women who are members of *Velugu* self-help groups, but this resulted from the inclusion of children's school enrollment as a non-negotiable condition of membership. By contrast, Galab *et al.* (2006) found that there was no positive correlation between self-help group membership and child's nutritional status, suggesting that the transmission mechanisms between women empowerment and different children's rights deprivations resulting from poverty are diverse and complex, and that there may be trade-offs between them in some cases.

Improved gender equality within the household may also have complex roles in relation to inter-generational transmissions of poverty. On one hand, a number of scholars emphasise the important effects of women empowerment in reducing chronic poverty. Bhargava *et al.* (2005) highlight the close association between long-term poverty and lower prioritisation of education, especially for girls, and norms of adolescent marriage and early pregnancy in Rajasthan, India. Similarly, Castaneda and Aldaz-Carroll (1999) argue that improving women's access to education and family planning to limit family size are critical for interrupting inter-generational poverty transfers in the Latin American context.

Finally, greater individual and household-level empowerment may spill over into women community-level empowerment and a more active role in demanding or even providing better child-related services. As women become more confident, mobile and knowledgeable about their citizenship rights, the hypothesis is that they may be more inclined to press service providers and authorities to become more accountable (Molyneux, 1985). While there is certainly a substantial body of literature that provides empirical evidence of this positive relationship (O'Connor *et al.*, 1999; Jackson and Pearson, 1998), there is also a growing recognition among analysts that women with positions of political power will not necessarily advocate for progressive social policies that will improve the lot of poor children and their families (Cornwall *et al.*, 2004).

Research Methods

Four *mandals*[4]—three rural and one urban—were selected across the three main agro-climatic regions of Andhra Pradesh on the basis of: (a) community poverty status and human development indicators and (b) a composite social capital index, capturing group membership, access to social support and involvement in collective action.[5] The four sites are:

1. Amrabad *mandal*, Mahabubnagar district, Telangana region (South).
2. Atlur *mandal*, Cuddapah district, Rayalseema region.
3. Seethampeta *mandal*, Srikakulam district, Coastal Andhra region.
4. Anantapur *mandal*, Anantapur district, Rayalaseema region.

Our qualitative data collection methodology included in-depth semi-structured interviews and focus group discussions (FGDs) with self-help group members and non-members across various caste groups, self-help group leaders at the village, *mandal* and district levels, local men and children in the community, service providers, local government representatives and line department officials. In the course of this study, a team of local research assistants conducted a total of 29 FGDs and 113 semi-structured interviews.

Findings

In order to assess the relationship between women empowerment as a result of self-help group participation and the impacts on child well-being,

4. *Mandals* are territorial and administrative units within the three-tiered structure of local governance in Andhra Pradesh. They are typically composed of 10–20 villages, and 5–10 *mandals* form a district.
5. The Young Lives measurement of maternal social capital is based on a shortened version of Adapted Social Capital Assessment Tool (A-SCAT Tool) developed by Harpham *et al.* (2003 quoted in Harpham *et al.*, 2006), with questions taking a yes/no format. Structural social capital was measured by asking about membership in formal and non-formal groups; social support was defined as material or other assistance received from formal and informal networks; and citizenship referred to involvement in collective initiatives.

each section below begins with a discussion of the evidence we found about different dimensions of women empowerment, before looking at the effects on children.

Psychological Empowerment

An important dimension of empowerment entails facilitating the disempowered to develop a positive sense of identity, self-value and confidence. Interestingly, this 'power within' dimension was highlighted more by upper-caste than lower-caste women. Whereas scheduled caste (SC) and scheduled tribe (ST) respondents focussed on their economic empowerment, backward caste (BC) and other caste (OC) women tended to emphasise changes in their physical mobility that the self-help group programmes had facilitated. This is probably because access to credit is relatively more important to lower-caste women than to their upper-caste counterparts, whose households can be expected to have more options for borrowing money through their social networks. It is also likely linked to the fact that BC and OC women typically face more constraints on their physical mobility.

It should be noted; however, that psychological empowerment does not automatically result from group membership but is closely linked to the type of group leadership and its commitment to capacity-building. In some sites, women members clearly appreciated their leaders, the time they invested in the group and the sense of unity that had been created by a shared sense of confidence in addressing life's challenges. However, in one village in Seethampeta *mandal*, we observed that self-help group members were unwilling to share information and seemed afraid of their leaders in the focus group format. When we followed up with semi-structured interviews, these women had scant awareness about basic group information such as whether the group was registered, or the loan amounts and repayment schedules. Moreover, they had no interaction with banks or local officials, and in fact were actively discouraged from engaging with the *Velugu* programme. Through further investigation we learned that two OC women had organised tens of independent groups in the area and were keeping a margin of the loans they secured from the banks. In this case, keeping their lower-caste 'clients' passive, ignorant and fearful of more active participation was in the organisers' best interests. As we discuss further, below, this suggests that if microcredit is to foster 'power within' among women participants, then developing effective accountability mechanisms among leaders will be critical.

In terms of links between women's psychological empowerment and child well-being, there has been less discussion in the theoretical literature than on other dimensions of empowerment. On the one hand, feminist analysis on the gendered division of labour would suggest that women's psychological empowerment will not necessarily translate into improved child well-being. It could be argued, for example, that overcoming internalised gendered oppression might lead some women to conclude that they should not have to shoulder primary responsibility for child care and that the burden of care work is standing in the way of personal self-fulfillment. Indeed, this attitude was clearly something that a number of male respondents feared. However, a broad body of empirical evidence suggests that as women become more confident and develop 'power within' they are most likely to address practical gender needs, including demanding better child-related services (Molyneux, 1985). This was the case in the overwhelming majority of our interviews with self-help group participants, where a new sense of self-value and self-esteem emerged as a necessary (but insufficient) condition for women to take action at the household and community levels to improve their children's well-being.

Empowered to Take Action

The following discussion analyses the relationship between self-help group members' access to economic and information resources and intra-household dynamics.

Financial Empowerment

A substantial number of our respondents confirmed that they invested the money they had access to as a result of self-help group membership—either from group savings or loans from banks or government programmes—in covering child-related expenses. These included school fees and supplies, access to health care services and dowry payments. Indeed, for many women, being able to support their children better was their *raison d'être* for group membership. This was also triangulated by interviews with members' families and government officials. These findings are also in keeping with the results from the DPIP mid-term assessment, which shows that very poor and poor DPIP self-help group members are more likely to invest greater amounts on both their sons' and daughters' education (see Table 4.1). Although this trend is reversed in the non-poor category, it seems likely that a threshold effect is at work. That is, non-poor women may have access to other financial resources and need not participate in self-help groups in order to be able to invest in their children's well-being.

Nevertheless, because of the small loan amounts and the infrequent availability of microcredit, the potential of women to make a significant difference to household consumption is still relatively limited. Indeed, although women were initially attracted to self-help groups because of the promise of income-generating opportunities, a number of them expressed their frustration at the paucity of loans, limited loan amounts and lack of employment opportunities. Among the self-help groups that we profiled, approximately 70 per cent of the groups affiliated to *Velugu* and DWCRA have received loans once (approximately Rs 2,000–2,500 per capita) but most of the new groups as well as OC groups had not received any loan. Among the independent groups, only approximately 40 per cent had received a loan, with the exception of two active women leaders in Seethampeta who had mobilised loans from bank authorities for most of the groups they had established. Moreover, while microfinance has been promoted as a mechanism to reduce the dependence of poor families on exploitative structures of debt repayment, our findings suggest that SHGs have not gone as far in dismantling these traditional structures of money exchange as was initially envisaged.

Another important limitation on the sustainability of women's financial empowerment through the self-help groups is the fact that a large majority of women used the money to cover specific household expenses rather than as seed capital for more sustainable livelihood options. The reason for this was not necessarily a dearth of entrepreneurial support, but often, a lack of market opportunities. Although we found one example of an independent all-OC self-help group in Amrabad who had used their savings to establish microenterprises such as tailoring, clothes and grocery shops, and other women in Atlur and Seethampeta had established themselves as moneylenders to other women, these were the exceptions rather than the rule and in large part related to the better socioeconomic positioning of the women involved.[6] Our interviews also suggested that participants as well as convenors of the *Velugu* programme in Anantapur had expected that compliance with the self-help group rules would be rewarded with income-generating opportunities, but they had largely been disappointed.[7] This mismatch between expectations and practice was also highlighted in the testimonies of a number of non-members who had previously been self-help group members but had withdrawn either because of their disappointment about limited access to loans or because they had been unable to cope with the repayment schedules.

In short, as we discuss further, one of the broader questions raised by our findings about the limitations of women's economic empowerment is whether the self-help group model has been scaled up at the expense of deepening and consolidating women empowerment and in turn the potential to reduce some of the manifestations of childhood poverty.

Intra-Household Decision-Making

Both women and men we interviewed noted that there had been a shift in the intra-household balance of power following women's participation in self-help groups. As a result of greater economic independence, they had been able to assert some decision-making power over issues such as their children's—and especially their daughters'—education, household consumption, access to health services and their children's marriage partners. Although husbands are still reported to have the final say on most matters and in some cases forced their wives to reverse their decisions where they had taken these without consulting their spouse. Therefore, participation in decision-making in and of itself is viewed as a significant change and should therefore not be underestimated.

6. In contrast to other SHGs where members were investing an average of Rs 30 each per month into a group savings pot, these members were saving a monthly average of Rs 600 each. This suggests that these women come from households with markedly better socioeconomic conditions (also confirmed by our quantitative data) and that there is therefore a need for analysts to pay greater attention to the caste and class positioning of examples of sustainable SHGs.

7. We encountered one exception: 'After establishing these groups we benefited a lot. We were sanctioned for laying the roads here...' (Anantapur, member).

Table 4.1

Average Education Expenditure (Rupees per Child) among Members of DPIP Self-Help Groups and Non-Members

Age	Boy		Girl	
	Non-member	Member	Non-member	Member
Poorest of the poor				
5–9	251.41	343.61	186.26	279.69
10–14	441.48	433.97	216.41	256.09
15–18	189.6	253.43	211.06	181.88
All	320.94	367.76	204.05	255.52
Poor				
5–9	380.71	392.52	210.7	424.44
10–14	464.26	522.2	288.23	368.08
15–18	341.96	629.79	183	216.49
All	410.12	504.24	239.85	369.48
Not-so-poor				
5–9	648.21	459.8	329.78	478.95
10–14	1,375.05	1,187.35	424.96	625.75
15–18	996.33	555.03	315.79	1,081.82
All	1,069.79	830.76	365.88	688.46
Non-poor				
5–9	1,367.26	509.05	556.33	236.42
10–14	1,398.56	724.88	931.42	696.87
15–18	1,740.95	1,198.56	2,033.96	552.86
All	1,455.51	719.98	1,125.87	541.31

Source: Dev *et al.*, 2006.

These changes notwithstanding, a number of respondents emphasised that changes in power relations within the family have been short-term and superficial. Rather than rethinking gender roles more fundamentally, some male partners appear to value women's participation in SHGs only for the loans that they might secure. Others similarly explained that their household clout diminished once loans had been utilised. In the case of rural women, some invested on livestock purchases, especially on milch animals, which provided more lasting, *albeit* modest, income. Children were sometimes called upon to take care of the livestock, but the time this needed was not perceived to be too burdensome. Urban women respondents involved in income-generating activities make the most substantial contribution to household income but they similarly denied that their children had to shoulder any significant additional work burden. This may be because the enterprises are largely home-based and thus facilitated women's ability to balance their domestic and financial roles without major household implications. Mothers' own-time allocation priorities also play a role.

Empowerment through Knowledge

Many of the women interviewed reported that their awareness of, and access to, information about child rearing practices and uptake of public services had improved as a result of their self-help group participation. Focus group discussions with members' male partners confirmed this finding, although some noted that women empowerment has also been enhanced through exposure to media and by affirmative action programmes for women instituted by local governments. Importantly, however, a closer analysis of our data revealed that women involved in *Velugu* and DWCRA self-help groups, and especially those supported by the international NGO, CARE, were more likely to have been exposed to new child-related knowledge than their independent counterparts. Broader social development focus of government- and donor-supported programmes is important in ensuring that women's empowerment contributes to a positive spillover effect on child well-being.

Our research highlighted, however, a number of important limitations to these broader social development programmes. First, SHG members tend to be mothers with older children, raising doubts about whether information on early child care and development is reaching women who need it most. The key obstacle to participation by mothers with young infants is the lack of child care possibilities to allow these women to attend meetings. Second, the training and capacity-building programmes offered to SHG women appear to be narrow in scope. Although many women noted that they had received training on how to handle the financial accounts of the group by banks and/or government agencies, many fewer had received vocational training and when they did a number of them complained that it was not in keeping with local resource realities. Most surprisingly, however, there was little mention of literacy training—indeed, some men pointed out that the programmes were using the rhetoric of literacy but in reality this was very superficial and women were only learning how to sign their names for loans. This would appear to be a serious weakness in the programme design if women are being conceptualised as the transmitters of new attitudes about familial development and knowledge about government services and programmes. It is even more concerning, given that women's overall literacy rate in Andhra Pradesh is just 33 per cent compared with a national average of 54 per cent for women. Equally important, although awareness-raising initiatives linked to SHGs seemed to advance children rights to survival and development to a certain extent, our research suggests that there have been only limited positive spillover impacts on children's rights to protection and participation.

In terms of protection issues, reducing exploitative forms of child labour has been identified as an important poverty alleviation goal in Andhra Pradesh. *Velugu* and DWCRA explicitly recognise that in addition to the matter of raising household incomes, citizens need to be made aware of the importance of education and of the long-term costs of child labour to human capital development. SHGs have been seen as an integral communication channel through which to spread this message. In the case of *Velugu* ensuring that children's school attendance is a non-negotiable condition of SHG membership, while in Amrabad *mandal* a local NGO, the Centre for Youth and Social Studies, works with SHGs as their main entry point in ensuring that school dropouts are enrolled in 'bridge schools'.[8] Mass communication methods, such as street theatre and role-

---

8. Bridge schools are a type of preparatory school, in which children who have dropped out of school or who have never been to school can attend before they rejoin mainstream schools. Extra coaching and guidance is provided for these children in the bridge schools to bring them up to the educational standard of children in regular schools. We found in Amrabad site that a considerable number of SHG members' children were attending such schools, suggesting that the message about the importance of education is indeed having an impact. This has been facilitated by government and other development agencies' prioritisation of child labour prevention efforts in the area; given that it is an important supply area for child domestic workers and agricultural labour.

play, have been used to convey the importance of investing in child's education. However, it should be noted that we did not find any evidence of clear monitoring systems within the SHG system and moreover, that according to Department of Education records, the proportion of girl child dropouts above fifth class ranges from 10 per cent (Cuddapah) to 50 per cent (Mahabubnagar).

In terms of HIV/AIDs we only encountered one group that had been exposed to HIV/AIDs prevention training and this was due to the private initiative of the group leader; similarly we found little discussion on violence against children or child trafficking. When we probed further about the issue of intra-household violence, a number of women noted that stigma prevents discussion about such issues and that women tend to be reluctant to 'bad-mouth' their husbands in public. This indicates that unless a broader conceptualisation of child's rights is explicitly integrated into the self-help group programmes, it would be misguiding to assume that as a result of women empowerment initiatives, these dimensions of children well-being will automatically be addressed. Lastly, we did not find any spillover effect between women's increased community participation and the development of more opportunities for children to have a voice in community affairs.

Empowered to Take Collective Action

Several women themselves cited good examples of joint action to tackle child poverty issues, including chipping in to support the costs of emergency health care for the child of a group member and challenging an abusive husband collectively rather than leaving it to local police. But we equally encountered a number of important barriers to the realisation of the 'power with' aspect of empowerment through self-help groups. The first difficulty that emerged repeatedly was a deficit of time. There was also recognition that developing group unity was neither easy nor automatic. For a sizeable number of women the group was useful for accessing credit but served no wider purpose. And in other cases, group leadership and purposive mobilisation by external government or donor agencies was critical for spurring on collective action. This was particularly evident in the case of Seethampeta *mandal* where the international NGO, CARE, appeared to play a crucial role in promoting women's action around public service uptake and monitoring.[9] Finally, it is worth noting that although involvement in some of these initiatives was initially mandatory, our results suggest that, over time, women did seem to develop a genuine interest in government programmes and what they could offer their children.

Empowerment that Transforms Unequal Structures

Only small minorities of SHG members interviewed were members of local village committees or participated actively in the *gram sabhas*. A number of respondents pointed out that, unlike SHG membership, meaningful participation in local politics is hampered by caste, class and gender barriers. Other women noted that meetings tend to be male-dominated affairs and thus there were limited opportunities for them to participate. Part of the problem here may rest with an overall emphasis within SHG programmes such as *Velugu* on quantitative expansion rather than qualitative improvements in group functioning. While *Velugu* programme coordinators emphasise that expanding the number of groups is important in terms of answering popular demand and maximising the outreach of SHG programmes to poor communities, it is important to note that they are incentivised to take this approach, as they receive a commission for placing new loans. Similar incentives, however, do not exist for social development and political empowerment components of SHGs, resulting in a prioritisation of the quantity of loans secured. An additional and related concern linked to the expansion focus is that *anganwadi*[10] workers are being asked by government officials to set up SHGs in the communities within which they work. However, the *anganwadi* workers we interviewed emphasised that they were already over-

9. Note, however, that close links to non-governmental agents were sometimes seen as an impediment to better relationships with governmental authorities, as one governmental key informant made clear: 'All the Self Help Groups are working under the control of private agencies. Their programmes and activities are not controlled by government authorities. If they come under the control of the Mandal level authorities, they may change more and more.'

10. *Anganwadis* are the primary community-level unit for implementing the government's Integrated Child Development Scheme (ICDS). The programmes implemented through the *anganwadi* target children aged 0–6 years, adolescent girls and lactating mothers. They include supplementary nutrition, immunisation, non-formal education, referral services and maternal and child health.

burdened with work (given limited resources and a large target population) and were thus not interested in having a leadership role in these groups.

The quality of linkages developed with service providers is another area of some concern. On the one hand there are clear positive examples: *angawadi*/village-level public health officers used their SHG contacts to fulfill their child vaccination programme targets and tended to interact more regularly with SHG members regarding child nutrition and health issues. On the other hand, there are also increasing expectations of SHGs fulfilling a community watchdog role *vis-à-vis* the distribution of ration cards from the public distribution system, the disbursement of widows' pensions, and the provision of services linked to government service programmes such as food preparation for school mid-day meals and meals for the National Rural Employment Guarantee Scheme.[11] Although this greater involvement in community affairs can be seen as a positive development, it simultaneously raises important questions about the time and capacity of members to meet these expectations. In the communities, where we carried out fieldwork, none of the women had received any training in capacity-building relating to these new functions. If local women lack the requisite capacities to effectively carry out this work, there is thus a risk that women empowerment initiatives may be undermined as a result of these new demands. Moreover, even though the SHGs are provided with nominal financial compensation for the meal preparation, it seems the government has identified this as a way of capitalising on women's cheap and underutilised labour.[12] This programme has not been operating for long, hence, it will be important to monitor whether SHG members see it as a valuable use of their time, and the impact that such participation is having, in turn, on their children.

11. This scheme was launched in February 2006 and assures 100 days of work per annum to all citizens. To prevent migration of people from rural areas during seasonal crises, the scheme provides work such as building community assets, roads, infrastructure etc., in one's home area. There are plans to involve SHG women to provide worksite child care facilities and to deliver drinking water to the workers for which they would be given some financial compensation.

12. The labour costs represent nearly 50 per cent of the total cost budgeted for each child under the mid-day meal programme. (The cost of mid-day meals is Rs 2.10 per child, with Re 1 allocated to cooking costs).

By and large, networking with local authorities did not seem to have penetrated to rank-and-file members. A number of reasons for this emerged from the focus group discussions and key informant discussions. Decision-makers are often located outside the village and thus there are more limited opportunities to lobby for change, especially for lower-caste/class women, many of whom work as daily labourers. While community leaders such as the *mandal* development officer, head of the *panchayat*, bank officials and NGO coordinators emphasised that they had regular (often monthly) contact with SHGs, this appears to have been only with SHG leaders.

Perhaps more importantly, members generally seemed to be unaware of these linkages, suggesting that even if leaders were representing 'the interests' of their members, the articulation of such interests was not being solicited in a participatory manner. This could be linked to the fact that a number of leaders are using their position of SHG leader as a springboard for wider political participation. Our fieldwork coincided with the period for electoral candidate registration, and in several sites, SHG leaders were registering their candidacies. Nevertheless, overall, there seemed to be very little evidence of the self-help groups having transformed into formal political life.

Conclusions and Policy Implications

The central motive of this paper was the need for a better understanding of the linkages between women empowerment through self-help groups and changes in child well-being. Overall, our research suggests that efforts to empower women through mobilisation into self-help groups have had some positive *albeit* limited effects on child well-being. There have been improvements in women intra-household decision-making power which have often translated into greater investment in child's nutrition, health and education; greater access to information about child caring practices and uptake of government services; and some collective efforts to monitor decentralised service delivery for children. By contrast, expectations that women self-help group participation would lead to significantly improved linkages with local authorities and a restructuring of existing power relations have been largely unmet. Moreover, positive changes at the individual, household and community level were unevenly distributed across groups, sites and individual women. This suggests that more attention in terms of both policy design and implementation is needed to ensure that certain prerequisites are in place if self-help groups are to fulfill their development and poverty-alleviation potential. Lastly, our hypothesised concerns that women's economic empowerment might result in reduced quantity and quality of caring time for children without broader changes in familial and state attitudes and practices towards child care were not borne out. However, this was largely due to self-help group programmes' limited provision of income-generating opportunities for women rather than an absence of competing tensions.

Sustainable Income-Generation Opportunities

The stated purpose of SHGs is economic empowerment through microcredit and microenterprises, but our findings revealed that loans tend to be infrequent and small, and are typically used by women to cover basic household needs rather than as seed money for more sustainable income-generation activities. If women are to be empowered to create more democratic household and community decision-making processes, however, more consistent support and context-appropriate capacity-building will be required so that women can better access income-generating opportunities. In this regard, the current DWCRA and *Velugu's* emphasis on expanding self-help group coverage rather than promoting group consolidation merits reconsideration.

Ensuring Expectations are in Line with Resource and Capacity Constraints

Expanding women's community involvement through the introduction of new watchdog and service delivery roles could be potentially beneficial to SHG members' social and political empowerment. However, government officials and donors need to be mindful that the fulfillment of these new roles will be contingent on the provision of related capacity-building initiatives, especially more substantive literacy programmes, and also adequate resources. If not, advances in women's empowerment may be undermined owing to under-delivery of these new activities and/or over-burdening women's time to the detriment of their own and their families' well-being. Internationally, there is now a considerable body of evidence about the toll that women's triple burden—juggling productive, reproductive and community labour—can have. It is therefore important to question whether initiatives to promote women involvement in service delivery and monitoring are underpinned by a commitment to more inclusive and effective service provision or are instead substituting for under-resourced public services.

In this vein, initiatives to introduce gender and child-sensitive budget monitoring will constitute critical new tools in advancing both analysis and policy practice in this area. In Andhra Pradesh, monitoring of resources flowing from government departments to child-related service provision could be complemented by focussing on the resources that are being channelled to child development through alternative service providers, particularly SHGs, to ensure that they are adequately funded to undertake these activities. Raising SHG leaders' and members' awareness of the potential to demand budgetary support could be a good way of taking advantage of these active grassroot structures to reach more children, in a more sustainable way. In particular, *mandal* and district level local bodies are mandated to allocate 15 per cent of their revenues to women and child welfare activities. SHGs could become active monitoring agents to ensure part of this money is used to support the child welfare activities they undertake.

Monitoring SHG Practices

Our findings underscored important differences across SHGs in terms of the empowerment opportunities—both financial and non-financial—that they provide to women. In part these emerged as differences between government/donor programmes and independent self-help groups, but we also noted significant differences across sites with greater penetration and activity rates in some villages than others. Clearly it is important for programmes to be adapted to context-specific realities and it would be inappropriate to advocate for a 'one-size-fits-all' approach. However, it also seems important to unpack discourses about the linkages between women's self-help groups and broader poverty-alleviation and social development goals, and ensure that a set of minimum standards or common code of practice including coordination of regular capacity-building programmes—such as literacy, legal literacy, child care practices, vocational training, and awareness about citizenship rights and government services—is monitored and evaluated on a regular basis. Rather than providing these services directly, the government, donor and NGO agencies involved in implementing self-help group programmes could play a coordination and linking role among other service providers and identify needs gaps.

Being Explicit about Tackling Childhood Poverty

Our findings suggest that spillover effects on women and children's broader well-being do not only derive from ripple effects, but often derive from deliberate efforts to provide information and foster awareness about citizenship rights and available public services. Specifically, a significant number of groups were involved in promoting child education and countering school dropouts and child labour; given an explicit programmatic emphasis on human capital development, only a small minority was concerned with child protection issues such as familial, school and community violence, trafficking and vulnerability to HIV/AIDS. Our results show that issues of family and community violence and sexuality are largely still shrouded in silence and with few exceptions SHGs have not yet emerged as a forum in which to address these issues. Similarly, while some members had used participation in SHGs as a springboard for involvement in community politics, there were no signs of a spillover effect on the importance of children's right to voice their views and to be heard. Taking lessons from and perhaps establishing linkages with the successful local youth parliaments in Karnataka state could be one possible way forward here.

Increasing Male Awareness of Ways to Tackle Childhood Poverty

Access to credit has equipped many women with greater influence within the household, but gender relations within the family remain unequal, with men still enjoying final decision-making power. Efforts to advance social justice will therefore require that government and non-government agencies involved in community mobilisation also pay attention to changing men's attitudes, including their responsibilities regarding their children's well-being. The reasons for aiming microcredit at women (women economic empowerment, altering intra-household distribution of power and resources, lower risk of non-payment, etc.) are sound, but the broader social development dimensions of DWCRA and *Velugu* are still largely framed within a 'women in development' paradigm rather than being informed by a gender equality perspective.

The Challenge of Political Empowerment

Finally, self-help groups have succeeded in mobilising women to be more frugal and better managers of scarce household resources, to avail themselves of government services and to serve as useful channels for the implementation of broader development and poverty-alleviation initiatives, but we found evidence in only a handful of cases that this type of participation was leading to greater involvement in other political spaces. As women participation in self-help groups is an important first step, but will remain limited in impact, unless supported by a longer-term investment in democratic deepening (including substantive decentralisation) and broader initiatives to address entrenched power structures.

References

Barrera, A. (1990). "The Role of Maternal Schooling and Its Interaction with Public Health Programs in Child Health Production", *Journal of Development Economics* 32: 69–91.

Batliwala, S. and D. Dhanraj (2004). "Gender Myths that Instrumentalise Women: A View from the Indian Frontline", in *Repositioning Feminisms in Development, Institute of Development Studies Bulletin* 35 (4): 11–18. University of Sussex.

Bhargava, P., K. Mathur and S. Rajagopal (2005). "Understanding Chronic Poverty in Rajastan", *CHIP Report* 16. London: CHIP. *http://www.childhoodpoverty.org/index.php?action=publicationdetails&id=97*

Castaneda, T. and E. Aldaz-Carroll (1999). "The Intergenerational Transmission of Poverty: Some Causes and Policy Implications", *Inter-American Development Bank Discussion Paper*.

Cornwall, A., E. Harrison and A. Whitehead (2004). "Repositioning Feminisms in Gender and Development", *Institute of Development Studies Bulletin* 35 (4).

Desai, S. and S. Alva (1998). "Maternal Education and Child Health: Is there a Strong Causal Relationship?", *Demography* 35(1): 71-81, February.

Dev, Mahendra, S. Galab, P. Prudhvikar Reddy, D. Sree Rama Raju, K.S. Reddy, C. Ravi, M. Gopinath Reddy, Suri Babu, G.K. Mitra (2006). *Mid-Term Appraisal of Andhra Pradesh District Poverty Initiatives Project*. Andhra Pradesh: Centre for Economic and Social Studies. May.

Durrant, V. and Z. Sathar (2000). "Greater Investments in Children through Women's Empowerment: A Key to Demographic Change in Pakistan", *Working Paper* 137, Washington DC: National Research Council. Committee on Population.

Ellis, F. (2000). *Rural Livelihoods and Diversity in Developing Countries*. Oxford: Oxford University Press.

Escobal, J., P. Suárez, S. Huttly, F. Lanata, M.E. Penny and E. Villar (2004). "Does Having a Newborn Child Affect Income Diversification Opportunities? Evidence from the Peruvian Young Lives Study", *Young Lives Working Paper* 24. London: Save the Children UK.

Galab, S., P. Antony, I. Wilson, N. Jones, A. McCoyn and R. Sreerama (2006). "Exploring Linkages Between Maternal Social Capital and Children's Nutritional Status in Andhra Pradesh", *Young Lives Working Paper*. London: Save the Children. UK.

Glewwe, P. (1999). "Why does Mother's Schooling Raise Child Health in Developing Countries: Evidence from Morocco", *Journal of Human Resources* 34 (1): 124–59.

Glick, P. (2002). "Women's Employment and its Relation to Children's Health and Schooling in Developing Countries: Conceptual Links, Empirical Evidence and Policies", *Cornell Food and Nutrition Policy Program Working Paper* No. 131. RAND.

Grootaert, C. (1998). "Social Capital: The Missing Link?", *World Bank Social Capital Initiative Working Paper* No. 3. Washington, DC: World Bank.

Haddad, L., J. Hoddinott and H. Alderman (1997). *Intrahousehold Resource Allocation in Developing Countries: Models, Methods, and Policies*. Washington, DC: International Food Policy Research Institute.

Harpham, T., M. Reichenhein, R. Oser *et al.* (2003). "Measuring Mental Health in a Cost-Effecive Manner", *Health Policy and Planning* 18: 344-349.

Harpham, T., Mary J. Dc Silva and Tran Tuan (2006). "Maternal Social Capital and Child Health in Vietnam", *Journal of Epidemiology and Community Health* 60(10): 865-871. London, UK.

Hobcraft, J. (1993). "Women's Education, Child Welfare and Child Survival: A Review of the Evidence", in *Health Transition Review* 3(2).

Jackson, C. and R. Pearson (1998). *Feminist Visions of Development: Gender Analysis and Policy*. Oxford: Routledge.

Kabeer, N. (1998). "'Money Can't Buy Me Love', Re-Evaluating Gender, Credit and Empowerment in Rural Bangladesh", *IDS Discussion Paper* No. 363, Brighton: Institute of Development Studies, University of Sussex. *www.ids.ac.uk/ids/bookshop/dp/Dp363.pdf*

Kabeer, N. (2001). "Conflicts Over Credit: Re-Evaluating the Empowerment Potential of Loans to Women in Rural Bangladesh", in *World Development* 63–84.

———. (2003). "Gender Mainstreaming in Poverty Eradication and the Millennium Development Goals: A Handbook for Policy-Makers and other Stakeholders", Commonwealth Secretariat.

Leslie, J. (1989). "Women's Time: A Factor in the Use of Child Survival Technologies?", *Health Policy and Planning* 4 (1): 1–16.

Marshall, J. (2003). "Children and Poverty—Some Questions Answered", *CHIP Briefing* 1, London: Save the Children UK. *www.savethechildren.org.uk/scuk_cache/scuk/cache/cmsattach/1660_CHIPBriefing1.pdf*

Mayoux, L. (2002). "Microfinance and Women's Empowerment: Rethinking 'Best Practice'", *Development Bulletin* 57: 67-81.

Mehrotra, S. (2004). "Improving Child Wellbeing in Developing Countries: What Do We Know? What can be done?", *CHIP Report 9*. London: CHIP.

Mooij, J. (2002). "Welfare Policies and Politics: A Study of Three Government Interventions in Andhra Pradesh, India", ODI *Working Paper* 181, London: Overseas Development Institute.

Molyneux, M. (1985). "Mobilization Without Emancipation? Women's Interests, State and Revolution in Nicaragua", *Feminist Studies* 11, Summer.

Mosedale, S. (2005). "Assessing Women's Empowerment: Towards a Conceptual Approach", *Journal of International Development* 7 (2): 243–57.

O'Connor, J., A. Schola Orloff and S. Shaver (1999). *States, Markets, Families: Gender, Liberalism and Social Policy: Australia, Canada, Great Britain and the US.* Cambridge: Cambridge University Press.

Robinson, M. (2007). "Decentralising Service Delivery", *IDS Bulletins* 38(1).

Schroeder, K. (2000). "Spatial Constraints on Women's Work in Tarija, Bolivia", *The Geographical Review* 90(2): 191–205.

Smith, Lisa C., U. Ramakrishnan, A. Ndiaye, L. Haddad and R. Martorell (2003). "The Importance of Women's Status for Child Nutrition in Developing Countries", *Research Report* 131, Washington, DC: International Food Policy Research Institute.

Thomas, D., J. Strauss and M. Henriques (1991). "How Does Mother's Education Affect Child Height?", *The Journal of Human Resources* 26(2): 183-211. (Spring).

UNICEF (2007). *Women and Children: The Double Dividend of Gender Equality. The State of the World's Children 2007*. New York: UNICEF.

Whitehead, A. and M. Lockwood (1999). "Gender in the World Bank's Poverty Assessments: Six Case Studies from Sub–Saharan Africa", *United Nations Research Institute for Social Development (UNRISD) Discussion Paper* No. 99, Geneva: UNRISD *ftp://ftp.unicc.org/unrisd/outgoing/dp/dp99.doc*

Wong, K.F. (2003). "Empowerment as a Panacea for Poverty—Old Wine in New Bottles? Reflection on the World Bank's Conception of Power", *Progress in Development Studies* 3(4): 307-22.

World Bank (2006). "What About Men And Gender? World Bank Publication Calls For *'Menstreaming'* Development".*http://web.worldbank.org/WBSITE/EXTERNAL/TOPICS/EXTGENDER/0,contentMDK:21101519~menuPK:336874~pagePK:64020865~ piPK:149114~theSitePK:336868,00.html. Accessed Feb 2007.*

5 Women Empowerment and Functioning of Formal and Informal Institutions

The Case of Indira Kranthi Patham of Andhra Pradesh

S. Galab, P. Prudhvikar Reddy and D. Sree Rama Raju

Context

The notion of empowerment has been captured by several researchers. Empowerment refers to the process by which those who have been denied the ability to make choices acquire such ability (Galab *et al.*, 2003). Empowerment is defined as the powerless gaining power to exercise greater control over the circumstances of their lives. It includes both control over resources and over ideology, extrinsic control and intrinsic capability in terms of greater self-confidence, self-efficacy and inner transformation of one's consciousness to overcome barriers' (Sen and Batliwala, 2000). The concept of empowerment can be explored through three closely interrelated dimensions *viz.*, agency, resources and achievements (Kabeer, 2003).

The informal institutions that govern the civil society and the formal institutions/organisations through which programmes of the government are implemented at the cutting edge level have a lot of bearing on the livelihoods of the poor. However, some of these institutions are not pro-poor in their dispensation. Policymakers are facing a big challenge in reorienting these institutions, both formal and informal, to make them sensitive to the needs of the poor. In this direction, the institution of poor women under Indira Kranthi Patham (IKP) tried to orient these institutions to cater to the needs of the poor and the poorest. This paper is an attempt in that direction.

Link between Institutions (Formal and Informal) and Poverty

The formal institutions include government schools, hospitals, public distribution system (PDS) shops, *anganwadi* and all other institutions of the line departments of the government, and the financial institutions like banks and cooperatives.

The effectiveness of government programmes meant for the reduction of poverty in all its forms by improving livelihoods of poor is mostly determined by the quality of functioning of formal institutions, mediating structures, which implement those programmes. The quality of services, the accessibility and proximity of these institutions influence the quality of functioning of these institutions. Proximity implies nearness of the institution to the poor. The accessibility could depend on the sensitivity of the institution to the needs of the poor.

Apart from the state institutions, a host of informal social institutions/socio-cultural practices condition the ability of different social groups to respond to the opportunities afforded by the programmes. Some of these institutions affect the livelihood choices and the capacity to pursue new opportunities. These institutions can be grouped into three types, *viz.*, institutions promoting caste based discrimination, institutions promoting gender based discrimination and institutions promoting violation of child rights.

Caste Based Discrimination

Untouchability is the caste-based discrimination promoting institution that is in practice in the society. The caste-based discrimination led to social alienation of scheduled castes (SCs). This constraints the participation of SCs in the networks that generate bridging social capital to tackle the conditioning factors that affect livelihoods of SCs. Thus, social capital formation and, consequently, livelihoods are affected negatively due to untouchability. Further, social alienation contributed negatively to the self-esteem and dignity of SCs. This, in turn, constrained the formation of human capital. Thus, the formation of capitals—social and human, and the conversion of these capitals into economic opportunities are constrained severely among SCs. Besides, the discriminatory practices suppress the legitimate demands of this community. Such practices obstruct the vertical socioeconomic mobility of these groups and limit their livelihood options.

Gender Based Discrimination

Jogin system, widow remarriage, polygamy and dowry are the institutions promoting gender discrimination. *Jogin/basvini/mathamma/devadasi* are the traditional and religious practices of dedicating girls from SCs at young age to local deity in temples and thereby institutionalising the practice of prostitution. The practice of dedicating girls to Hindu gods and goddesses at the places of worship has been prevalent in certain parts of the state, particularly among the Madiga community (a scheduled caste). These girls are forced to serve the sexual urges of the landed gentry. Thus, this system has been producing traditional sex workers. Children of *jogins/basvin/mathamma/devadasi* identify with their mothers and hence become single-parent care children. The customers who visit their respective mothers subject them to sexual abuse. Child poverty is another manifestation of this system. Self-esteem and dignity of the families under this system has been at stake. This system coupled with untouchability has been constraining the formation of social and human capital that ultimately affected livelihoods negatively. This system perpetuates poverty and social marginalisation. Widow remarriages provide economic and social security to women. Polygamy and dowry are the manifestation of the patriarchic social values of the society. These institutions have been down sliding the self-esteem and dignity of women. The rising cost of marriages and such other unproductive expenditure often financed by borrowing at high rates of interest, resulted in high indebtedness and eventual dispossession of assets. Despite the increase in school enrollment rates of girls, the poor men and women continue to prefer education of boys' *vis-à-vis* girls. The excessive consumption of alcohol is another important reason attributed by the groups for the growing debt burden.

Violation of Child Rights

Child marriage as a practice is prevalent in the society. The age at marriage, on an average, is found to be 21 years and 17 years for males and females, respectively. Incidence of child marriage is higher, by and large, among SCs and scheduled tribes (STs) compared to backward caste (BC) and other caste (OC); and poor over non-poor in all the project areas, except for Adilabad. Child marriages have affected health and education of women and children. These marriages have serious implications for human development—affects family size, maternal and child health, educational status and earnings profile. Thus, child marriages have constrained the formation of human capital and thereby affecting livelihoods of the poor negatively. Child labour is another institution in the labour market. This is an indication of child poverty which is highly prevalent among the poor. However, a significant proportion of children among non-poor are also involved in child labour. This institution has to be understood beyond the issue of poverty.

Women Empowerment under Indira Kranthi Patham (IKP)

The IKP, earlier *Velugu*, is meant to eradicate poverty in all its forms, including child labour, through establishing of strong and vibrant poor people's institutions—women's self-help groups (SHGs) and their federations—forging alliances between these institutions and non-poor organisations, state, corporate sector and non-governmental organisations (NGOs) to tackle the conditioning factors that are perpetuating poverty, and supporting demand-driven economic projects to increase and consolidate economic gains on sustainable basis. It seeks to not only mobilise communities but also provides support to facilitate linkages with the credit institutions to open investment opportunities for the poor in economic activities. The formation of women SHGs and their federations at village and *mandal* level meant for generating micro-processes to influence the institutions, formal and informal, and policies for improving the livelihoods of the poor, is central to IKP. One of the major expected outcomes of the project is empowerment of women. The project adopts the following framework with regard to women empowerment. Empowerment consists of four dimensions of power that operates at the personal, intra-household and community levels. It includes 'power from within', 'power to', 'power with' and 'power over' (Wong, 2003). 'Power within' refers to personal psychological power, and empowerment is the process whereby someone develops a sense of self-confidence and self-respect that was previously lacking. It is critical in terms of overcoming internalised oppressions, which often underpin more tangible and structural forms of power. 'Power to' is the capacity to make decisions and take action to change one's life's circumstances. This is typically linked to notions of human capital development stemming from access to economic resources, information, education and other services. 'Power with' focusses on collective action, and the ability to solve problems and claim citizenship rights through cooperation and networks. 'Power over', however, can be viewed as both negative and positive. It can be negative in the sense that it entails forcing others to do something against their will, but such power may be necessary to overcome unequal power structures and bring about more fundamental social, political and economic transformation (Kabeer, 2001; Mosedale, 2005).

Considerable emphasis is laid on access to information and social capital in the project since this is an important element of empowerment strategy. The poor usually have no access to information regarding various programmes and institutions and, as a result, they are deprived of the benefits from these initiatives. Simultaneously, improving the density and quality of social relations among women leads to an enhancement in individual as well as in community social capabilities of women. As a result of the increasing level of awareness and social capital that is being generated in the project, it is assumed that women are becoming more empowered.

The project aims at reducing poverty in the project areas through:

- Nurturing self-managed grassroot organisations of the poor and their federations at village, *mandal* and district levels and building their capacity to manage their affairs and enable them to access commercial credit.
- Building the capacity of local institutions (government departments, local bodies and NGOs) to be inclusive of the needs of the poor.
- Supporting investments in sub-projects proposed by grassroots institutions of the poor to accelerate their entry and expand their involvement in social and economic activities.
- Improving access to education for girls to reduce the incidence of child labour among the poor.

- Improving livelihood opportunities to the poor and reduce the percentage of people living below the poverty line.
- Qualitatively change the lives of the poor and eliminate large-scale distress migration.
- Achieving gender equity through the enhanced role of women at household and community levels.
- Achieving changes in entrenched caste and power relations.
- To increase the stake of the poor in social systems through individual and collective actions.

IKP, Women Empowerment and Institutions

The assessment of IKP has indicated that the project interventions have contributed to the four dimensions of women empowerment mentioned above. The last two dimensions of empowerment are considered to examine their impact on the functioning of the formal and informal institutions that reflect unequal power structures.

Empowered to Take Collective Action

The 'power with' dimension of empowerment reflects the role of civil society and social capital in shaping development outcomes (Grootaert, 1998; Wong, 2003). The women groups and their federations engaged themselves to make the formal institutions to be inclusive of poor. The initiatives are in order. There are a number of line departments and other institutions like banks and cooperatives working for the development of village communities. Sensitising these institutions to work for the poor and the downtrodden in a focussed manner is an important task that IKP has taken on itself. The most important aspect of financial convergence is with banks in providing assistance of microfinance to various SHGs. This is the single most important achievement due to convergence efforts.

Child labour is one of the core issues that District Poverty Initiatives Project (DPIP) addressed in earnest, and the results have been very encouraging. Community mobilisation against child labour has been organised in a big way in all the study areas by creating awareness and making it non-negotiable among SHG member households. In addition to this, provision of educational infrastructure in the form of bridge/

residential schools for children in all the districts gave an incentive to their parents to withdraw their children from work and put them back into these schools, thereby mainstreaming them into regular schools. In Chittoor, an institution called *Ammavadi* was initiated on the lines of Integrated Child Development Services (ICDS) centre with the assistance of DPIP. The primary intention for starting such an institution for children below five years is to facilitate elder siblings (above five years) who are staying at home to take care of their younger ones, to attend school. This has paved way for parents to go for work leaving children in *Ammavadi* and elder siblings to attend the school thus reducing child labour.

In the health sector, IKP took proactive role in involving primary health centres (PHCs) and other paramedical staff in addressing the health needs of the poor and the poorest. In Mahabubnagar, the officials working towards eradication of Tuberculosis (TB) were sensitised on the vast social capital that the IKP has in the form of hundreds of self-help groups, village organisation (VOs), *mandal samakhyas* (MSs) and dedicated field workers and activists operating from the villages (Table 5.2).

Empowerment that Transforms Unequal Structures

There is growing attention among analysts of power as to why greater participation of the poor and marginalised is making only slow inroads into a more fundamental transformation of unequal power structures, including caste, class and gender relations. Some scholars attribute this to a disproportionate focus on positive forms of power and insufficient attention to its negative manifestations, including 'power over', among development practitioners. But, the women groups of IKP have focussed on addressing the social institutions/practices that are generating unequal social structures. The initiatives that were taken up by women groups in this regard provide substantial evidence to this. Some of the major initiatives are in order.

IKP efforts in Mahabubnagar against untouchability are quite noteworthy. The extension of Social Discrimination Project (SDP), which was started during South Asia Poverty Alleviation Project (SAPAP) in IKP, is evidence to this. The *jogini/basavini/mathamma* is a practice prevalent in some of the project districts. DPIP along with 'ASRAYA' (an NGO based at Narayanpet working for *jogini* eradication for long time) formed a district

Jogini Vyavastha Vyathirekha Porata Samiti (JVVPS), which took up this cause in a serious manner. As a result, members of MSs and village Dalit organisations formed a joint action committee (JAC) with a few members of Andhra Pradesh Jogini Vyavastha Vyathirekha Porata Samiti to fight against *jogini* system. Eradication of *jogini* (the practice of dedicating girls drawn mostly from SCs and to some extent BCs to Hindu gods and goddesses) is one of the mandatory objectives of DPIP. The JAC took up this issue by performing *Kalajatharas* (road shows) in the region to generate awareness on the evils of the system and its legal abolition in 1988. They also interacted with the government institutions, revenue officials, police officials and activists and involved them in its prevention. DPIP officials conducted *Kalajatharas* for five days to sensitise people on the evils of the system and about the act in *Kurumuthy Jathara* which is the biggest *Jathara* (goes on for 45 days) in the region where lakhs of people gather. It is here that the JAC was able to prevent at least 80 probable cases of young girls being inducted into the system. DPIP staff at village/*mandal* level kept vigil all through the 45 days to curb this practice. DPIP is also involved in this region in forming SHGs for *joginis* and their rehabilitation (housing) is taken up with the help of SC Corporation. *Jogini* women were also elected to SHG leadership positions.

There are a number of other social issues like alcohol consumption, domestic violence, bonded labour, child education, child marriages etc., where DPIP has intervened. In all the districts, the awareness campaign against the ill-effects of liquor consumption on the household health and economy was taken up in a big way among all the SHG members and made non-negotiable. SHG members in turn brought pressure on their menfolk to give up drinking. SHG/VO/MS members have taken concrete action against brewing of alcohol with the help of the Excise Department and to a large extent these efforts have met with success. There is a perceptible change in the attitude of the village folk towards alcohol consumption and there is widespread realisation that this habit ruins the households. Even though the same degree of success has not been reported against other evils like child marriages, domestic violence etc., and the awareness is being generated constantly among the SHG members.

The issues in question are whether all groups have taken up these initiatives wherever they have encountered the manifestations of unequal structures and malfunctioning of formal institutions and whether the initial enthusiasm in this regard is sustained.

Objectives

In the above backdrop, this paper addresses itself to the following specific objectives:

- How far the collective actions undertaken by VO of women contributed to the better functioning of formal institutions?
- How far the collective actions undertaken by the VOs succeeded in eliminating the informal institutions that contributed to the prevalence of unequal social structures? and
- Which groups have undertaken the collective actions to influence the formal and informal institutions?

The study was carried out in the districts of Srikakulam, Ananatapur and Adilabad to investigate the impact of IKP on women empowerment and functioning of formal and informal institutions. An attempt is made to see whether the increased participation has had an impact on public institutions—both formal (such as education and health) and informal (such as practices regarding child labour, education of girl child, untouchability etc.). It also seeks to understand whether the increased empowerment and participation of women has given women increased power to bring about change at the community level. It will consider both the provision of quality public services by local government, and changes in socially undesirable practices. In order to test the hypothesis that there has been an improvement in education, health services and services of *anganwadi* in those areas where VOs have taken an active role in addressing these issues, the following two-stage least square regression (2SLS) is run. Similarly, with regard to the social issues, the collective actions of VOs might have contributed in reduction of evil practices like child marriages, child labour and untouchability. Same statistical tool has been adapted for estimation of the impact of the VOs.

The equation looks as follows:

$$\Delta Service\ i = \beta_D D_i + \sum_{j=1}^{j} \beta_j X_{ji} + \varepsilon_i$$

(i) Where D is a dummy which takes the value of 1 if the VO undertook action on this issue, and χ is a vector of variables which might affect the provision of services to that village: socioeconomic characteristics during the year 2003; distance to district headquarters etc. A significant coefficient of D provides a test of whether action taken by VOs has a significant impact. Finally, to test the hypothesis that there has been a reduction in socially undesirable practices in those areas where VOs have taken an active role in addressing these issues, the following regression is run:

$$\Delta \, Practice \; i = \beta_D D_i + \sum_{j=1}^{J} \beta_j X_{ji} + \varepsilon_i$$

Where D is a dummy which takes the value of 1 if the VO undertook action on this issue, and χ is a vector of variables which might affect changing attitudes with regard the that practice regardless of VO action: socioeconomic characteristics in 2003, heterogeneity of village in 2003 etc. A significant coefficient of D provides a test of whether action taken by VOs has a significant impact.

Functioning of Formal Institutions

The regression analysis indicate a significant positive impact on the functioning of the formal institutions in terms of accessing drinking water, quality of drinking water, quality of education, sanitation condition, quality of internal roads, access to communication, and also appropriation of various benefits from the government, wherever VOs have undertaken actions to address these problems/issues. For instance, when the problems relating to the access to drinking water as well as quality of drinking water are brought to the notice of VOs, and VO, initiate action to address these issues, the results show a positive and significant impact (at 1 per cent level in case of access to drinking water and at 5 per cent level in case of quality of water) (Table 5.3). In other words, the access and quality of drinking water has improved significantly wherever VOs involved. Similar highly significant results (at 1 per cent level) were noticed with respect to the quality of education and quality of internal roads (Table 5.3). VOs have also impacted significantly (at 5 per cent level) on the improvement of sanitation conditions (which is an indirect indicator of health), in accessing better communication and on appropriation of government benefits. Thus, the involvement of VOs had a positive and significant impact on the functioning of the most of the formal institutions at the village level. It also amounts that irrespective of the fact whether the Panchayati Raj Institutions (PRIs) or other institutions initiate action on the functioning of these formal institutions, the involvement of VOs had a positive and significant effect. Village characteristics such as size of the village had a negative impact on quality of education, quality of internal roads, while proportion of SC/ST population of the village had positive impact on access to education. None of the other village characteristics considered for the analysis had any impact (Table 5.3).

The household level data on the percentage of dropouts of boys, girls, and percentage of households reporting better performance of the schools (Table 5.1) which are all indicators of functioning of the schools, show an improvement in all these indicators both for programme participants as well as non-participants; which is in corroboration with the regression results demonstrating the robustness of the analysis. In the light of the above scenario, an attempt has been made to evaluate: whether there is any difference in change (due to programme) in percentage of dropouts and any change in the percentage of households reporting improvement in the performance of schools? The analysis indicates a higher level of decline in the dropouts among the girls in general, particularly in Adilabad indicating the improved service delivery of educational institutions. In other words, enrollment in the schools has gone up both for the participants and non-participants (though high in case of participants) in the project period indicating the positive impact of the programme. Apart from the validation of the performance of the educational institutions, the perceptions of the respondents was also captured and 80 per cent of the respondent participant households reported better performance of the primary schools in the end-term evaluation of DPIP as against 77 per cent in mid-term evaluation conducted in 2004. Across the districts, 87 per cent of the participant households (as against 80 per cent of non-participants) in Srikakulam, followed by Anantapur (81 per cent) and 78 per cent and Adilabad (against 75 per cent of non-participants) reported better performance of primary schools. Thus, there is a clear indication of the improved service delivery of education institutions due to project interventions such as creating awareness among women members on the importance of education, which lead to demand for better quality services from the educational institutions.

It is apt to examine the characteristics of the VOs, which have initiated collective action. The regression results indicate that the higher the age of the VO, higher the collective action for betterment of services like access to communication, appropriation of government benefits and quality of internal roads. Similarly, the number of SHGs in the VO did have a positive impact on the quality of internal roads, i.e. higher the number of SHGs in the VO, better the action on quality of internal roads. Those VOs which convene monthly meetings as well as meeting more than once in a month have initiated positive and significant action on the regularity of the government employees at the village level. Similarly, the VOs which are undertaking more number of government programmes have taken up action for attaining the better quality of education which is highly significant (Table 5.5).

Social Institutions

Social institutions that are examined include: child marriages, child labour, domestic violence, and atrocities against women. The action of VOs had a positive and highly significant contribution in arresting the child marriages. The age of the VO made significant and positive contribution i.e., older the VO, higher the impact (Table 5.4). However, other characteristics of the VO as well as village considered for the analysis had any impact in arresting the child marriages. Another important institution that has been influenced by the VO is on atrocities against women. That is, wherever VO initiated action; atrocities against women have declined significantly. Proportion of gross irrigated area and proportion of SC/ST population of the village and age of the VO have played a positive and significant role in arresting the atrocities against women. However, even without the influence of the characteristics of either village or VO, the actions initiated by the VO yielded highly significant results in reducing the undesirable practices like atrocities against women (Table 5.5). Thus, it is clear that the institutions/practices which are within the domain of the group members/poor people can be controlled with the interventions of the VO. Finally, it can be concluded that the IKP has resulted in women empowerment thus affecting the performance of formal and informal institutions positively.

Table 5.1

Changes in Education Indicators

Indicator	*Round*	*All Households*				*Srikakulam*			*Anantapur*			*Adilabad*			*Districts*			*Poverty Status*			
		All	*Participants*	*Non-Participants*	*Significant*	*Participants*	*Non-Participants*	*Significant*	*Participants*	*Non-Participants*	*Significant*	*Participants*	*Non-Participants*	*Significant*	*SKIM*	*ANTP*	*ADB*	*POP*	*Poor*	*NSP*	*NP*
% of dropouts among boys	FUS-2	10.20	7.65	8.82		9.22	11.57		11.57	5.69	**	9.22	7.06		10.39	8.24	8.04	14.12	10.20	9.61	7.65
	FUS-1	13.14	19.41	12.94		6.27	18.04		19.02	15.69		11.57	7.65		11.96	17.45	9.61	16.27	14.90	12.75	11.57
	Diff	-2.94	-11.76	-4.12		2.94	-6.47		-7.45	-10.00	**	-2.35	-0.59		-1.57	-9.22	-1.57	-2.16	-4.71	-3.14	-3.92
% of dropouts among girls	FUS-2	14.29	7.96	11.43		12.45	6.33		14.08	4.90	**	18.16	14.29		9.18	8.78	16.12	15.71	12.04	10.82	11.22
	FUS-1	16.12	13.06	14.49		11.84	14.69		19.18	9.18		21.84	10.20		13.27	14.08	15.92	16.94	17.35	13.88	14.29
	Diff	-1.84	-5.10	-3.06		0.61	-8.37		-5.10	-4.29		-3.67	4.08	*	-4.08	-5.31	0.20	-1.22	-5.31	-3.06	-3.06
% of dropouts – all	FUS-2	11.10	7.80	9.50		9.90	8.20		12.80	5.50	***	12.50	9.40		9.00	8.70	10.80	13.60	10.40	9.50	8.90
	FUS-1	14.10	14.90	12.50		7.60	14.10		17.30	11.50		16.50	8.60	*	10.60	14.40	12.50	15.90	15.00	11.40	12.30
	Diff	-3.00	-7.10	-3.00		2.30	-5.90		-4.50	-6.00	*	-4.00	0.80		-1.60	-5.70	-1.70	-2.30	-4.60	-1.90	-3.40
% of HHs reporting better performance of primary schools	FUS-2	84.00	78.90	80.70		86.80	79.90		81.10	84.20		77.70	75.10		83.20	82.80	76.30	83.40	83.10	79.10	81.00
	FUS-1	77.80	76.60	74.90		78.40	69.70		78.90	73.80		79.70	71.10		73.80	76.00	75.00	78.40	78.70	73.80	73.90
	Diff	6.20	2.30	5.80		8.40	10.20		2.20	10.40		-2.00	4.00		9.40	6.80	1.30	5.00	4.40	5.30	7.10

Note: FUS – Follow-up survey,
POP – Poorest of poor,
NSP – Not so poor,
NP – Non-poor.

Table 5.2

Changes in Access to Health Services

Indicator	Round	All Households				Srikakulam			Anantapur			Adilabad			Districts			Poverty Status			
		All	*Participants*	*Non-Participants*	*Significant*	*Participants*	*Non-Participants*	*Significant*	*Participants*	*Non-Participants*	*Significant*	*Participants*	*Non-Participants*	*Significant*	*SKIM*	*ANTP*	*ADB*	*POP*	*Poor*	*NSP*	*NP*
% of deliveries in public hospital	FUS-2	21.89	17.14	27.08	*	20.51	40.00		14.29	12.12		16.13	28.57	*	29.73	13.24	22.03	21.25	20.97	25.58	18.75
	FUS-1	16.92	15.24	18.75		10.26	17.14		17.14	12.12		19.35	28.57		13.51	14.71	23.73	16.25	20.97	16.28	6.25
	Diff	4.97	1.90	8.33		10.25	22.86		-2.85	0.00		-3.22	0.00		16.22	-1.47	-1.70	5.00	0.00	9.30	12.50
% of deliveries in private hospital	FUS-2	30.85	29.52	32.29		25.64	25.71		25.71	36.36		38.71	35.71		25.68	30.88	37.29	28.75	27.42	34.88	43.75
	FUS-1	29.35	28.57	30.21		30.77	42.86		20.00	18.18		35.48	28.57		36.49	19.12	32.20	25.00	22.58	46.51	31.25
	Diff	1.50	0.95	2.08		-5.13	-17.15		5.71	18.18		3.23	7.14		-10.81	11.76	5.09	3.75	4.84	-11.63	12.50
% of deliveries in hospitals	FUS-2	52.24	46.67	58.33	*	46.15	65.71		40.00	48.48		54.84	60.71	*	55.41	44.12	57.63	50.00	48.39	60.47	56.25
	FUS-1	45.77	43.81	47.92		41.03	57.14		37.14	30.30		54.84	57.14		48.65	33.82	55.93	41.25	43.55	60.47	37.50
	Diff	6.47	2.86	10.41		5.12	8.57		2.86	18.18		0.00	3.57		6.76	10.30	1.70	8.75	4.84	0.00	18.75
% of persons treated in public hospitals	FUS-2	11.70	6.20	9.30		8.30	7.70		12.00	10.70		7.80	9.30		8.00	11.20	8.60	10.60	10.40	9.70	8.00
	FUS-1	6.70	5.40	7.30		4.60	6.80		7.60	5.60	*	11.10	8.70		5.70	6.40	9.80	6.40	9.40	7.60	7.90
	Diff	5.00	0.80	2.00		3.70	0.90		4.40	5.10		-3.30	0.60		2.30	4.80	-1.20	4.20	1.00	2.10	0.10
% of persons treated in private hospitals	FUS-2	46.00	46.20	44.80		45.80	45.40		42.20	40.40		53.70	42.70		45.60	41.20	47.80	42.50	48.60	45.00	43.50
	FUS-1	27.40	23.30	27.00	***	26.60	18.40		32.40	22.40	***	37.60	27.30	***	22.20	26.60	31.90	26.30	34.70	27.40	27.10
	Diff	18.60	22.90	17.80	***	19.20	27.00		9.80	18.00	*	16.10	15.40	*	23.40	14.60	15.90	16.20	13.90	17.60	16.40

Table 5.3

Formal Institutions

Description of the Items	*Access to Drinking Water*	*Significant*	*Quality of Drinking Water*	*Significant*	*Access to Education*	*Significant*	*Quality of Education*	*Significant*	*Sanitation Condition*	*Significant*	*Access to Approach Road*	*Significant*	*Quality of Internal Roads*	*Significant*	*Access to Communication*	*Significant*	*On Govt. Employees*	*Significant*	*Appropriation. of Benefits*	*Significant*
Action undertaken by VO	0.303	**	0.258	*	0.168		0.439	**	0.296	*	0.99		2.959	**	1.951	*	0.367		0.577	
	(2.72)		(2.34)		(1.56)		(3.56)		(2.50)		(1.14)		(3.07)		(2.49)		(1.11)		(2.05)	*
Size of village	-.000		.000		-.000		-.000	*	-.000		0.000		-.001	*	-.000		0.000		-.000	
	(-.57)		(1.18)		(-0.98)		(-2.06)		(-0.11)		(1.62)		(-2.56)		(-0.90)		(0.69)		(-1.28)	
Proportion of SC/ST population	0.003		0.002		0.004	*	0.005		0.001		0.002		0.006		0.002		-.005	*	0.001	
	(1.35)		(0.56)		(2.07)		(1.61)		(0.21)		(0.48)		(11.11)		(0.42)		(-2.24)		(0.18)	
Proportion of gross irrigated area	-.001		0.002		-.002		-.001		-.002		-.005		-.011		0.007		-.003		.005	
	(0.33)		(0.52)		(-0.53)		(-.035)		(-0.57)		(-0.74)		(-1.36)		(1.02)		(-1.06)		(1.53)	
Proportion of female contestants	0.001		0.004		0.000		-.001		0.001		-.007		-.009		-.013	*	0.002		-.006	
	(0.48)		(1.26)		(0.37)		(-0.20)		(0.40)		(-1.47)		(-1.50)		(-2.19)		(0.84)		(-2.23)	
Proportion of SC/ST contestants	0.001		0.005		0.002		-.002		-.007	*	-.000		-.014		-.005		-.002		-.006	
	(0.43)		(1.56)		(0.86)		(-.045)		(-2.06)		(-0.01)		(-1.81)		(-0.98)		(-1.04)		(-1.54)	
Fare to district headquarters	0.004		-.006		0.002		-.004		-.000		-.001		0.000		0.009		0.000		0.003	
	(1.62)		(-1.94)		(0.76)		(-1.30)		(-0.14)		(-0.18)		(0.06)		(1.73)		(0.37)		(0.99)	
No. of groups per 100 population	-.005		-.002		-.002		-.012		-.024		0.022		0.003		-.012		-.000		0.18	
	(0.21)		(-0.13)		(-.023)		(-0.95)		(-1.76)		(0.87)		(0.12)		(-.057)		(-0.03)		(1.37)	
Srikakulam	-.041		0.62	**	0.887	**	0.423		-.412		0.661		-.046		-.085		-.617	**	-.252	
	(0.21)		(2.91)		(6.13)		(0.19)		(-1.83)		(1.91)		(-0.10)		(-0.20)		(-3.41)		(-0.93)	
District dummy 2	0.033		0.359		0.246		0.015		-.623	**	0.464		-.232		-.401		-.521	**	0.088	
	(1.67)		(1.90)		(1.71)		(0.08)		(-3.44)		(1.17)		(-0.52)		(-1.04)		(-3.67)		(0.41)	
Sample size	157		161		88		158		206		183		221		161		119		114	
R-Square	0.153		0.153		0.491		0.143		0.098		0.077						0.205		2.264	
Prob >F statistic	0.006		0.004		0.000		0.01		0.025		0.055		0.101		0.028		0.011		0.001	

contd...

...contd...

Description of the Items	Access to Drinking Water	Significant	Quality of Drinking Water	Significant	Access to Education	Significant	Quality of Education	Significant	Sanitation Condition	Significant	Access to Approach Road	Significant	Quality of Internal Roads	Significant	Access to Communication	Significant	On Govt. Employees	Significant	Appropriation. of Benefits	Significant
VO age in months	-.000		0.004		0.002		0.004		-.007	*	0.004		0.007	*	0.014	**	0.003		0.011	**
	(-0.10)		(1.12)		(0.48)		(1.39)		(-2.45)		(1.24)		(2.19)		(4.91)		(0.88)		(2.99)	
SC/ST SHGs	-.005		-.005		0.003		-.007		0.007		0.009		-.012		0.006		0.011		-.010	
	(-0.50)		(-0.51)		(0.24)		(-0.71)		(0.97)		(1.11)		(-1.47)		(0.82)		(1.17)		(-0.95)	
Total SHGs in VO	0.006		0.004		-.006		0.008		0.006		0.004		0.014	*	-.005		-.005		0.000	
	(0.82)		(0.65)		(-0.71)		(1.22)		(1.03)		(0.64)		(2.24)		(-0.84)		(-0.70)		(0.05)	
Meeting more than once in a month	-016		-.165		0.023		-.009		-.038		0.015		-.011		-.046		0.344	*	-.015	
	(-0.16)		(-1.31)		(0.23)		(-0.10)		(-0.46)		(0.17)		(-0.13)		(-0.60)		(2.25)		(-0.15)	
Meeting once in a month	-.066		-.193	*	-.080		-.294	*	0.138		0.056		-.098		-.012		0.234	**	-.258	
	(-0.46)		(-2.00)		(-0.57)		(-2.15)		(1.25)		(0.46)		(-0.86)		(-0.10)		(2.79)		(-1.68)	
VO committees	-.002		-.165		-.021		0.026		-.105		-.035		-.040		-.024		-.101		0.118	
	(-0.03)		(-1.31)		(-0.26)		(0.38)		(-1.68)		(-0.53)		(-0.64)		(-0.41)		(-1.55)		(1.51)	
No. of Govt. programmes undertaken	-.082		0.035		0.019		0.099	**	0.011		-.002		0.006		-.007		-.022		-.003	
	(-1.89)		(0.90)		(0.46)		(2.75)		(0.31)		(-0.06)		(0.19)		(-0.21)		(-0.64)		(-0.06)	
Srikakulam	-.519	**	-.139		0.064		0.153		-.133		0.022		-.079		0.223	*	-.022		0.074	
	(-3.80)		(-1.09)		(0.50)		(1.21)		(-1.20)		(0.18)		(-0.69)		(2.10)		(-0.17)		(0.48)	
Anantapur	-.138		0.102		0.0931		0.371	**	0.047		0.189	*	0.147		0.166	*	0.181	*	0.49	
	(-1.47)		(1.06)		(0.87)		(3.87)		(0.56)		(2.06)		(1.80)		(2.14)		(2.11)		(0.44)	
Sample size	221		230		123		219		284		261		301		223		151		162	
R-Square	0.1000		0.094		0.022		0.166		0.065		0.039		0.062		0.119		0.105		0.101	
Prob >F statistic	0.007		0.009		0.978		0.000		0.029		0.337		0.026		0.001		0.068		0.055	

Note: Figures in parentheses are t values.

** indicates 1 per cent significant level and * indicates 5 per cent significant level.

Table 5.4

Informal Institutions

Description of the Items	*Child Marriages*	*Significant*	*Child Labour*	*Significant*	*Domestic Violence*	*Significant*	*Atrocities Against Women*	*Significant*
Action undertaken by VO	1.281 (2.69)	**	0.055 (0.36)		0.881 (1.80)		0.463 (2.92)	*
Size of village	-.000 (-1.47)		0.000 (0.25)		0.000 (0.09)		-.000 (-0.90)	
Proportion of SC/ST population	0.006 (1.50)		0.003 (0.78)		0.007 (1.88)		-.002 (-0.48)	
Proportion gross irrigated area	0.007 (1.09)		-.007 (-1.30)		0.003 (0.57)		0.023 (3.70)	**
Proportion of female contestants	-.008 (-1.64)		0.003 (0.59)		-.000 (-0.01)		0.000 (0.01)	
Proportion of SC/ST contestants	-.001 (-0.11)		0.003 (0.73)		-.003 (0.89)		0.015 (2.51)	*
Fare to district headquarters	0.002 (0.56)		0.003 (0.86)		-.009 (-3.04)	**	0.005 (0.92)	
No. of groups per 100 population	-.032 (-1.50)		-.013 (-0.65)		-004 (-0.23)		0.061 (1.82)	
Srikakulam	-.161 (-.44)		-1.018 (-3.16)	**	-.611 (-1.43)		0.726 (1.64)	
District dummy 2	0.542 (2.22)	*	0.146 (0.66)		-089 (-0.32)		1.189 (2.73)	*
Sample size	0.000		196		108		25	
R-Square			0.164		0.131		0.782	

contd...

...contd...

Description of the Items	*Child Marriages*	*Significant*	*Child Labour*	*Significant*	*Domestic Violence*	*Significant*	*Atrocities Against Women*	*Significant*
Prob >F statistic			0.000		0.001		0.003	0
VO age in months	0.016 (4.54)	**	0.009 (2.83)	**	0.008 (2.26)	*	0.027 (3.58)	**
SC/ST SHGs	-.004 (-0.37)		-.013 (-1.40)		0.000 (0.01)		-.039 (-1.52)	
Total SHGs in VO	-.001 (-0.18)		0.009 (1.45)		0.012 (1.52)		.039 (1.82)	
Meeting more than once in a month	-.112 (-1.08)		0.063 (0.72)		-.039 (-0.33)		0.335 (1.32)	
Meeting once in a month	-.234 (-1.50)		-.063 (-0.51)		-.288 (-1.25)		-.359 (-0.96)	
VO committees	0.039 (0.52)		-.021 (-0.33)		0.072 (0.86)		-.415 (-1.83)	
No. of government programmes undertaken	-.014 (-0.35)		-.038 (-1.12)		0.078 (1.61)		-.194 (-1.55)	
Srikakulam	-.138 (-0.84)		-.427 (-3.38)	**	0.100 (0.37)		0.437 (0.96)	
Anantapur	-.055 (-0.61)		-.135 (-1.66)		0.216 (2.14)	**	0.346 (1.56)	
Sample size	187		270		150		33	
R-Square	0.148		0.101		0.174		0.511	
Prob >F statistic	0.001		0.000		0.001		0.026	

Note: Figures in parentheses are t values.

** indicates 1 per cent significant level and * indicates 5 per cent significant level.

Table 5.5

No Action Taken by VO/MS

	No Action Taken by VO/MS					*Action Taken by VO/MS*				
Description of Variables	*Observations*	*Mean*	*Std. Dev.*	*Min.*	*Max.*	*Observations*	*Mean*	*Std. Dev.*	*Min.*	*Max.*
Access to drinking water	149	0.72	0.57	0.10	4.60	73	1.07	0.70	0.20	3.10
Prop. of VOs taken action	149	0.00	0.00	0.00	0.00	73	1.00	0.00	1.00	1.00
Village size	135	399	472	37	2540	72	457	446	51	1784
% of SC/ST population	135	34.61	30.53	0.00	100.00	72	42.08	27.67	0.00	100.00
% of gross irrigated area	134	18.83	16.46	0.00	59.99	72	17.83	14.63	0.00	50.47
% of female contestants in elections	135	27.24	15.67	0.00	70.00	70	25.89	17.82	0.00	100.00
% of SC/ST contenstants in elections	135	37.99	34.52	0.00	106.67	70	47.56	31.70	0.00	120.00
Fare to district HQ	110	35.27	15.92	5.00	100.00	56	34.84	21.42	0.00	100.00
No. of groups per 100 population in the village	130	9.79	5.76	0.80	28.00	71	8.61	4.56	2.44	20.19
Prop. of villages in Srikakulam district	149	0.23	0.42	0.00	1.00	73	0.01	0.12	0.00	1.00
Prop. of villages in Anantapur district	149	0.52	0.50	0.00	1.00	73	0.62	0.49	0.00	1.00
VO age in months	149	42	10	8	66	73	43	9	15	59
SC/ST SHGs per VO	149	4.50	5.37	0.00	29.00	73	4.88	4.18	0.00	21.00
Total no. of SHGs per VO	148	10.38	6.79	1.00	39.00	73	9.74	5.93	1.00	31.00
No. of VOs have meeting in less than one month	149	0.07	0.26	0.00	1.00	73	0.03	0.16	0.00	1.00
No. of VOs have meeting every month	149	0.15	0.36	0.00	1.00	73	0.08	0.28	0.00	1.00
Prop. of VO committees	149	0.52	0.50	0.00	1.00	73	0.41	0.50	0.00	1.00
No. of government programes per VO	149	0.64	0.90	0.00	4.00	73	0.62	0.76	0.00	3.00
Quality of drinking water	136	1.06	0.67	0.20	3.10	95	1.25	0.78	0.20	3.00
Prop. of VOs taken action	136	0.00	0.00	0.00	0.00	95	1.00	0.00	1.00	1.00

contd...

...contd...

Description of Variables	No Action Taken by VO/MS					Action Taken by VO/MS				
	Observations	Mean	Std. Dev.	Min.	Max.	Observations	Mean	Std. Dev.	Min.	Max.
Village size	124	364	412	45	2540	87	463	462	37	1800
% of SC/ST population	124	34.04	31.12	0.00	100.00	87	34.69	26.28	0.00	100.00
% of gross irrigated area	123	21.26	16.25	0.00	59.99	87	18.30	15.53	0.00	50.60
% of female contestants in elections	124	26.93	15.94	0.00	71.43	85	29.27	17.12	0.00	100.00
% of SC/ST contestants in elections	124	36.80	34.62	0.00	106.67	85	38.58	31.29	0.00	120.00
Fare to district HQ	94	34.73	18.22	5.00	100.00	78	33.56	16.39	0.00	90.00
No. of groups per 100 population in the village	118	9.43	5.17	0.80	24.44	84	8.85	5.08	1.83	21.62
Prop. of villages in Srikakulam district	136	0.26	0.44	0.00	1.00	95	0.07	0.26	0.00	1.00
Prop. of villages in Anantapur district	136	0.50	0.50	0.00	1.00	95	0.68	0.47	0.00	1.00
VO age in months	136	41.90	10.40	8.00	87.00	95	42.95	9.51	21.00	66.00
SC/ST SHGs per VO	136	4.31	5.07	0.00	29.00	95	4.23	3.92	0.00	18.00
Total no. of SHGs per VO	135	10.50	6.03	2.00	30.00	95	10.13	6.96	1.00	39.00
No. of VOs have meeting in less than one month	136	0.11	0.31	0.00	1.00	95	0.04	0.20	0.00	1.00
No. of VOs have meeting every month	136	0.21	0.41	0.00	1.00	95	0.07	0.26	0.00	1.00
Prop. of VO committees	136	0.55	0.50	0.00	1.00	95	0.52	0.50	0.00	1.00
No. of government programmes per VO	136	0.58	0.95	0.00	4.00	95	0.75	0.84	0.00	4.00
Access to education	103	0.60	0.46	0.20	2.50	22	0.69	0.68	0.20	2.60
Prop of VOs taken action	103	0.00	0.00	0.00	0.00	22	1.00	0.00	1.00	1.00
Village size	94	302	345	16	1900	22	464	560	37	1784
% of SC/ST population	94	32.11	29.48	0.00	100.00	22	36.21	37.30	0.00	100.00
% of gross irrigated area	94	21.73	16.46	0.00	59.14	22	17.01	17.34	0.00	50.00

contd...

...contd...

Description of Variables	No Action Taken by VO/MS					Action Taken by VO/MS				
	Observations	Mean	Std. Dev.	Min.	Max.	Observations	Mean	Std. Dev.	Min.	Max.
% of Female contestants in elections	93	25.44	17.80	0.00	71.43	22	30.92	15.82	0.00	57.89
% of SC/ST contestants in elections	93	32.93	31.87	0.00	100.00	22	43.23	39.07	0.00	100.00
Fare to district HQ	74	35.42	17.15	2.00	120.00	18	42.67	16.42	17.00	100.00
No. of groups per 100 population in the village	91	10.35	5.82	0.80	28.00	22	8.87	7.07	1.16	22.45
Prop. of villages in Srikakulam district	103	0.29	0.46	0.00	1.00	22	0.23	0.43	0.00	1.00
Prop. of villages in Anantapur district	103	0.46	0.50	0.00	1.00	22	0.55	0.51	0.00	1.00
VO age in months	103	40.83	11.58	8.00	87.00	22	41.64	10.24	25.00	61.00
SC/ST SHGs per VO	103	4.58	5.17	0.00	27.00	22	4.23	3.05	0.00	11.00
Total no. of SHGs per VO	101	9.95	5.79	2.00	33.00	22	8.59	5.32	1.00	21.00
No. of VOs have meeting in less than one month	103	0.12	0.32	0.00	1.00	22	0.05	0.21	0.00	1.00
No. of VOs have meeting every month	103	0.22	0.42	0.00	1.00	22	0.27	0.46	0.00	1.00
Prop. of VO committees	103	0.50	0.50	0.00	1.00	22	0.45	0.51	0.00	1.00
No. of Government programmes per VO	103	0.56	0.86	0.00	4.00	22	0.64	1.00	0.00	3.00
Quality of education	135	0.86	0.56	0.10	2.40	87	1.15	0.69	0.10	2.70
Prop. of VOs taken action	135	0.00	0.00	0.00	0.00	87	1.00	0.00	1.00	1.00
Village size	123	331	371	16	2540	85	532	481	37	1900
% of SC/ST population	123	33.81	29.97	0.00	100.00	85	28.68	20.77	0.00	100.00
% of gross irrigated area	123	22.91	16.86	0.00	77.72	85	16.99	13.20	0.00	50.00
% of female contestants in elections	123	27.08	18.36	0.00	100.00	84	30.16	16.86	0.00	72.73
% of SC/ST contestants in elections	123	38.07	33.75	0.00	100.00	84	28.76	21.25	0.00	100.00
Fare to district HQ	95	36.48	20.21	0.00	120.00	69	36.36	16.31	2.00	125.00

contd...

...contd...

Description of Variables	*No Action Taken by VO/MS*					*Action Taken by VO/MS*				
	Observations	*Mean*	*Std. Dev.*	*Min.*	*Max.*	*Observations*	*Mean*	*Std. Dev.*	*Min.*	*Max.*
No. of groups per 100 population in the village	120	9.21	5.22	0.80	28.00	83	8.12	5.05	1.16	21.62
Prop. of villages in Srikakulam district	135	0.21	0.41	0.00	1.00	87	0.08	0.27	0.00	1.00
Prop. of villages in Anantapur district	135	0.52	0.50	0.00	1.00	87	0.82	0.39	0.00	1.00
VO age in months	135	40.76	10.97	8.00	87.00	87	42.18	10.03	19.00	66.00
SC/ST SHGs per VO	135	4.19	4.85	0.00	27.00	87	3.93	3.49	0.00	18.00
Total no. of SHGs per VO	132	9.80	5.69	1.00	33.00	87	10.44	6.59	2.00	39.00
No. of VOs have meeting in less than one month	135	0.11	0.32	0.00	1.00	87	0.01	0.11	0.00	1.00
No. of VOs have meeting every month	135	0.20	0.40	0.00	1.00	87	0.15	0.36	0.00	1.00
Prop. of VO committees	135	0.49	0.50	0.00	1.00	87	0.63	0.49	0.00	1.00
No. of Government programmes per VO	135	0.59	0.83	0.00	4.00	87	0.86	1.08	0.00	4.00
Sanitation condition	173	1.67	0.92	0.20	3.70	114	1.88	0.71	0.30	4.10
Prop. of VOs taken action	173	0.00	0.00	0.00	0.00	114	1.00	0.00	1.00	1.00
Village size	157	333	327	16	1784	107	485	532	40	2540
% of SC/ST population	157	32.89	30.71	0.00	100.00	107	34.70	29.31	0.00	100.00
% of gross irrigated area	155	20.40	17.58	0.00	77.72	107	20.59	16.28	0.00	52.08
% of female contestants in elections	156	28.44	19.12	0.00	100.00	106	29.81	16.05	0.00	68.18
% of SC/ST contestants in elections	156	35.15	33.53	0.00	120.00	106	39.32	30.63	0.00	100.00
Fare to district HQ	127	39.03	21.86	5.00	125.00	91	36.25	15.44	0.00	100.00
No. of groups per 100 population in the village	152	9.16	4.91	0.80	24.44	103	8.96	5.49	1.16	28.00
Prop. of villages in Srikakulam district	173	0.27	0.45	0.00	1.00	114	0.16	0.37	0.00	1.00

contd...

...contd...

Description of Variables	*No Action Taken by VO/MS* Observations	*Mean*	*Std. Dev.*	*Min.*	*Max.*	*Action Taken by VO/MS* Observations	*Mean*	*Std. Dev.*	*Min.*	*Max.*
Prop. of villages in Anantapur district	173	0.46	0.50	0.00	1.00	114	0.55	0.50	0.00	1.00
VO age in months	173	42.70	9.89	8.00	87.00	114	40.25	10.49	15.00	66.00
SC/ST SHGs per VO	173	3.97	4.57	0.00	27.00	114	4.88	5.06	0.00	29.00
Total no. of SHGs per VO	170	10.48	5.87	1.00	30.00	114	11.00	6.91	1.00	39.00
No. of VOs have meeting in less than one month	173	0.09	0.28	0.00	1.00	114	0.11	0.31	0.00	1.00
No. of VOs have meeting every month	173	0.23	0.42	0.00	1.00	114	0.14	0.35	0.00	1.00
Prop. of VO committees	173	0.55	0.50	0.00	1.00	114	0.46	0.50	0.00	1.00
No. of government programmes per VO	173	0.69	0.95	0.00	4.00	114	0.76	0.91	0.00	4.00
Access to approach road	168	1.28	0.91	0.10	4.10	96	1.75	1.27	0.20	5.80
Prop. of VOs taken action	168	0.00	0.00	0.00	0.00	96	1.00	0.00	1.00	1.00
Village size	152	399	481	45	2540	91	333	247	16	1100
% of SC/ST population	152	30.42	28.99	0.00	100.00	91	34.73	29.39	0.00	100.00
% of gross irrigated area	150	22.28	17.61	0.00	77.72	91	18.50	15.10	0.00	50.35
% of female contestants in elections	151	27.72	18.81	0.00	100.00	90	28.41	16.91	0.00	72.73
% of SC/ST contestants in elections	151	32.99	33.31	0.00	106.67	90	36.65	30.12	0.00	100.00
Fare to district HQ	122	39.07	20.49	0.00	120.00	75	33.36	17.03	2.00	125.00
No. of groups per 100 population in the village	147	9.31	5.39	0.80	28.00	87	8.65	4.68	1.16	24.00
Prop. of villages in Srikakulam district	168	0.26	0.44	0.00	1.00	96	0.19	0.39	0.00	1.00
Prop. of villages in Anantapur district	168	0.49	0.50	0.00	1.00	96	0.61	0.49	0.00	1.00
VO age in months	168	40.98	9.86	8.00	66.00	96	42.66	10.05	15.00	66.00
SC/ST SHGs per VO	168	3.82	4.45	0.00	27.00	96	4.68	5.00	0.00	29.00

contd...

...contd...

Description of Variables	No Action Taken by VO/MS					Action Taken by VO/MS				
	Observations	Mean	Std. Dev.	Min.	Max.	Observations	Mean	Std. Dev.	Min.	Max.
Total no. of SHGs per VO	166	10.10	6.17	1.00	39.00	95	11.03	6.50	1.00	33.00
No. of VOs have meeting in less than one month	168	0.09	0.29	0.00	1.00	96	0.08	0.28	0.00	1.00
No. of VOs have meeting every month	168	0.19	0.39	0.00	1.00	96	0.16	0.36	0.00	1.00
Prop. of VO committees	168	0.52	0.50	0.00	1.00	96	0.52	0.50	0.00	1.00
No. of government programmes per VO	168	0.66	0.88	0.00	3.00	96	0.65	0.89	0.00	4.00
Quality of internal road	169	1.48	0.85	0.10	3.40	135	1.88	1.32	0.30	5.90
Prop. of VOs taken action	169	0.00	0.00	0.00	0.00	135	1.00	0.00	1.00	1.00
Village size	151	278	233	16	1500	133	523	527	49	2540
% of SC/ST population	151	34.42	30.77	0.00	100.00	133	33.83	27.34	0.00	100.00
% of gross irrigated area	149	19.56	17.05	0.00	77.72	133	19.33	15.46	0.00	50.60
% of female contestants in elections	150	25.44	18.05	0.00	100.00	132	30.81	17.15	0.00	100.00
% of SC/ST contenstants in elections	150	34.31	33.63	0.00	106.67	132	39.88	30.77	0.00	120.00
Fare to district HQ	124	38.22	21.98	2.00	125.00	111	34.70	18.10	0.00	100.00
No. of groups per 100 population in the village	145	9.61	5.03	0.80	28.00	130	8.39	5.05	1.37	24.00
Prop. of villages in Srikakulam district	169	0.22	0.42	0.00	1.00	135	0.13	0.34	0.00	1.00
Prop. of villages in Anantapur district	169	0.47	0.50	0.00	1.00	135	0.62	0.49	0.00	1.00
VO age in months	169	40.92	9.98	8.00	66.00	135	43.13	9.65	15.00	66.00
SC/ST SHGs per VO	169	4.37	4.80	0.00	27.00	135	4.36	4.59	0.00	29.00
Total no. of SHGs per VO	167	9.97	5.38	1.00	27.00	134	10.93	7.10	1.00	39.00
No. of VOs have meeting in less than one month	169	0.10	0.30	0.00	1.00	135	0.06	0.24	0.00	1.00

contd...

...contd...

Description of Variables	No Action Taken by VO/MS					Action Taken by VO/MS				
	Observations	Mean	Std. Dev.	Min.	Max.	Observations	Mean	Std. Dev.	Min.	Max.
No. of VOs have meeting every month	169	0.20	0.40	0.00	1.00	135	0.16	0.36	0.00	1.00
Prop. of VO committees	169	0.51	0.50	0.00	1.00	135	0.51	0.50	0.00	1.00
No. of government programmes per VO	169	0.72	0.95	0.00	4.00	135	0.73	0.92	0.00	4.00
Acess to communication	177	1.13	0.93	0.10	3.90	49	1.54	1.11	0.30	3.60
Prop of VOs taken action	177	0.00	0.00	0.00	0.00	49	1.00	0.00	1.00	1.00
Village size	163	377	411	40	1900	49	307	290	16	1100
% of SC/ST population	163	35.22	32.11	0.00	100.00	49	43.15	32.38	0.00	100.00
% of gross irrigated area	163	18.30	16.31	0.00	77.72	49	17.10	14.76	0.00	50.00
% of female contestants in elections	162	25.58	17.34	0.00	100.00	48	32.73	16.22	0.00	64.71
% of SC/ST contestants in elections	162	36.91	33.93	0.00	120.00	48	45.15	34.47	0.00	100.00
Fare to district HQ	127	40.50	22.10	0.00	125.00	42	35.33	13.46	9.00	90.00
No. of groups per 100 population in the village	159	9.22	5.39	0.80	28.00	48	10.07	5.71	3.17	24.44
Prop. of villages in Srikakulam district	177	0.17	0.38	0.00	1.00	49	0.20	0.41	0.00	1.00
Prop. of villages in Anantapur district	177	0.54	0.50	0.00	1.00	49	0.59	0.50	0.00	1.00
VO age in months	177	40.53	10.19	8.00	66.00	49	47.71	7.91	30.00	66.00
SC/ST SHGs per VO	177	4.34	4.86	0.00	27.00	49	5.29	5.33	0.00	29.00
Total no. of SHGs per VO	174	10.15	6.23	1.00	39.00	49	10.88	6.63	1.00	29.00
No. of VOs have meeting in less than one month	177	0.07	0.26	0.00	1.00	49	0.08	0.28	0.00	1.00
No. of VOs have meeting every month	177	0.18	0.39	0.00	1.00	49	0.16	0.37	0.00	1.00
Prop. of VO committees	177	0.54	0.50	0.00	1.00	49	0.55	0.50	0.00	1.00
No. of government programmes per VO	177	0.76	0.99	0.00	4.00	49	0.67	0.80	0.00	2.00

contd...

...contd...

Description of Variables	*No Action Taken by VO/MS*					*Action Taken by VO/MS*				
	Observations	*Mean*	*Std. Dev.*	*Min.*	*Max.*	*Observations*	*Mean*	*Std. Dev.*	*Min.*	*Max.*
Government employees' absence from their duties	131	0.59	0.38	0.10	1.70	22	0.84	0.63	0.10	2.40
Prop. of VOs taken action	131	0.00	0.00	0.00	0.00	22	1.00	0.00	1.00	1.00
Village size	123	423	451	45	1900	22	259	158	49	590
% of SC/ST population	123	32.62	27.47	0.00	100.00	22	29.93	30.11	0.00	100.00
% of gross irrigated area	123	17.84	15.72	0.00	77.72	22	17.40	15.82	0.00	50.60
% of female contestants in elections	123	29.16	18.77	0.00	100.00	22	23.15	15.77	0.00	57.14
% of SC/ST contestants in elections	123	35.04	32.77	0.00	100.00	22	46.05	30.07	0.00	100.00
Fare to district HQ	105	39.96	19.30	0.00	120.00	16	34.50	23.33	2.00	100.00
No. of groups per 100 population in the village	122	8.66	5.03	1.37	24.44	22	10.99	5.87	1.16	22.45
Prop. of villages in Srikakulam district	131	0.11	0.32	0.00	1.00	22	0.09	0.29	0.00	1.00
Prop. of villages in Anantapur district	131	0.56	0.50	0.00	1.00	22	0.68	0.48	0.00	1.00
VO age in months	131	40.81	10.69	8.00	66.00	22	41.64	8.62	22.00	61.00
SC/ST SHGs per VO	131	4.13	4.52	0.00	18.00	22	4.05	3.53	0.00	13.00
Total no. of SHGs per VO	129	9.69	6.16	1.00	39.00	22	8.82	6.13	1.00	27.00
No. of VOs have meeting in less than one month	131	0.04	0.19	0.00	1.00	22	0.09	0.29	0.00	1.00
No. of VOs have meeting every month	131	0.16	0.37	0.00	1.00	22	0.32	0.48	0.00	1.00
Prop. of VO committees	131	0.47	0.50	0.00	1.00	22	0.32	0.48	0.00	1.00
No. of government programmes per VO	131	0.78	0.96	0.00	4.00	22	0.50	0.86	0.00	3.00
Appropriation of benefits of government programmes for the poor	123	0.61	0.44	0.10	2.40	41	0.90	0.50	0.10	1.80
Prop. of VOs taken action	123	0.00	0.00	0.00	0.00	41	1.00	0.00	1.00	1.00
Village size	119	362	283	45	1900	41	611	583	50	1800

contd...

...contd...

Description of Variables	No Action Taken by VO/MS					Action Taken by VO/MS				
	Observations	*Mean*	*Std. Dev.*	*Min.*	*Max.*	*Observations*	*Mean*	*Std. Dev.*	*Min.*	*Max.*
% of SC/ST population	119	27.54	20.57	0.00	100.00	41	29.40	25.32	1.11	100.00
% of gross irrigated area	118	23.79	16.25	0.00	77.72	41	16.42	13.06	0.00	50.00
% of female contestants in elections	119	30.80	17.06	0.00	100.00	40	26.95	17.40	0.00	57.14
% of SC/ST contestants in elections	119	30.33	25.50	0.00	100.00	40	36.13	31.76	0.00	100.00
Fare to district HQ	87	39.45	21.67	0.00	120.00	32	35.16	15.48	11.00	80.00
No. of groups per 100 population in the village	117	8.19	4.15	1.37	24.44	41	7.69	5.32	1.83	21.57
Prop. of villages in Srikakulam district	123	0.15	0.35	0.00	1.00	41	0.12	0.33	0.00	1.00
Prop. of villages in Anantapur district	123	0.64	0.48	0.00	1.00	41	0.76	0.43	0.00	1.00
VO age in months	123	39.26	8.80	15.00	58.00	41	44.22	9.68	23.00	66.00
SC/ST SHGs per VO	123	3.90	4.26	0.00	27.00	41	3.32	3.53	0.00	14.00
Total no. of SHGs per VO	121	9.98	5.72	2.00	27.00	41	9.59	8.04	1.00	39.00
No. of VOs have meeting in less than one month	123	0.09	0.29	0.00	1.00	41	0.02	0.16	0.00	1.00
No. of VOs have meeting every month	123	0.19	0.39	0.00	1.00	41	0.22	0.42	0.00	1.00
Prop. of VO committees	123	0.48	0.50	0.00	1.00	41	0.66	0.48	0.00	1.00
No. of government programmes per VO	123	0.60	0.92	0.00	4.00	41	0.61	0.83	0.00	3.00
Child marriages	130	0.97	0.75	0.10	3.60	59	1.53	0.85	0.30	3.20
Prop. of VOs taken action	130	0.00	0.00	0.00	0.00	59	1.00	0.00	1.00	1.00
Village size	119	404	386	50	2540	59	466	534	40	1800
% of SC/ST population	119	28.77	23.13	0.00	100.00	59	41.75	31.28	0.00	100.00
% of gross irrigated area	118	20.14	15.37	0.00	77.72	59	14.99	13.27	0.00	50.00
% of female contestants in elections	119	28.59	16.57	0.00	100.00	57	26.90	17.00	0.00	100.00

contd...

...contd...

Description of Variables	No Action Taken by VO/MS *Observations*	*Mean*	*Std. Dev.*	*Min.*	*Max.*	Action Taken by VO/MS *Observations*	*Mean*	*Std. Dev.*	*Min.*	*Max.*
% of SC/ST contestants in elections	119	32.63	28.06	0.00	106.67	57	43.81	33.75	0.00	120.00
Fare to district HQ	87	39.56	23.19	5.00	125.00	51	38.49	15.33	2.00	90.00
No. of groups per 100 population in the village	118	8.63	4.61	1.16	21.57	59	9.72	5.20	2.44	24.44
Prop. of villages in Srikakulam district	130	0.12	0.33	0.00	1.00	59	0.03	0.18	0.00	1.00
Prop. of villages in Anantapur district	130	0.62	0.49	0.00	1.00	59	0.59	0.50	0.00	1.00
VO age in months	130	39.56	9.12	15.00	61.00	59	46.86	9.68	17.00	66.00
SC/ST SHGs per VO	130	3.85	3.74	0.00	16.00	59	4.78	4.06	0.00	21.00
Total no. of SHGs per VO	128	10.02	5.78	1.00	30.00	59	10.39	6.91	2.00	39.00
No. of VOs have meeting in less than one month	130	0.08	0.27	0.00	1.00	59	0.02	0.13	0.00	1.00
No. of VOs have meeting every month	130	0.15	0.35	0.00	1.00	59	0.10	0.30	0.00	1.00
Prop. of VO committees	130	0.55	0.50	0.00	1.00	59	0.56	0.50	0.00	1.00
No. of government programmes per VO	130	0.72	1.01	0.00	4.00	59	0.76	0.75	0.00	2.00
Child labour	156	1.74	0.99	0.10	4.40	115	2.03	1.11	0.30	6.30
Prop. of VOs taken action	156	0.00	0.00	0.00	0.00	115	1.00	0.00	1.00	1.00
Village size	141	396	384	45	2540	113	432	483	16	1800
% of SC/ST population	141	34.17	27.89	0.00	100.00	113	40.25	31.08	0.00	100.00
% of gross irrigated area	140	19.92	15.41	0.00	59.99	113	15.96	15.56	0.00	77.72
% of female contestants in elections	141	27.63	16.24	0.00	68.18	111	27.85	18.48	0.00	100.00
% of SC/ST contestants in elections	141	37.24	32.50	0.00	106.67	111	43.17	32.55	0.00	120.00
Fare to district HQ	106	37.65	19.51	0.00	120.00	101	38.17	22.11	2.00	125.00
No. of groups per 100 population in the village	133	8.30	4.93	0.80	28.00	112	9.80	5.12	2.44	24.44

contd...

...contd...

Description of Variables	*No Action Taken by VO/MS*					*Action Taken by VO/MS*				
	Observations	*Mean*	*Std. Dev.*	*Min.*	*Max.*	*Observations*	*Mean*	*Std. Dev.*	*Min.*	*Max.*
Prop. of villages in Srikakulam district	156	0.17	0.38	0.00	1.00	115	0.04	0.20	0.00	1.00
Prop. of villages in Anantapur district	156	0.58	0.49	0.00	1.00	115	0.55	0.50	0.00	1.00
VO age in months	156	40.09	9.74	8.00	62.00	115	44.43	10.01	17.00	66.00
SC/ST SHGs per VO	156	4.40	4.77	0.00	29.00	115	4.94	4.37	0.00	21.00
Total no. of SHGs per VO	155	10.15	5.66	1.00	29.00	115	10.40	6.44	2.00	39.00
No. of VOs have meeting in less than one month	156	0.10	0.30	0.00	1.00	115	0.04	0.20	0.00	1.00
No. of VOs have meeting every month	156	0.13	0.34	0.00	1.00	115	0.17	0.37	0.00	1.00
Prop. of VO committees	156	0.54	0.50	0.00	1.00	115	0.47	0.50	0.00	1.00
No. of government programmes per VO	156	0.78	1.02	0.00	4.00	115	0.83	0.87	0.00	4.00
Domestic violence	102	0.87	0.72	0.10	3.30	49	1.23	0.67	0.20	2.80
Prop. of VOs taken action	102	0.00	0.00	0.00	0.00	49	1.00	0.00	1.00	1.00
Village size	95	419	440	49	2540	48	575	551	45	1800
% of SC/ST population	95	38.15	29.03	0.00	100.00	48	37.72	26.67	0.00	100.00
% of gross irrigated area	95	18.96	15.43	0.00	77.72	48	15.28	12.83	0.00	50.00
% of female contestants in elections	93	27.98	17.65	0.00	100.00	48	25.37	14.25	0.00	47.06
% of SC/ST contestants in elections	93	43.44	33.67	0.00	100.00	48	36.90	31.78	0.00	100.00
Fare to district HQ	70	40.59	23.98	0.00	120.00	41	37.24	11.52	2.00	80.00
No. of groups per 100 population in the village	94	8.45	5.29	1.16	28.00	48	8.35	5.15	2.67	24.44
Prop. of villages in Srikakulam district	102	0.03	0.17	0.00	1.00	49	0.02	0.14	0.00	1.00
Prop. of villages in Anantapur district	102	0.59	0.49	0.00	1.00	49	0.76	0.43	0.00	1.00
VO age in months	102	40.24	10.84	8.00	62.00	49	45.27	9.83	23.00	66.00
SC/ST SHGs per VO	102	4.05	4.04	0.00	18.00	49	5.31	5.33	0.00	29.00

contd...

...contd...

Description of Variables	No Action Taken by VO/MS					Action Taken by VO/MS				
	Observations	Mean	Std. Dev.	Min.	Max.	Observations	Mean	Std. Dev.	Min.	Max.
Total no of SHGs per VO	101	8.29	5.28	1.00	22.00	49	11.86	7.86	2.00	39.00
No. of VOs have meeting in less than one month	102	0.05	0.22	0.00	1.00	49	0.00	0.00	0.00	0.00
No. of VOs have meeting every month	102	0.15	0.36	0.00	1.00	49	0.10	0.31	0.00	1.00
Prop. of VO committees	102	0.39	0.49	0.00	1.00	49	0.63	0.49	0.00	1.00
No. of government programmes per VO	102	0.65	0.87	0.00	3.00	49	0.88	0.81	0.00	3.00
Atrocities against women	24	0.36	0.13	0.20	0.90	9	0.77	0.51	0.30	1.60
Prop. of VOs taken action	24	0.00	0.00	0.00	0.00	9	1.00	0.00	1.00	1.00
Village size	24	451	437	91	1900	9	773	761	200	1784
% of SC/ST population	24	34.01	25.84	0.00	99.17	9	18.79	10.88	2.00	32.02
% of gross irrigated area	24	25.67	16.10	0.00	50.47	9	26.58	12.95	7.90	43.03
% of female contestants in elections	23	35.89	23.42	0.00	100.00	9	21.29	5.80	14.29	28.57
% of SC/ST contestants in elections	23	40.38	32.76	0.00	100.00	9	9.99	13.15	0.00	35.71
Fare to district HQ	18	35.50	15.07	0.00	53.00	8	41.38	13.23	11.00	50.00
No. of groups per 100 population in the village	24	6.90	4.02	1.68	17.58	9	8.61	4.20	3.48	13.00
Prop. of villages in Srikakulam district	24	0.08	0.28	0.00	1.00	9	0.00	0.00	0.00	0.00
Prop. of villages in Anantapur district	24	0.75	0.44	0.00	1.00	9	1.00	0.00	1.00	1.00
VO age in months	24	38.67	10.07	15.00	55.00	9	47.11	8.08	34.00	60.00
SC/ST SHGs per VO	24	4.67	6.81	0.00	29.00	9	3.11	3.22	0.00	8.00
Total no. of SHGs per VO	24	8.83	6.81	1.00	29.00	9	9.44	6.73	2.00	19.00
No. of VOs have meeting in less than one month	24	0.08	0.28	0.00	1.00	9	0.00	0.00	0.00	0.00
No. of VOs have meeting every month	24	0.08	0.28	0.00	1.00	9	0.11	0.33	0.00	1.00
Prop. of VO committees	24	0.50	0.51	0.00	1.00	9	0.44	0.53	0.00	1.00
No. of government programmes per VO	24	0.54	0.72	0.00	2.00	9	0.11	0.33	0.00	1.00

References

Ashley, C. and D. Carney (1999). *Sustainable Livelihoods: Lessons from Early Experience.* London: Department for International Development (DFID).

Dev Mahendra *et al.* (2003). "Andhra Pradesh District Poverty Initiatives Project (APDPIP): Effectiveness of Seeds of Change in Sustainable Livelihood Framework", Report prepared for the SERP (GoAP), Hyderabad: Centre for Economic and Social Studies.

———. (2007). *End-Term Appraisal of Andhra Pradesh District Poverty Initiatives Project.* Hyderabad: Centre for Economic and Social Studies.

Galab, S. and N.C. Rao (2003). "Women's Self-Help Groups, Poverty Alleviation and Empowerment", *Economic and Political Weekly,* 38 (12 & 13): 1274-1282.

Galab, S. and E. Revathi (2009). "Women Empowerment and Child Development: An Inter State and Intra State Analysis", in S. Mahendra Dev, C. Ravi, M. Venkatanaraya (eds.), *Human Development in Andhra Pradesh Experiences, Issues and Challenges.* Hyderabad: Centre for Economic and Social Studies.

Grootaert, C. (1998). "Social Capital: The Missing Link?", *World Bank Social Capital Initiative Working Paper* No. 3. Washington, DC: World Bank.

Kabeer, N. (2001). "Conflicts Over Credit: Re-Evaluating the Empowerment Potential of Loans to Women in Rural Bangladesh", in *World Development* 1: 63–84.

———. (2003). *Gender Equality, Poverty Eradication and the Millennium Development Goals: Promoting Women's Capabilities and Participation. www.unescap.org /esid/ committee2003/genderequality.pdf*

Mosedale, S. (2005). "Assessing Women's Empowerment: Towards a Conceptual Approach", *Journal of International Development* 7(2): 243–57.

Murray, C. (2001). "Livelihoods Research: Some Conceptual and Methodological Issues", *Background Paper* 5. Manchester: Chronic Poverty Research Centre, University of Manchester.

Norton, A. and M. Foster (2001). "The Potential of using Sustainable Livelihoods Approaches in Poverty Reduction Strategy Papers", *Working Paper* 148. London: Overseas Development Institute (ODI).

Scoones, I. (1998). "Sustainable Rural Livelihoods: A Framework of Analysis", *Working Paper* 72. Sussex, London: Institute of Development Studies.

Sen, G. and S. Batliwala (2000). "Empowering Women for Reproductive Rights", in H.B. Presser and G. Sen (eds.), *Women's Empowerment and Demographic Processes: Moving Beyond Cairo.* Oxford: Oxford University Press.

Wong, K.F. (2003). "Empowerment as a Panacea for Poverty—Old Wine in New Bottles? Reflection on the World Bank's Conception of Power", *Progress in Development Studies* 3(4): 307–22.

6 Indira Kranthi Patham and Poverty Reduction in Andhra Pradesh

S. Mahendra Dev, S. Galab,
C. Ravi and G. Alivelu

Introduction

The formation of self-help groups (SHGs) and their federations at the village, *mandal* and district levels for generating micro-processes to influence the institutions, formal and informal, and policies for improving the livelihoods of the poor, is central to Andhra Pradesh District Poverty Initiatives Project (APDPIP), which is now called Indira Kranthi Patham (IKP). This project aims at enhancing assets, capabilities and the ability of the poor to deal with shocks and risks. It recognises that the livelihood strategies and income levels of the poor are inadequate not only due to lack of financial capital but also due to low/lack of physical and human capabilities. It assumes that empowerment of poor women should come prior to the access to financial capital for the better utilisation of existing resources and expanding the resource base to address the issues relating to poverty. The APDPIP was launched in 2000 in backward *mandals* of six districts of the state. The evaluation of APDPIP was carried out using household sample surveys conducted in 2000, 2003 and 2006. The surveys conducted in 2003 and 2006 were panel surveys. The panel survey compared to cross-section surveys enables to unpack more issues especially relating to 'mobility' in poverty.

Context

Of late, there is a growing concern regarding the mobility of the households in regard to their poverty status overtime. This concern has emerged due to two significant dynamics of poverty *viz*., chronic poverty (remaining in poverty for long time); and the drivers and the barriers contributing to remaining in poverty, moving out of poverty, and falling into poverty differ. Thus, the public policies to tackle these three dimensions of poverty also differ (Krishna, 2004). In this context, analysis based on the panel data can be robust and throw more light on these issues. The panel data collected to assess the contribution of Indira Kranthi Patham (IKP) to poverty reduction in the project area of Andhra Pradesh at two points of time, 2003 and 2006 provides an opportunity to analyse the contribution of IKP to these dimensions of poverty.

Research Issues

Against the above backdrop, this paper addresses itself to the following specific issues:

1. How far IKP has contributed to poverty reduction?
2. What is the contribution of IKP to the mobility in poverty between 2003 and 2006?
3. What is the role of different factors for poverty, escaping poverty and falling into poverty?
4. How far IKP contributed in reducing poverty, escaping poverty and falling into poverty?

Methodology

A total of 2,641 households spread across the 256 main villages and 306 habitations were covered in the surveys to assess the contribution to the poverty reduction. The present study is based on the panel survey (2003 and 2006) data. The sample of households includes both the participants and non-participants of the programme. The surveys of 2003 and 2006 used comparable questionnaires to collect detail household consumption expenditure. The consumption expenditure data was used to categorise all the sample households into three income groups, *viz*., very poor, moderately poor and non-poor. Very poor are those living below 75 per cent of poverty—these are hardcore poor; moderately poor are those between 75 per cent of poverty line and poverty line, the rest are categorised as non-poor. State level official poverty line of 1999-2000 was adjusted for inter-district price differential and moved with consumer price index for agricultural labour to arrive at the price indices for 2003 and 2006. The poverty status of each household was determined for each year using the district-specific poverty lines. But the estimation of poverty is beyond the scope of the paper. However, the contribution of the programme to poverty reduction is assessed—in terms of changes in consumption expenditure, changes in the incidence of poverty and mobility in poverty from one expenditure group to another between 2003 and 2006—between participant and non-participant households using the double difference (DD) method. In the analysis we see the changes in these parameters for the participant households between 2003 and 2006 to assess the improvements in the consumption expenditure, decline in the incidence of poverty and mobility in poverty. These improvements cannot be attributed to DPIP alone due to the fact that there could be improvement in these parameters for the non-participant households between 2003 and 2006, independent of the participation in DPIP. This is due to non-DPIP interventions. Hence, the improvements in these parameters of the participant households should be corrected for the increase of the non-participant households. This is what is called double difference (difference-in-differences) method. This can be denoted as follows:

$$\Delta P_{DPIP=}\Delta P_{PART} - \Delta P_{NONPART}$$

Where ΔP_{DPIP} represents the improvement in the poverty status due to DPIP;

ΔP_{PART} represents the improvements in the poverty status due to DPIP and NON-DPIP; and

$\Delta P_{NONPART}$ represents improvements in poverty status due to NON-DPIP

The analysis has been conducted at two levels, *viz.*, descriptive and econometric analysis. The analysis based on this method is in order.

Descriptive Analysis

Changes in the distribution of consumption expenditure, changes in poverty status; mobility in poverty status and the factors that differentiate the three dimensions of mobility in poverty (remained in poverty, escaping poverty and falling into poverty) have been considered for the descriptive analysis.

Changes in Poverty

The cumulative distribution of households according to monthly per capita expenditure (MPCE) groups for the participant and non-participant households in 2003 and 2006 clearly indicates faster decline in the percentage of households at the lower end of MPCE distribution of the participant households. The percentage of households below Rs 270 declined from 9.8 to 3.6 for the participant households, while it declined from 10 to 4 for the non-participant households. Similar pattern emerged for the immediate MPCE group with a cut-off of Rs 320. However, the changes in the distribution flatten at later stages indicating similar gains for participant and non-participant households (Table 6.1). This distribution affects the poverty status of the households. The percentage of decline in the poverty ratios between 2003 and 2006 is negligible in the project area and the same is true for the very poor and moderately poor (Table 6.2). A disaggregated poverty ratios for the different social groups unfold that the incidence of poverty has declined by 6 per cent for all the poor and it has declined by less than 1 per cent among very poor and 9 per

Table 6.1

Cumulative Frequency Distribution of the Sample Participant and Non-Participant Households by MPCE Groups

MPCE Class	*Participants*		*Non-Participants*		*% Decline in Cumulative Frequency*	
	2003	*2006*	*2003*	*2006*	*Participants*	*Non-Participants*
< Rs. 235	5.1	1.8	5.6	2.7	-65.8	-52.5
< 270	9.8	3.6	10.0	4.0	-63.6	-60.0
< 320	19.5	7.4	18.9	7.8	-62.2	-58.6
< 365	28.7	12.9	29.0	12.9	-55.0	-55.6
< 410	39.2	20.0	39.9	20.0	-48.9	-49.9
< 455	48.0	29.3	48.1	28.9	-39.0	-40.0
< 510	57.6	41.2	58.0	37.9	-28.5	-34.5
< 580	68.1	54.0	68.8	51.2	-20.8	-25.6
< 690	78.8	69.4	77.9	67.2	-12.0	-13.7
< 890	87.7	84.3	88.1	82.3	-3.9	-6.6
< Rs. 1155	94.3	91.9	94.4	91.0	-2.5	-3.5
All	100.0	100.0	100.0	100.0	0.0	0.0

cent among moderately poor among scheduled castes (SCs). However, the respective figures are 7 per cent for all the poor, 4 per cent for the very poor and 8 per cent for the moderately poor among the other castes (OCs). The poverty reduction is much faster for the backward castes (BCs) compared to OCs. Scheduled tribes (STs) and OC groups did not gain much in this regard.

Table 6.2

Changes in Poverty between 2003 and 2006 for the Participant and Non-Participant Sample Households

Poverty Category	*Year*		*% Change*
	2003	*2006*	
Very poor			
Participant households	7.29	7.72	5.9
Non-participant households	3.92	4.29	9.4
Programme impact			-3.5
Moderately poor			
Participant households	15.63	14.78	-5.4
Non-participant households	8.62	8.29	-3.8
Programme impact			-1.6
All poor			
Participant households	22.92	22.5	-1.8
Non-participant households	12.54	12.58	0.3
Programme impact			-2.2
Non-poor			
Participant households	77.08	77.5	0.5
Non-participant households	87.46	87.42	0.0
Programme impact			0.6

Mobility and Correlates of Mobility in Poverty

The mobility of all poor households in terms of escaping poverty found to be very limited due to the project between 2003 and 2006. However, moderately poor moving out of poverty and very poor moving to moderately poor is slightly higher among the participant households compared to the non-participant households. This indicates that the

Table 6.3

Changes in Poverty between 2003 and 2006 for the Participant and Non-Participant Sample Households by Social Groups

Category	Very Poor			Moderately Poor			All Poor			Non-Poor		
	2003	2006	% Change	2003	2006	% Change	2003	2006	% Change	2003	2006	% Change
SC												
Participant households	15.04	6.5	-56.8	25.2	10.98	-56.4	40.24	17.48	-56.6	29.67	41.06	38.4
Non-participant households	12.73	5.45	-57.2	20	12.12	-39.4	32.73	17.57	-46.3	34.55	37.58	8.8
Programme impact			0.4			-17.0			-10.2			29.6
ST												
Participant households	8.47	5.56	-34.4	18.52	14.29	-22.8	26.99	19.85	-26.5	32.28	35.45	9.8
Non-participant households	8.4	4.2	-50.0	14.29	10.08	-29.5	22.69	14.28	-37.1	41.18	37.82	-8.2
Programme impact			15.6			6.6			10.6			18.0
BC												
Participant households	4.44	2.45	-44.8	11.94	4.9	-59.0	16.38	7.35	-55.1	37.67	34.15	-9.3
Non-participant households	6.52	4.18	-35.9	14.88	8.36	-43.8	21.4	12.54	-41.4	34.95	31.44	-10.0
Programme impact			-8.9			-15.1			-13.7			0.7
OC												
Participant households	4	2	-50.0	8.67	6.67	-23.1	12.67	8.67	-31.6	34	28.67	-15.7
Non-participant households	6.59	3.59	-45.5	9.58	2.99	-68.8	16.17	6.58	-59.3	31.74	23.95	-24.5
Programme impact			-4.5			45.7			27.7			8.9

programme has not contributed considerably to the poor households to move out of poverty. The percentage of very poor in 2003, moving to moderately poor and to non-poor in 2006 has increased by 2 per cent and 3 per cent respectively and remained very poor has decreased by 5 per cent for the sample participant households in case of SCs due to IKP. Interestingly, the programme has not contributed positively to the mobility in poverty for the moderately poor households belonging to the same caste. However, only the very poor participant households moving to moderately poor have increased by 9 per cent due to the programme in case of STs. But, among the BCs, the percentage of all poor escaping poverty has increased by 4 and the percentage of remained poor has decreased by 3 for the participant households due to the programme. However, the moderately poor compared to the very poor gained more from the programme in the mobility due to the programme. Interestingly, all the category of poor households among the OCs have moved positively in poverty due to the programme (Table 6.4). The correlates of mobility in poverty unfolds that caste affiliation of the household did not have relationship with the mobility in poverty. The households with larger family size remained to be poor and those with smaller family size could move out of poverty and continued to be non- poor. Similarly, the households with higher proportion of workers could move out of poverty and continue to be non-poor and those with lower proportion of workers remained to be poor. Relatively larger piece of cultivated land enabled the households to move out of poverty and enabled to continue to be non-poor. The households who remained to be non-poor had high number of milch and draught animals. Relatively higher levels of women empowerment in public and private spaces facilitated the households to move out of poverty and to remain to be non-poor. Similarly, households who moved out of poverty and remained to be non-poor had relatively higher women's borrowing capacity (Table 6.5).

Table 6.4

Percentage Distribution of Very Poor, Moderately Poor and Non-Poor Households of 2003 by their Mobility in 2006 by Social Groups

	SC			*ST*			*BC*		
	Participant	*Non-Participant*	*Diff.*	*Participant*	*Non-Participant*	*Diff.*	*Participant*	*Non-Participant*	*Diff.*
% of very poor in 2003	15.04	12.73		8.47	8.4		4.44	6.52	
Of which:									
% remained VP	13.51	19.05	-5.54	15.63	10.00	5.63	20.69	12.82	7.87
% moved to MP	16.22	14.29	1.93	18.75	10.00	8.75	17.24	7.69	9.55
% moved to NP	70.27	66.67	3.60	65.63	80.00	-14.37	62.07	79.49	-17.42
% of moderately poor in 2003	25.20	20.00		18.52	14.29		11.94	14.88	
Of which:									
% remained MP	17.74	15.15	2.59	22.86	17.65	5.21	11.54	16.85	-5.31
% became VP	6.45	6.06	0.39	7.14	11.76	-4.62	1.28	7.87	-6.59
% moved to NP	75.81	78.79	-2.98	70.00	70.59	-0.59	87.18	75.28	11.90
% of all poor in 2003	40.24	32.73		26.99	22.69		16.38	21.40	
Of which:									
% remained poor	26.26	25.93	0.33	31.37	25.93	5.44	19.63	23.44	-3.81
% escaped poverty	73.74	74.07	-0.33	68.63	74.07	-5.44	80.37	76.56	3.81
% of non-poor in 2003	59.75	67.28		73.02	77.31		83.61	78.60	
Of which:									
% remained non-poor	88.44	86.49	1.95	84.42	89.13	-4.71	95.05	90.43	4.62
% fallen to VP	4.76	2.70	2.06	3.99	2.17	1.82	1.65	2.77	-1.12
% fallen to MP	6.80	10.81	-4.01	11.59	8.70	2.89	3.30	6.81	-3.51

contd...

...contd...

	OC			*All*		
	Participant	*Non-Participant*	*Diff.*	*Participant*	*Non-Participant*	*Diff.*
% of very poor in 2003	4.00	6.59		7.29	7.72	
Of which:						
% remained VP	0.00	9.09	-9.09	15.38	13.58	1.80
% moved to MP	16.67	27.27	-10.60	17.31	12.35	4.96
% moved to NP	83.33	63.64	19.69	67.31	74.07	-6.76
% of moderately poor in 2003	8.67	9.58		15.63	14.78	
Of which:						
% remained MP	15.38	6.25	9.13	17.04	15.48	1.56
% became VP	0.00	6.25	-6.25	4.48	7.74	-3.26
% moved to NP	84.62	87.50	-2.88	78.48	76.77	1.71
% of all poor in 2003	12.67	16.17		22.92	22.50	
Of which:						
% remained poor	15.79	22.22	-6.43	25.08	24.15	0.93
% escaped poverty	84.21	77.78	6.43	74.92	75.85	-0.93
% of non-poor in 2003	87.33	83.84		77.09	77.50	
Of which:						
% remained non-poor	92.37	96.43	-4.06	91.18	90.77	0.41
% fallen to VP	2.29	2.86	-0.57	2.73	2.71	0.02
% fallen to MP	5.34	0.71	4.63	6.09	6.52	-0.43

Table 6.5

Social and Economic Characteristics of Households by their Mobility in Poverty

Category of Households	*Remained VP*		*Moved from VP to MP*		*Moved from VP to NP*	
	Participant	*Non-Participant*	*Participant*	*Non-Participant*	*Participant*	*Non-Participant*
% of SC	31.25	36.36	33.33	30.00	37.15	23.33
% of ST	31.25	9.09	33.33	10.00	30.00	13.33
% of BC	37.50	45.45	27.78	30.00	25.71	51.67
% OC	0.00	9.09	5.56	30.00	7.14	11.67
HH size	6.31	5.09	6.00	5.00	5.26	4.55
Land possessed	2.00	1.86	1.77	1.75	2.42	1.38
Cultivated	1.50	0.64	1.74	1.75	2.30	1.14
Number of activities	2.81	3.27	2.94	2.50	2.83	2.38
Average no. milch animals	0.75	0.82	1.22	0.00	0.60	0.27
Average no. draught animals	0.50	0.00	0.44	0.40	0.50	0.25
Average no. of small ruminants	3.13	1.55	2.89	0.00	2.93	0.85
% primary	22.87	7.97	26.51	17.00	25.57	20.09
% secondary	20.88	10.82	14.74	12.50	16.13	11.31
% female literacy	35.83	11.36	28.24	18.33	31.35	24.69
% literates	43.75	18.79	41.25	29.50	41.70	31.39
Number of groups member of	0.94	0.09	0.89	0.10	1.00	0.02
Number of other groups member of	0.31	0.18	0.50	0.10	0.37	0.13
Number of Govt. progs. (livelihood) accessed	1.94	0.09	1.28	0.20	1.56	0.43
Number of Govt. progs. (cash/kind) accessed	2.25	1.18	2.39	0.70	1.61	1.33
Index of participation in social action	0.44	0.31	0.62	0.44	0.47	0.37
Index of autonomy	0.30	0.30	0.48	0.44	0.37	0.35
Index of control/coersion	0.71	0.76	0.68	0.61	0.71	0.67
Borrowing capacity (informal)	1745	1868	2522	1775	3644	3693
Borrowing capacity (SHG)	1688	0	2972	0	2940	192
Borrowing capacity (formal)	0	0	56	100	700	140
Average MPCE in 2003	206	194	209	185	211	200
Average MPCE in 2006	224	215	337	332	573	595
% change in MPCE	8.48	10.94	61.41	79.71	171.77	197.05

contd...

...contd...

Category of Households	Remained MP		From MP became VP		Moved from MP to NP	
	Participant	Non-Participant	Participant	Non-Participant	Participant	Non-Participant
% of SC	28.95	20.83	40.00	16.67	26.85	21.85
% of ST	42.11	12.50	50.00	16.67	28.00	10.08
% of BC	23.68	62.50	10.00	58.33	38.86	56.30
% OC	5.26	4.17	0.00	8.33	6.29	11.76
HH size	6.05	5.75	6.50	4.08	5.15	4.70
Land possessed	4.20	2.51	2.47	1.71	3.10	4.51
Cultivated	3.86	2.15	2.18	1.00	2.89	2.31
Number of activities	2.97	2.63	3.60	2.42	2.81	2.77
Average no. milch animals	0.53	1.00	1.10	0.75	0.65	0.52
Average no. draught animals	0.53	0.25	0.40	0.33	0.58	0.55
Average no. of small ruminants	3.16	2.79	1.30	1.92	2.39	1.32
% primary	19.93	22.73	15.96	24.67	23.87	22.33
% secondary	14.24	13.22	11.36	9.26	20.43	17.86
% female literacy	24.89	19.10	21.92	20.00	33.04	30.78
% literates	34.17	35.96	27.32	33.93	44.30	40.19
Number of groups member of	0.95	0.04	1.00	0.00	1.00	0.01
Number of other groups member of	0.18	0.13	0.20	0.25	0.40	0.13
Number of Govt. progs. (Livelihood) accessed	1.29	0.29	1.60	0.00	1.87	0.34
Number of Govt. progs. (cash/kind) accessed	2.40	1.58	2.60	1.08	1.67	1.14
Index of participation in social action index	0.32	0.50	0.76	0.28	0.48	0.37
Index of autonomy	0.45	0.45	0.60	0.19	0.46	0.36
Index of control/ coersion	0.70	0.69	0.70	0.76	0.75	0.69
Borrowing capacity (informal)	3714	7081	2810	979	5696	4979
Borrowing capacity (SHG)	3645	417	1750	83	4690	261
Borrowing capacity (formal)	0	625	1200	125	1047	1097
Average MPCE in 2003	298	301	300	297	299	298
Average MPCE in 2006	326	331	234	218	598	608
% change in MPCE	9.61	9.69	-22.24	-26.47	100.30	104.17

contd...

...contd...

Category of Households	Remained NP		Moved from NP to VP		Moved from NP to MP	
	Participant	Non-Participant	Participant	Non-Participant	Participant	Non-Participant
% of SC	12.97	13.01	23.33	13.64	14.92	22.64
% of ST	23.23	11.11	36.67	9.09	47.76	15.09
% of BC	51.74	57.59	30.00	59.09	26.87	60.38
% OC	12.06	18.29	10.00	18.18	10.45	1.89
HH size	4.70	4.16	6.17	5.32	5.64	5.00
Land possessed	4.14	3.27	3.96	1.74	3.99	1.64
Cultivated	3.74	3.01	3.74	1.51	3.80	1.56
Number of activities	2.57	2.38	3.00	2.82	2.70	2.47
Average no. milch animals	1.73	1.18	0.93	0.59	1.34	0.83
Average no. draught animals	0.82	0.60	0.47	0.45	0.96	0.60
Average no. of small ruminants	2.56	1.74	2.13	0.95	2.16	2.00
% primary	21.62	20.43	28.97	17.52	27.37	18.04
% secondary	27.32	25.02	18.43	24.33	18.28	16.77
% female literacy	34.70	31.41	41.17	26.06	33.33	30.96
% literates	48.94	45.45	47.40	41.85	45.65	34.81
Number of groups member of	0.96	0.01	1.03	0.00	1.09	0.00
Number of other groups member of	0.23	0.09	0.43	0.09	0.21	0.13
Number of Govt. progs. (Livelihood) accessed	1.67	0.77	0.97	1.32	2.25	1.19
Number of Govt. progs. (cash/kind) accessed	1.12	0.73	1.77	1.23	1.76	1.38
Index of participation in social action index	0.54	0.38	0.58	0.42	0.73	0.48
Index of autonomy	0.44	0.42	0.50	0.32	0.48	0.41
Index of control/ coersion	0.74	0.71	0.73	0.70	0.74	0.75
Borrowing capacity (informal)	10385	7785	1923	1939	1911	2752
Borrowing capacity (SHG)	4334	158	3000	0	2418	500
Borrowing capacity (formal)	1939	1898	333	0	1060	4
Average MPCE in 2003	679	700	619	1457	490	641
Average MPCE in 2006	775	786	239	228	337	336
% change in MPCE	14.19	12.28	-61.42	-84.37	-31.27	-47.55

Note: VP - very poor;

MP - moderately poor;

NP - non-poor.

Econometric Analysis

The determinants of poverty and mobility in poverty of the households have been identified through logistic regression analysis.

The following models have been formulated to estimate the role of different factors:

$$PS_{2006} = a+b\ X_{2003} + c\ PTdpip+Ui$$

$$RIP = a+b\ X_{2003} + c\ PTdpip+Ui$$

$$MOP = a+b\ X_{2003} + c\ PTdpip+Ui$$

$$FIP= a+b\ X_{2003} + c\ PTdpip+Ui$$

$$PS_{2006} = a+b\ X_{2003} + c\ PTdpip+dV+Ui$$

$$RIP = a+b\ X_{2003} + c\ PTdpip+dV+Ui$$

$$MOP = a+b\ X_{2003} + c\ PTdpip+dV+Ui$$

$$FIP = a+b\ X_{2003} + c\ PTdpip+dV+Ui$$

Where:

- PS2006= poverty status of the households in 2006 and it takes value '1' if the household is in poverty and takes value '0' if the household is out of poverty;
- RIP= remained in poverty between 2003 and 2006 and it takes value '1' if the household remained in poverty and takes value '0' if the household has not remained in poverty;
- MOP= moved out of poverty between 2003 and 2006 and it takes value '1' if the household moved out of poverty and takes value '0' if the household does not move out of poverty;
- FIP= fallen in poverty between 2003 and 2006 and it takes value '1' if the household fallen into poverty and takes value '0' if the household does not fall into poverty;
- X2003= a vector of characteristics of the households in 2003, *viz.*, caste affiliation, household size, percentage of workers in household, land cultivated (in acres), number of milch/draught animals/small ruminants held by the household, literacy levels of the head of the household, female literacy, members in the other groups, number of government programmes (livelihood) accessed by the household,

number of government programmes (cash/kind) accessed, women's political participation, women's participation in social action, women's autonomy, control/coercion husband, borrowing capacity (in rupees);

- PTdpip = participation in DPIP and it takes value '1' if the women participates in DPIP and it takes value '0' if the women doesn't participate in DPIP;
- V=village dummies.

All the equations contain the characters of the households in 2003.These are considered as initial conditions that determine poverty. Their relationship with poverty is well researched. However, their relationship with mobility in poverty (remaining poverty, moving out of poverty and falling in poverty) using panel data has not been attempted so far. Moreover, the poverty status and mobility in poverty can be influenced by the variations in the determinants of poverty across the villages. These variations are controlled by introducing village dummies. This allows the household factors alone to play in determining reduction and mobility in poverty.

The probit regression results are presented in Table 6.6. The results indicate that SC and ST households have higher probability of being poor, while non-poor SC, ST and BC households have higher probability of falling into poverty. Larger household size increases the chances of being poor as well as chances of a non-poor households falling to poverty. Female literacy is significant in enhancing the likelihood of moving out of poverty as well as reducing chances of a non-poor household falling into poverty. Cultivated land and milch animals are found to be significant. The size of cultivated land not only reduces the probability of being poor but also increases the chances of moving out of poverty. Similarly, possession of milch animals reduces the chances of being poor and increases the chances of moving out of poverty. Possession of draught animals does not seem to be significant for being poor or for falling into poverty. However, the chance of moving out of poverty seems to be reduced with possession of milch animals. Access to livelihood based public programmes is found to enhance the chances of moving out of poverty. The indicator of women's borrowing capacity seems to be a significant determinant of mobility. It reduces the chances of being poor, increases chances of moving out of poverty and reduces the chances of falling into poverty. Women's autonomy is found to be significant. Women's autonomy enhances chances of moving out of poverty significantly. Participation in *gram panchayats* reduces the chances of being poor, falling into poverty and increases the chances of moving out of poverty. Controlling for all the above, participation in DPIP programme is found to reduce the chances of being poor and increase the chances of moving out of poverty.

Table 6.6

Probit Estimates for Poverty Status in FUS, Escaping Poverty, and Falling into Poverty

Variable	*Poor FUS*		*Escaped Poverty*		*Fallen into Poverty*	
	Coef.	*Sig.*	*Coef.*	*Sig.*	*Coef.*	*Sig.*
Social group of household (ref: others)						
SC	0.456	*	0.014		0.529	*
ST	0.222		0.013		0.165	
BC	0.268		0.289		0.376	
HH size	0.159	*	-0.189		0.137	
% female literates	-0.004	*	0.011	*	0.000	
% workers	0.004		-0.006		0.006	
Cultivated land (hectares)	-0.072	*	0.045		-0.086	*
Number of activities	-0.048		0.186		-0.034	
Number of milch animals	-0.006		-0.210	*	-0.032	
Number of draught animals	0.001		0.223		0.114	
Number of small ruminants	0.005		-0.036		-0.003	
Number of groups women are members of	-0.070		-0.879		-5.589	*
Number of government programmes accessed (livelihood)	-0.011		0.153		0.018	
Number of Government programmes (cash/kind) accessed	0.155	*	0.030		0.296	*
Borrowing capacity (Rs)	-0.024	*	0.004		-0.038	*
Women attend *panchayat* meetings	-0.373		0.230		-0.524	

contd...

...contd...

Variable	*Poor FUS*		*Escaped Poverty*		*Fallen into Poverty*	
	Coef.	*Sig.*	*Coef.*	*Sig.*	*Coef.*	*Sig.*
Women participate in social actions	-0.129		-0.090		-0.217	
Women autonomy	-0.234		-0.262		-0.367	*
Index of control/coercion	0.469	*	-0.771		0.457	
Participation in IKP (ref: non-participant)						
Participant	0.937		-0.473		1.091	
Interaction of participation with						
SC	-0.368		-0.116		-0.501	
ST	0.063		-0.272		0.095	
BC	-0.463	*	-0.304		-0.696	*
HH size	-0.048		0.006		-0.045	
% female literates	0.002		-0.006		0.000	
% workers	-0.006		0.000		-0.008	
Cultivated land (hectares)	0.053	*	-0.017		0.071	*
Number of activities	0.134		-0.195		0.074	
Number of milch animals	-0.029		0.178		-0.003	
Number of draught animals	-0.170	*	-0.012		-0.230	*
Number of small ruminants	-0.002		0.025		0.002	
Number of groups women are members of	0.270		1.047	*	5.936	
Number of Government programmes accessed (livelihood)	0.013		-0.130		-0.005	
Number of Government programmes (cash/kind) accessed	0.000		-0.209	*	-0.182	*
Borrowing capacity (Rs)	-0.022	*	0.032	*	-0.014	
Women attend *panchayat* meetings	-0.324		0.172		-0.315	
Women participate in social actions	-0.073		0.525		0.150	
Women autonomy	0.390	*	0.330		0.628	*
Index of control/coercion	-0.729	*	1.355	*	-0.468	
Constant	-2.062	*	1.566	*	-2.408	*

Conclusions

Poverty, being an outcome of multiple deprivations, empowerment of poor is considered a critical factor for reducing poverty (Radhakrishna, and Ray, 2005). It is well recognised that SHGs are appropriate grass-root level institutions for addressing the barriers to move out of poverty. Our analysis shows that IKP has significant impact on status and mobility in poverty. Our results also indicate that women's empowerment can be a useful instrument in reducing poverty and also in reducing the chances of falling into poverty.

References

Krishna, Anirudh (2004). "Escaping Poverty and Becoming Poor: Who gains, Who Loses and Why?", *World Development* 32(1): 121-36.

Radhakrishna, R. and Shovan Ray (ed.) (2005). *Handbook of Poverty in India—Perspectives, Policies and Programmes*. Oxford University Press.

7 DPIP Outcomes

Assets, Livelihoods and Security

S. Galab, G.K. Mitra,
P. Prudhvikar Reddy and G. Alivelu

Livelihood has been defined by Blaikie *et al.* (1994) as 'the command an individual, family, or other social group has over an income and/or bundles of resources that can be used or exchanged to satisfy its needs.' A livelihood comprises capabilities, assets and activities required for a means of living. Assets like land, livestock, farm and non-farm equipment can be used directly or indirectly to generate economic activities for living. Sustainable livelihood security is a complex social concept. According to Dahl (1993/94), livelihood can be described as means for living on sustenance. Security indicates protection, assurance, or a secure condition. The livelihood is sustainable if it can bear the weight of present activities for a long period, or maintain or keep efforts or activities going continuously. Sustainable livelihood security has to be determined by standards of ecological security, social equity, and economic efficiency.

The District Povertys Initiatives Project (DPIP) in Andhra Pradesh attempted to improve access to credit for the poor to come out of poverty. It aimed at enhancing the asset base and capabilities of the poor to undertake economic activities for escaping poverty. The project has made interventions in the land market to improve access to land for the poor. Increased access to credit may increase the ability of the poor to access land and or undertake investments on land from improving productivity of land. The access to credit results in the enhancement of the productive assets such as livestock, farm and non-farm enterprise equipment. These changes ultimately would result in widening the livelihood choices of the poor. Thus the changes in livelihood choices might bring changes in the level and composition of household income. The changes in the level and composition of income in turn lead to improvements in the levels and composition of consumption basket of the poor for improving the well-being of the poor. The study is conducted across three districts of Andhra Pradesh—Srikakulam, Anantapur and Adilabad and across the economic categories for two points of time—Follow up Survey I and II.

Changes in Landholdings and Other Agricultural Assets

Proportion of households possessing own land has increased, across all households from 64 per cent in FUS-I to 83 per cent in FUS-II. It is true across all the districts, though the increase in the percentage of households possessing own land is high in Srikakulam (from 58 per cent in FUS-I to 85 per cent in FUS-II) (Table 7.1). Further, the participants have clear title of the land possessed due to programme interventions. Total land possessed per household is higher among the participants (3.02 acres) against the non-participants (2.68 acres). The data reveal that total land possessed per household has increased marginally among the participants, while there is a considerable decline amongst the non-participants (18 cents) across all the districts. Further, the quality of land possessed by the participants is much better than that of the non-participants. This is reflected in the per unit value of land (Rs 1.11 lakh for participants and Rs 1.03 lakh for non-participants). This could be particularly observed in Srikakulam and Anantapur (Table 7.1).

The proportion of households having agricultural implements is slightly higher for participants (87 per cent) while it is 84 per cent in the case of non-participants. Though there is a decline in the proportion of households having agricultural implements from FUS-I to FUS-II, this decline is more pronounced amongst the non-participants (3 per cent decline) than the participants (1 per cent decline). Similar results hold good in Anantapur and Adilabad. This implies that the programme has enabled the participants to retain their assets even though they do not acquire any new assets. The value of the implements owned by the participants also is at higher level, when compared to the non-participants, particularly so in Anantapur. This is particularly due to high value of irrigation assets for the participants over the non-participants (Rs 15,540 *versus* Rs 12,208) (Table 7.1).

The composition of livestock shows an improvement in draught and milch animals, among the participants between FUS-I and FUS-II, while small ruminants declined marginally. The case of milch animals shows that the percentage of households having milch animals is high among participants compared to non-participants (70 per cent *versus* 67 per cent) in FUS II. While more number of participants possessed milch animals over FUS-I, there was not any improvement amongst the non-participants. Similar increase of 4 per cent over FUS-I was noticed in case of draught animals also. However, in Adilabad district, the number of participant households possessing small ruminants increased in FUS-II, while there is a marginal decline in the households possessing milch animals. Average number of milch animals per household is slightly higher for participant households (1.45 per cent) and for non-participants (1.35 per cent). This is true across Srikakulam and Anantapur. However, possession of average number of draught animals is significantly higher for participant households as against non-participants. Thus, it reveals that the share of milch and draught animals is slightly higher for participants in Srikakulam and Anantapur, for Adilabad, there is a slight increase in draught animals and marginal decline in the case of milch animals (Table 7.2). The data clearly indicate that the financial capital in terms of levels of savings and credit is high for the participants over the non-participants indicating positive changes in the levels of living of the people.

Livelihoods, Institutions and Vulnerability

The conversion of productive assets into income is influenced by the market institutions that fetch prices for the outputs flown from the economic activities. Similarly, the vulnerability of the households in terms of shocks/risks also determines the utilisation of productive assets to generate income.

Income

The assets should be utilised to undertake livelihood activities that generate income to the households. The annual total income per household for the participants of DPIP recorded a substantial increase from Rs 32,934 in FUS-I to Rs 45,792 in FUS-II (an increase of 39 per cent) as against 12 per cent in case of non-participants (Table 7.5). Even when income is adjusted for the inflation of 10-15 per cent, the rise is much more for participants. The composition of income reveals that there is substantial decrease in the proportion of income flowing from the wage labour from 34 per cent in FUS-I to 29 per cent in FUS-II, as against 35 per cent to 33 per cent for non-participants showing a net decline (rate of increase of participants minus rate of increase of non-participants) of 3 per cent for participants. Though it is true for all the districts, the decrease in Anantapur is the highest, showing a net decline of 13 per cent. This shows that the dependency on migration and agriculture labour as source of livelihood declined among the participants. On the other hand, the source of income from self-employed activities has increased considerably for participants in FUS-II over FUS-I. Of the self-employed activities (agriculture, allied activities and other non-farm activities) registered a net increase of 6 per cent. Across the districts, income from self-employed related sources has increased substantially in Anantapur, lowest in Adilabad as against the decline in income from high risk-prone activities like casual labour. This indicates that the participants have withdrawn from high-risk prone activities (migration, casual labour) and shifted to less risk prone activities (self-cultivation, allied activities and allied non-farm activities). Thus, the level and quality of income of poor, has been enhanced due to the programme (see Tables 7.3, 7.4, 7.5 and 7.6).

Household Consumption

The increased incomes should bring changes in the level and composition of consumption basket. The data on average per capita per month consumption of food items in all the districts reveal that it increased from Rs 246 per month in FUS-I to Rs 281 in FUS-II for participants while it is Rs 250 in FUS-I to Rs Rs 290 in FUS-II for non-participants (Table 7.10). Across the districts, the average per capita consumption of all food items by the participants show that there has been an increase over FUS-I, with the rate of increase being highest in Srikakulam (Table 7.7) followed by Anantapur (Table 7.8) and Adilabad (Table 7.9). Between participants and non-participants, it is in Anantapur district in FUS-I and II that the participant households' per capita consumption of food items is more than that of the non-participants.

The composition of consumption basket among the participants has undergone change, reflecting improvement in the quality of consumption of commodities. There is a clear shift from food to non-food items, and among food items, shift is more towards non-cereals. A substantial increase over FUS-I was noticed in the consumption of *gur* and sugar, fruits and vegetables, milk and milk products, edible oils and eggs among the participants across all the districts. Again, within the districts the consumption of *gur* and sugar and fruits and vegetables is more in Srikakulam when compared to Anantapur, while the consumption of milk and milk products is high in Adilabad (Table 7.10). The intake of milk and milk products, *gur* and sugar is particularly high for participants compared to non-participants, which indicates better nutritional status for the participants. Thus, the per capita consumption expenditure and quality of consumption has gone up considerably for the poor due to the programme. The expenditure on non-food also reveals a substantial improvement over FUS-I especially among the participants from Rs 4,455 to Rs 6,430 (Table 7.11). Across districts, it is in Adilabad district that the expenditure on non-food is more for the participants as against non-participants (the increase for participants is Rs 2,579 as against Rs 1,598 for non-participants). The expenditure on education increased from Rs 576 to Rs 973 and the expenditure on health increased from Rs 2,072 in FUS-I to Rs 3,292 in FUS-II for the participants as a whole (Table 7.11). Across the districts, a significant increase in the budget share is noticed in Adilabad as against the other two districts. The budget share on alcohol and tobacco has declined over FUS-I across all categories. (Tables 7.7, 7.8, 7.9, 7.10 and 7.11).

Food Security and Vulnerability

According to World Food Summit (1996), 'Food security exists when all people, at all times, have physical and economic access to sufficient, safe and nutritious food to meet their dietary needs and food preferences for an active and healthy life'. Food security depends principally on three variables: availability of food, access to food and a nutritious diet, and proper use of food to ensure maximal nutrition and hygiene. These variables are influenced by other factors, particularly poverty. In turn, this is influenced by access to pasture, the infrastructure (transportation and communication), population growth, conflict, environmental and climatic factors, and by economic factors (national and international). Other factors include opportunities for appropriate training and job skills and the quality of public health and health care provision (Cohen, 2005). The food security system consists of three instruments: procurement prices/minimum support prices, buffer stocks and the public distribution system. In order to ensure remunerative prices to farmers, the Government of India has been intervening in the food grain market through its minimum support price/ procurement policy. The importance of building up a buffer stock of food grains is to provide food security to the country (Dev *et al.*, 2003). Various committees have suggested the optimal size of the buffer stock which varies from 15 to 25 million tonnes, depending on the season. The Expenditure Reforms Commission recommended 17 million tonnes as the total average stock to be maintained for distribution and as a buffer (GoI, 2000). State policies have an important role to play in ensuring food security by maintaining relative stability of prices, and adequate availability of food in all regions while accounting for reasonable price differences due to transport and storage costs, and returns to labour and capital involved (Vijay, 2003).

The term vulnerability refers to the relationship between poverty, risk and efforts/ability to manage risk. Risks and the inability to manage these effectively could force people below the poverty line, and those already living below poverty line deeper into poverty. On the other hand, reducing vulnerability through effective and efficient risk management would contribute positively to economic growth. Therefore, any effort towards poverty eradication/reduction needs to be based upon a good understanding of the risks, constraints and opportunities faced by the poor. Further, these efforts should help people manage risk and prevent them from sliding into poverty.

The poor in developing countries are especially vulnerable to a wide range of shocks/risks like natural disasters, drought, crop failure or illness that could affect individuals, households or whole communities and lead to a reduction in their well-being. Risks, if not effectively managed, often impact to reduce the size of the asset bundle and/or change the type of living that can be pursued. The ability of the poor to cope with and recover from shocks/risks is central to sustainable livelihoods. The DPIP project aims at improving the ability of the poor to deal with such shocks/risks through direct and indirect interventions.

In the year 2004, the project introduced risk mitigation programmes like comprehensive insurance programme and development of weather based insurance schemes. Besides, DPIP aims at strengthening the capability of the poor to utilise various government programmes like employment guarantee programme, public distribution system (PDS) and other social security programmes. Clearly, neither covariate risks like drought and cyclone nor idiosyncratic risks such as death of family members and accident are under the control of the project; the objective is only to improve the capacity of the poor in encountering such shocks/risks. Household level data are used to identify different types of risks and how these risks have affected the livelihoods of the poor.

Food Security

Around 2 per cent of the households in the DPIP area said that they went without two square meals a day, during the *kharif* season as against 8 per cent in FUS-I. This had happened both for participant and non-participant households, though the percentage reporting food insecurity is less for the participant households compared to non-participant households. Across the districts, the percentage of households reporting food insecurity is higher in Anantapur followed by Srikakulam. However, the reporting of food insecurity is much steeper in Srikakulam. Further, the percentage of households reporting food insecurity is slightly lower among poor households comprising the poorest of the poor (PoP) and poor (hovering around 4 per cent) compared to the non-poor (NP) covering both not so poor (NSP) and non-poor (around 6 per cent). This gives an indication about the support extended by the programme to the targeted groups through rice credit line (RCL), food security line (FSL) and providing easy access to credit to overcome difficult situations. (Table 7.12)

Then the question arises as to what are the important factors that might have led to the improved food security. The analysis of expenditure on food in the programme areas would enable us to answer this question. PDS is the main source of food grains for the poor and the budget share of quantities purchased during the period of survey is clearly at a slightly higher level now compared to FUS-I. This leads to the inference that the people in the programme area access PDS more regularly, perhaps due to easy access to credit. At the district level too, in Srikakulam and Adilabad there has been an improvement in the access of PDS now as compared to FUS-I. Among the economic category of households, the increase in the budget share of PDS items is seen in the case of PoP. All these point to the fact that the prices of food grains in PDS are cheaper compared to open market and the programme participants are now well aware of the safety nets provided by the government and how to avail of them, so that more food is secured. Participants lifted 17.7 kgs per month on an average per household from PDS as against 16.4 kgs by the non-participants. It can be construed as an indirect contribution of the project that better awareness, employment and easy access to credit, have given them the capability to purchase a greater quantity of the ration allowed to them. The expenditure on food items also supports these conclusions. Participant households are spending higher amount on food items over non-participants (Table 7.13). However, there is a decline in expenditure on cereals and pulses across all classes, especially in Anantapur, while the spending on meat and milk products increased considerably. This is evident from the fact that over 88 per cent of the respondent households were accessing PDS against 74 per cent of non-participant households. Percentage of households accessing food from PDS has increased in FUS-II over FUS-I. Acquiring food grains through PDS, RCL and FSL at relatively cheaper prices by the programme participants might have generated some surplus which can be spent on more nutritious food items like eggs, meat and fish. Acquisition of food grains through PDS, RCL and FSL is more in FUS-II compared to FUS-I. Increase in the budget share of these items over FUS-I is evidence to this across all categories of households, especially in Srikakulam and in Anantapur districts. The significant increase in the budget share on total food in the DPIP area when compared to FUS-I period is a clear indication that the participants now have more food security. (Table 7.13)

Risks/Shocks Encountered

The risks faced by the households and the average loss due to risks for the participants and the non-participants should be understood first before assessing the impact on the capability of the participating households to deal with the multiple risks they are exposed to. According to 27 per cent of the respondent households, drought was the most severe risk faced by them followed by flood or pest; health problems and death of family members in the DPIP area. Thus, nature related shocks (covariate) like drought, floods and pests are the most serious shocks experienced by the households. However, a considerable proportion of households also reported other shocks which are miscellaneous, reflecting the individual nature of risks at the household level. Nonetheless, there has been a significant reduction in the proportion of households experiencing nature related problems, health and other shocks when compared to FUS-I. A significant reduction in health and other shocks could be due to increased levels of awareness on heath care in the DPIP areas. By and large, these have been observed in the case of programme participants in DPIP-SHGs and also across all economic categories of households. At the district level, 61 per cent of the reporting households in Anantapur encountered drought, while it was only 24 per cent in Srikakulam and 4 per cent in Adilabad. Thus, drought continued to be a major problem in Anantapur. Similarly, the risk of flood and pests dominates in Adilabad district, though the percentage of households affected is now lower compared to FUS-I (27 per cent *versus* 34 per cent). To sum up, covariate risks (nature related) dominated in all the sample districts compared to idiosyncratic risks. (Table 7.14)

Impact of the Risks/Shocks

The impact of risks/shocks may result in loss of income, additional expenditures and food insecurity. On an average, the participant households suffered losses up to Rs 11,004 irrespective of the type of risk/shocks encountered as against Rs 35,975 in FUS-I indicating an improvement in the strategies of the participants. Among the districts, people in Anantapur suffered more losses followed by Adilabad and Srikakulam. Among the events, the highest losses are due to drought in Anantapur and in Srikakulam while they are due to flood and pests in Adilabad. However, the losses incurred are much lower compared to FUS-I in all the districts. (Table 7.14)

Among the poor households, the poorest of the poor suffered more losses (Rs 9,618) as against Rs 8,146 in the case of poor households. Drought is the reason for higher losses among both the PoP and poor. Lack of employment opportunities resulting in the loss of wage income during the drought period is probably the main reason for loss of income. However, compared to FUS-I, they could minimise the losses. The importance of generating alternative employment opportunities (perhaps with more emphasis on National Rural Employment Guarantee Programme) and economising the household expenditure may reduce the losses in the event of risks/shocks. The other important causes of loss of income are flood and pests. Replication of pest management practices and widespread dissemination of these practices would go a long way in minimising such losses. Finally, the poor are also incurring losses because of additional expenditure due to the health problems. The increased coverage of comprehensive insurance programme in addition to sensitising the SHGs to access public health services may improve the situation of the poor. The data indicate that the total loss associated with health problems is relatively lower among the participants compared to the non-participants (Rs 941 *versus* Rs 1,281). Thus, it is clear that the members of DPIP SHGs are well aware of preventive health care and access public health services when required. (Table 7.14)

Coping Mechanisms

It is important to examine how the households have coped with the risk events in general and whether participation in the project has enabled women and their households to minimise the long-term impact of the shocks and any reduction in their income. It is also interesting to analyse how far the participants in the project have been able to shift from 'bad' coping mechanisms to 'good' coping mechanisms.

The rural households in the study area have adopted various strategies to reduce the impact of shocks. Thirty-one per cent of respondents of DPIP-SHGs resorted to borrowing as a first measure; while it was 29 per cent for the non-participants. Recurring drought, floods and cyclones in the study area have made the rural population extremely vulnerable and the immediate need for cash, particularly, to buy essential commodities, health and education requirements had forced them to borrow money from friends, relatives and others. Borrowing is considered to be a better coping mechanism in such a situation rather than reducing consumption or selling household assets. Interestingly, a higher percentage of participants in the programme area borrowed money to tide over the crisis compared to non-participants, which indicates that the borrowing capacity of the participants is much more than of non-participants. In other words, creditworthiness of the participants members has increased, which is a direct evidence of the programme impact. Similarly, creditworthiness is slightly higher for the members of newly formed DPIP groups compared to the members of the DWCRA converted groups. It also indicates that the members of the newly formed DPIP groups have internalised the principles of DPIP to a greater degree and are practicing better available options. Across the districts, a higher percentage of people in Anantapur are opting for borrowing followed by Srikakulam and Adilabad. When compared to FUS-I, there is a steep decline in borrowing when the contingency arises in Srikakulam but the decline is much less in Adilabad and Anantapur. Thus, people in Anantapur continue to resort to good coping mechanisms compared to the other districts. The poor (31 per cent) and poorest of the poor also rely heavily on borrowings, which is a direct contribution of the project. (Table 7.15)

The next widely reported response to manage the risk is to use savings. Around 9 per cent of the respondent households among participants and non-participants used savings as the first resort to cope with the shocks. Use of savings in times of need is also one of the good coping mechanisms and is widely seen among the participants in the programme. This supports the notion that in addition to any possible incentive which the programme may provide for local governments to respond effectively to emergencies, an individual's ability to accumulate savings, together with greater borrowing capacity associated with programme participation are key factors leading to such outcomes which have been observed. The increase in the use of savings is also noticed in Anantapur indicating that the programme impact in this district continued to be better compared to other districts. However, in Adilabad, a considerable proportion of population resorted to seeking more wage employment in order to deal with the risks and this increased from 9 per cent in FUS-I to 14 per cent in FUS-II. This also shows the positive response at times of distress, which could be an indirect contribution of the project. In Anantapur, the proportion of respondents resorting to intra-household mechanisms (reduce consumption) is higher compared to respondent families in other districts. It is to be noted that those resorting to intra-household mechanisms showed a decline as compared with the mid-term appraisal (MTA) period, but there is an increase in the good practice of mechanisms in this district i.e., resorting to borrowings and use of savings. A negligible percentage of households resorted to migration which has declined, though only marginally, as compared to FUS-I. This is particularly true in Anantapur, PoP and poor which is an encouraging sign. (Table 7.15)

Thus, with regard to assets and livelihoods favourable changes have taken place with respect to possession of land between FUS-I and FUS-II across all the districts and economic categories including participants and non-participants. Further, the level and quality of income of poor has been enhanced due to the interventions of the programme. The composition of livestock shows an improvement in possession of draught and milch animals, among the participants between FUS-I and FUS-II, while small ruminants declined marginally. There is clear evidence that the dependency on migration and agriculture labour as source of livelihood declined among the participants. On the other hand, the source of income from self-employed activities has increased considerably for participants in FUS-II over FUS-I. The participants have withdrawn from high risk-prone activities and shifted to less risk-prone activities. Thus, the level and quality of income of poor, has been enhanced due to the programme. The composition of consumption basket among the participants has undergone change, reflecting improvement in the quality of consumption of commodities. There is a clear shift from food to non-food items, and among food items, shift is more towards non-cereals. This indicates that the programme interventions resulted in creation of more assets and more livelihood opportunities to the participants. In case of food security and vulnerability, interventions by the project (direct and indirect) have helped the most vulnerable sections of the people in the programme areas to cope by adopting different strategies that made them withstand the distress events.

Table 7.1

Changes in Land and Other Agricultural Assets

Indicator	Round	All Households				Srikakulam			Anantapur			Adilabad			Districts			Poverty Status			
		All	Participants	Non-Pparticipants	Sig.	Participants	Non-Participants	Sig.	Participants	Non-Participants	Sig.	Participants	Non-Participants	Sig.	SKLM	ANTP	ADB	PoP	Poor	NSP	NP
% of HHs having land	FUS-II	83.82	85.69	81.8		85.29	81.58		88.31	79.69		83.4	84.35	**	83.64	83.93	83.86	85.87	82.14	83.86	80.18
	FUS-I	83.61	85.83	81.21		81.93	80.53		88.31	80.86		87.14	82.17	**	81.31	84.52	84.71	85.33	82.14	82.81	82.88
% of HHs having own land	FUS-II	82.93	84.96	81.16		86.7	82.82		84.29	79.95		83.8	80.87	**	84.73	81.88	82.23	83.75	81.93	82.47	83.85
	FUS-I	64.32	70.66	58.78		65.96	50.51		74.86	64.24		71.51	60.77	***	58.09	68.95	65.76	64.36	67.03	61.44	61.46
Total land in acres per HH	FUS-II	2.8607	3.0228	2.6864		3.3547	2.5182		3.1504	2.824		2.5637	2.6722		2.9834	2.9846	2.6167	3.1175	2.7043	2.7186	2.5636
	FUS-I	2.9341	3.0003	2.863		3.3405	2.7253		3.11	3.1017		2.5513	2.711		3.0674	3.1058	2.6293	3.0968	2.8666	2.8354	2.6406
Total land values in Rs/HH	FUS-II	107477	111231	103440		91565	90966		131975	74429		109305	146035		91299	102745	127241	124661	107371	85747	77158
	FUS-I	85232	83008	87624		50147	78439		69725	67570		129130	117532		62706	68630	123467	87591	85827	84616	72533
% of HHs having implements	FUS-II	85.25	86.91	83.8		87.4	89.74		86.17	79.16		87.11	82.96	**	88.6	82.3	84.91	85.76	85.99	83.54	84.29
	FUS-I	87.47	88.3	86.74		88.47	86.92		88.18	87.35		88.24	85.93		87.68	87.73	87.01	88.83	86.55	85.83	88.48
Value of implements per HH	FUS-II	2564	3181	1998		3209	3114		4346	1659		2026	1173		3160	2913	1586	3066	1812	2882	2160
	FUS-I	2753	4060	1556		4724	1537		3505	1958		3899	1158	**	3078	2680	2485	3423	1961	3289	1151
% of HHs having irrigation assets	FUS-II	6.84	7.29	6.44		8.78	6.67		6.86	5.47		6.15	7.26		7.7	6.08	6.74	6.5	7.03	7.22	6.77
	FUS-I	8.17	8.95	7.49		11.44	8.72		7.43	6.83		7.82	7.02		10.05	7.1	7.39	8.88	7.86	7.42	7.81
Value of (Rs) irrigation assets per HH	FUS-II	15766	12100	20084		9370	26517		15540	12208		12847	18667	**	16898	14059	15757	16108	15528	15787	14786
	FUS-I	11677	10353	13236		9974	16000		11413	8467		9873	13733		12620	10104	11803	11246	14821	9561	8000

Table 7.2

Changes in Durables, Livestock and Other Assets

Indicator	Round	All Households				Srikakulam			Anantapur			Adilabad			Districts			Poverty Status			
		All	Participants	Non-Participants	Sig.	Participants	Non-Participants	Sig.	Participants	Non-Participants	Sig.	Participants	Non-Participants	Sig.	SKLM	ANTP	ADB	PoP	Poor	NSP	NP
Avg. no. of	FUS-II	1.40	1.45	1.35		1.76	1.55		1.53	1.38		1.10	1.14		1.66	1.46	1.12	1.32	1.48	1.41	1.51
milch	FUS-I	1.32	1.40	1.22		1.35	1.47		1.73	1.23		1.10	0.97		1.41	1.51	1.04	1.23	1.42	1.27	1.52
animals	Diff.	0.09	0.04	0.14		0.41	0.08		-0.20	0.16		0.01	0.16		0.26	-0.04	0.08	0.10	0.06	0.14	-0.02
Avg. no. of	FUS-II	0.99	1.11	0.84	***	1.13	0.57	***	1.23	0.79		0.98	1.14	***	0.87	1.03	1.05	0.96	1.07	0.95	0.97
draught	FUS-I	0.88	1.02	0.71	**	1.03	0.72	***	1.15	0.59		0.87	0.84	***	0.89	0.90	0.86	0.92	0.88	0.85	0.75
animals	Diff.	0.11	0.10	0.13	*	0.10	-0.15		0.08	0.20		0.11	0.30		-0.02	0.14	0.19	0.03	0.19	0.10	0.22
Average no.	FUS-II	2.38	2.22	2.59		1.84	2.82		2.58	2.71		2.16	2.23		2.30	2.63	2.19	2.20	1.93	3.21	2.70
of small	FUS-I	2.25	2.10	2.43		2.34	2.17		1.82	2.88		2.20	2.17		2.26	2.29	2.19	1.90	1.86	3.21	2.67
ruminants	Diff.	0.14	0.12	0.16		-0.50	0.65		0.76	-0.17		-0.04	0.06		0.04	0.34	0.00	0.29	0.06	0.00	0.03
HHs owning	FUS-II	68.40	69.80	66.80		75.40	72.90		75.30	68.20		59.70	59.50		74.20	72.10	59.60	64.90	71.80	66.50	79.40
milch	FUS-I	66.40	65.90	67.00		68.00	69.20		69.60	69.00		60.40	62.90		68.60	69.30	61.50	64.90	65.00	67.00	77.80
animals	Diff.	2.00	3.90	-0.20		7.40	3.70		5.70	-0.80		-0.70	-3.40		5.60	2.80	-1.90	0.00	6.80	-0.50	1.60
% of HHs	FUS-II	46.40	51.60	40.10	***	53.30	29.90	***	56.30	40.30		45.50	49.10	***	42.40	49.10	47.00	46.00	50.00	43.20	44.40
owning draught	FUS-I	41.50	47.90	33.50	***	50.80	31.80	***	51.90	30.20		41.60	38.80	***	41.90	42.20	40.40	42.80	42.30	39.20	38.10
animals	Diff.	4.90	3.70	6.60		2.50	-1.90		4.40	10.10		3.90	10.30		0.50	6.90	6.60	3.20	7.70	4.00	6.30
% of HHs	FUS-II	18.70	19.60	17.60		18.00	17.80		19.00	18.60		21.40	16.40		17.90	18.80	19.30	19.80	16.70	21.00	14.30
owning	FUS-I	18.10	20.30	15.30		20.50	13.10		20.90	15.50		19.50	17.20	**	17.00	18.50	18.50	18.80	15.00	20.50	19.00
small animals	Diff.	0.60	-0.70	2.30		-2.50	4.70		-1.90	3.10		1.90	-0.80		0.90	0.30	0.80	1.00	1.70	0.50	-4.70
% of	FUS-II	97.30	97.70	96.90		99.20	97.20		98.10	98.40		96.10	94.80		98.30	98.30	95.60	96.20	97.40	98.30	100.00
HHs having	FUS-I	98.00	97.70	98.30		98.40	99.10		98.10	98.40		96.80	97.40		98.70	98.30	97.00	96.50	99.10	98.90	98.40
livestock assets	Diff.	-0.70	0.00	-1.40		0.80	-1.90		0.00	0.00		-0.70	-2.60		-0.40	0.00	-1.40	-0.30	-1.70	-0.60	1.60

Table 7.3

Percentage Distribution of Workers by Industry/Occupation During FUS-I

Sector	Srikakulam			Anantapur			Adilabad			All		
	Partici-pants	Non-Parti-cipants	Total	Partici-pants	Non-Parti-cipants	Total	Partici-pants	Non-Parti-cipants	Total	Partici-pants	Non-Parti-cipants	Total
Agriculture (cultivation)	27.6	29.3	28.3	41.8	35.8	38.4	67.2	54.2	63.2	48.0	38.4	43.9
Agriculture casual labour	40.3	34.9	38.0	32.9	38.3	35.9	13.6	22.0	16.2	27.1	33.2	29.7
Salaried agriculture worker	0.0	0.4	0.2	0.7	0.5	0.6	1.9	1.9	1.9	1.0	0.8	0.9
Own business	2.3	3.7	2.9	4.9	4.5	4.7	2.2	3.0	2.4	2.9	3.9	3.3
Self-employed in household industry	1.5	1.0	1.3	4.6	3.4	3.9	1.3	1.2	1.3	2.3	2.1	2.2
Self-employed in services (other than business)	3.9	5.3	4.5	3.1	3.3	3.2	2.2	3.2	2.5	3.0	3.9	3.4
Non-agriculture casual labour	11.5	13.8	12.5	3.9	6.3	5.2	3.1	5.8	3.9	5.9	8.5	7.0
Salaried work	6.2	5.9	6.1	4.9	5.4	5.2	6.3	7.4	6.7	5.9	6.1	6.0
Common property resources (CPR)	4.6	3.3	4.0	0.0	0.0	0.0	0.4	0.4	0.4	1.6	1.1	1.4
Livestock management	2.1	2.3	2.2	3.3	2.6	2.9	1.8	0.8	1.5	2.3	2.1	2.2

Table 7.4

Percentage Distribution of Workers by Industry/Occupation During FUS-II

Sector	*Srikakulam*			*Anantapur*			*Adilabad*			*All*		
	Partici-pants	*Non-Parti-cipants*	*Total*	*Partici-pants*	*Non-Parti-cipants*	*Total*	*Partici-pants*	*Non-Parti-cipants*	*Total*	*Partici-pants*	*Non-Parti-cipants*	*Total*
Agriculture (cultivation)	28.4	32.6	30.2	25.7	24.6	25.1	65.5	51.2	61.1	43.8	33.9	39.6
Agriculture casual labour	44.2	39.9	42.3	43.6	46.5	45.2	14.7	24.3	17.6	31.2	38.8	34.4
Salaried agriculture worker	0.4	0.2	0.3	0.2	0.4	0.3	1.9	1.2	1.7	1.0	0.5	0.8
Own business	2.0	1.8	1.9	3.1	3.5	3.3	2.5	2.0	2.3	2.5	2.6	2.5
Self-employed in household industry	1.5	0.6	1.1	5.3	3.8	4.5	2.7	2.4	2.6	3.1	2.5	2.8
Self-employed in services (other than business)	3.4	4.1	3.7	5.6	5.2	5.4	2.8	4.5	3.3	3.7	4.7	4.1
Non-agriculture casual labour	13.1	9.8	11.7	5.8	4.2	4.9	2.0	5.7	3.2	6.3	6.3	6.3
Salaried work	4.8	7.8	6.1	5.4	7.3	6.5	5.8	6.3	5.9	5.4	7.2	6.2
Common property resources (CPR)	0.3	1.4	0.8	0.5	0.2	0.3	0.1	0.3	0.2	0.3	0.6	0.4
Livestock management	1.8	1.7	1.8	4.8	4.2	4.5	2.0	2.2	2.1	2.7	3.0	2.8
	100	100	100	100	100	100	100	100	100	100	100	100

Table 7.5

Changes in Average Per Household Annual Income

(Rs/annum)

Sector	*FUS-I*			*FUS-II*			*Percentage Change*		
	Partici-pants	*Non-Parti-cipants*	*All*	*Partici-pants*	*Non-Parti-cipants*	*All*	*Partici-pants*	*Non-Parti-cipants*	*All*
Srikakulam									
Agriculture (cultivation)	17854	29195	23596	33661	32618	33191	88.5	11.7	40.7
CPR	262	516	391	224	448	325	-14.3	-13.2	-16.8
Livestock	607	546	576	597	71	369	-1.6	-86.9	-36.0
Self-employed in non-agriculture	1935	2799	2374	2964	2656	2825	53.2	-5.1	19.0
Other non-farm	3532	3214	3371	1012	751	894	-71.4	-76.6	-73.5
Agricultural labour	4890	3889	4382	6165	5085	5678	26.1	30.7	29.6
Non-agriculture casual labour	3484	2791	3133	2634	2265	2468	-24.4	-18.8	-21.2
Salaried	2047	4579	3332	3293	3593	3428	60.9	-21.5	2.9
Migration	526	923	728	1212	1213	1212	130.3	31.4	66.6
Other income	193	175	184	75	66	71	-61.1	-62.5	-61.5
Total income	35330	48628	42064	51836	48766	50461	46.7	0.3	20.0
Anantapur									
Agriculture (cultivation)	2084	5944	4823	13039	6780	9575	525.8	14.1	98.5
CPR	133	35	64	250	169	206	87.7	379.1	221.9
Livestock	880	450	575	2666	1995	2357	202.9	343.6	309.9
Self-employed in non-agriculture	4146	3657	3799	9851	6601	8052	137.6	80.5	111.9
Other non-farm	5056	4501	4662	4670	3408	3971	-7.6	-24.3	-14.8
Agricultural labour	5934	5568	5674	7880	8374	8154	32.8	50.4	43.7
Non-agriculture casual labour	2379	2501	2466	2393	2135	2250	0.6	-14.6	-8.7
Salaried	1412	3104	2612	3435	3465	3452	143.2	11.6	32.1
Migration	482	597	564	447	1037	773	-7.4	73.7	37.2
Other income	20	44	37	31	86	61	51.1	96.2	65.7
Total income	22527	26401	25276	44662	34050	38851	98.3	29.0	53.7

contd...

...contd...

Sector	FUS-I			FUS -II			Percentage Change		
	Partici-pants	*Non-Parti-cipants*	*All*	*Partici-pants*	*Non-Parti-cipants*	*All*	*Partici-pants*	*Non-Parti-cipants*	*All*
Adilabad									
Agriculture (cultivation)	15498	12736	14365	18730	17163	18192	20.9	34.8	26.6
CPR	1061	761	938	618	534	589	-41.7	-29.9	-37.2
Livestock	1497	1019	1301	2676	996	2196	78.7	-2.3	68.7
Self-employed in non-agriculture	3591	4992	4166	4499	6585	5215	25.3	31.9	25.2
Other non-farm	2290	3515	2793	1630	3516	2278	-28.8	0.0	-18.4
Agricultural labour	4181	4277	4220	4563	3809	4304	9.1	-10.9	2.0
Non-agriculture casual labour	2180	5519	3550	2693	2985	2793	23.5	-45.9	-21.3
Salaried	5341	5880	5562	5380	5898	5558	0.7	0.3	-0.1
Migration	359	240	310	138	168	149	-61.4	-29.7	-52.0
Other income	90	191	131	114	91	106	27.1	-52.2	-19.2
Total income	36088	39130	37336	41041	41745	41380	13.7	6.7	10.8
All districts									
Agriculture (cultivation)	13495	14874	14243	22060	17957	20218	63.5	20.7	41.9
CPR	576	367	463	390	355	374	-32.3	-3.3	-19.1
Livestock	1046	623	816	2236	1119	1819	113.8	79.8	122.9
Self-employed in non-agriculture	3114	3724	3445	5451	5299	5383	75.1	42.3	56.3
Other non-farm	3326	3852	3612	2254	2562	2392	-32.2	-33.5	-33.8
Agricultural labour	4809	4721	4761	5987	6115	6044	24.5	29.5	27.0
Non-agriculture casual labour	2691	3348	3047	2592	2397	2505	-3.7	-28.4	-17.8
Salaried	3320	4260	3830	4170	4135	4154	25.6	-2.9	8.5
Migration	445	609	534	573	871	707	28.6	42.9	32.3
Other income	112	122	117	79	80	79	-29.8	-33.8	-32.2
Total income	32934	36499	34869	45792	40890	43675	39.0	12.0	25.3

Table 7.6

Changes in Percentage Distribution of Household Income by Source

Sector	*FUS-I*			*FUS-II*		
	Participants	*Non-Participants*	*All*	*Participants*	*Non-Participants*	*All*
Srikakulam						
Agriculture (cultivation)	50.54	60.04	56.09	64.94	66.89	65.78
CPR	0.74	1.06	0.93	0.43	0.92	0.64
Livestock	1.72	1.12	1.37	1.15	0.15	0.73
Self-employed in non-agriculture	5.48	5.76	5.64	5.72	5.45	5.60
Other non-farm	10.00	6.61	8.01	1.95	1.54	1.77
Agricultural labour	13.84	8.00	10.42	11.89	10.43	11.25
Non-agriculture casual labour	9.86	5.74	7.45	5.08	4.65	4.89
Salaried	5.79	9.42	7.92	6.35	7.37	6.79
Migration	1.49	1.90	1.73	2.34	2.49	2.40
Other income	0.55	0.36	0.44	0.14	0.13	0.14
Total income	100.00	100.00	100.00	100.00	100.00	100.00
Anantapur						
Agriculture (cultivation)	9.25	22.51	19.08	29.20	19.91	24.65
CPR	0.59	0.13	0.25	0.56	0.50	0.53
Livestock	3.91	1.70	2.27	5.97	5.86	6.07
Self-employed in non-agriculture	18.40	13.85	15.03	22.06	19.39	20.73
Other non-farm	22.44	17.05	18.44	10.46	10.01	10.22
Agricultural labour	26.34	21.09	22.45	17.64	24.59	20.99
Non-agriculture casual labour	10.56	9.47	9.75	5.36	6.27	5.79
Salaried	6.27	11.76	10.34	7.69	10.18	8.88
Migration	2.14	2.26	2.23	1.00	3.04	1.99
Other income	0.09	0.17	0.15	0.07	0.25	0.16
Total income	100.00	100.00	100.00	100.00	100.00	100.00

contd...

...contd...

Adilabad						
Agriculture (cultivation)	42.95	32.55	38.48	45.64	41.11	43.96
CPR	2.94	1.95	2.51	1.51	1.28	1.42
Livestock	4.15	2.61	3.49	6.52	2.39	5.31
Self-employed in non-agriculture	9.95	12.76	11.16	10.96	15.77	12.60
Other non-farm	6.35	8.98	7.48	3.97	8.42	5.50
Agricultural labour	11.59	10.93	11.30	11.12	9.12	10.40
Non-agriculture casual labour	6.04	14.10	9.51	6.56	7.15	6.75
Salaried	14.80	15.03	14.90	13.11	14.13	13.43
Migration	0.99	0.61	0.83	0.34	0.40	0.36
Other income	0.25	0.49	0.35	0.28	0.22	0.26
Total income	100.00	100.00	100.00	100.00	100.00	100.00
All districts						
Agriculture (cultivation)	40.98	40.75	40.85	48.18	43.92	46.29
CPR	1.75	1.01	1.33	0.85	0.87	0.86
Livestock	3.18	1.71	2.34	4.88	2.74	4.16
Self-employed in non-agriculture	9.45	10.20	9.88	11.90	12.96	12.33
Other non-farm	10.10	10.55	10.36	4.92	6.27	5.48
Agricultural labour	14.60	12.93	13.65	13.07	14.95	13.84
Non-agriculture casual labour	8.17	9.17	8.74	5.66	5.86	5.73
Salaried	10.08	11.67	10.98	9.11	10.11	9.51
Migration	1.35	1.67	1.53	1.25	2.13	1.62
Other income	0.34	0.33	0.34	0.17	0.20	0.18
Total income	100.00	100.00	100.00	100.00	100.00	100.00

Table 7.7

Average Per Capita Consumption of Food Items in Srikakulam District

(Rs/month)

Commodity	*FUS-I*			*FUS-II*			*Percentage Change*		
	Participants	*Non-Participants*	*All*	*Participants*	*Non-Participants*	*All*	*Participants*	*Non-Participants*	*All*
Rice	92.62	101.34	96.46	94.31	103.95	98.51	1.8	2.6	2.1
Wheat	0.73	1.41	1.03	2.07	2.27	2.16	186.0	61.4	110.5
Bajra/jowar	2.10	1.58	1.87	0.34	0.49	0.41	-83.9	-68.7	-78.3
Maize	0.46	0.03	0.27	0.27	0.62	0.42	-41.6	2098.2	55.4
Other cereals	1.51	1.13	1.34	3.68	4.54	4.05	143.9	303.0	202.6
All cereals	97.42	105.48	100.97	100.66	111.87	105.55	3.3	6.1	4.5
Pulses/gram	10.64	13.58	11.93	15.86	16.09	15.96	49.1	18.5	33.8
Gur and sugar	8.74	10.91	9.69	18.81	20.13	19.39	115.3	84.5	100.0
Milk and milk products	23.36	26.72	24.84	18.95	23.30	20.84	-18.9	-12.8	-16.1
Edible oils	21.93	23.79	22.75	25.05	26.89	25.85	14.2	13.0	13.6
Eggs, meat and fish	27.34	31.09	28.99	38.85	40.06	39.38	42.1	28.9	35.8
Fruits and vegetables	26.59	31.64	28.82	48.34	50.61	49.33	81.8	59.9	71.2
Other food	15.86	18.15	16.87	17.36	21.87	19.32	9.4	20.5	14.5
Non-cereal food	134.47	155.88	143.90	183.21	198.95	190.07	36.3	27.6	32.1
All food	231.89	261.36	244.87	283.88	310.82	295.61	22.4	18.9	20.7

Table 7.8

Average Per Capita Consumption of Food Items in Anantapur District

(Rs/month)

Commodity	*FUS-I*			*FUS-II*			*Percentage Change*		
	Participants	*Non-Participants*	*All*	*Participants*	*Non-Participants*	*All*	*Participants*	*Non-Participants*	*All*
Rice	86.3	87.2	86.8	81.4	77.8	79.5	-5.6	-10.9	-8.4
Wheat	6.2	3.3	4.7	6.3	5.7	6.0	1.2	69.8	27.6
Bajra/jowar	7.4	7.3	7.4	4.5	4.6	4.5	-40.1	-36.9	-38.4
Maize	0.2	0.3	0.3	0.1	0.2	0.2	-59.1	-38.9	-46.9
Other cereals	9.2	10.2	9.7	7.1	5.5	6.3	-22.6	-46.2	-35.7
All cereals	109.4	108.4	108.9	99.4	93.7	96.4	-9.1	-13.5	-11.4
Pulses/gram	18.2	14.1	16.0	19.8	19.4	19.6	8.7	37.5	22.3
Gur and sugar	12.0	11.7	11.8	16.2	15.1	15.6	35.4	28.9	32.0
Milk and milk products	15.9	14.9	15.4	25.1	22.7	23.8	57.8	52.0	54.9
Edible oils	16.6	17.3	17.0	23.0	23.7	23.4	38.3	37.1	37.6
Eggs, meat and fish	22.9	23.2	23.0	32.2	34.1	33.2	40.7	47.3	44.2
Fruits and vegetables	19.5	18.4	18.9	32.0	33.0	32.5	63.9	79.5	72.0
Other food	16.5	13.2	14.7	22.2	21.4	21.8	34.5	62.2	47.8
Non-cereal food	121.6	112.8	116.9	170.5	169.4	169.9	40.2	50.2	45.4
All food	231.0	221.2	225.8	269.9	263.1	266.3	16.8	19.0	18.0

Table 7.9

Average Per Capita Consumption of Food Items in Adilabad District

(Rs/month)

Commodity	FUS-I			FUS-II			Percentage Change		
	Participants	Non-Participants	All	Participants	Non-Participants	All	Participants	Non-Participants	All
Rice	67.8	70.1	68.5	66.0	72.7	68.1	-2.6	3.7	-0.6
Wheat	4.7	5.3	4.9	7.8	7.5	7.7	66.3	42.6	58.3
Bajra/jowar	15.6	14.0	15.1	18.6	16.3	17.9	19.2	16.3	18.4
Maize	0.5	0.6	0.5	0.5	0.1	0.4	1.1	-77.1	-26.2
Other cereals	0.7	0.6	0.7	1.1	0.8	1.0	48.5	44.1	47.4
All cereals	89.3	90.5	89.7	94.0	97.4	95.0	5.3	7.7	6.0
Pulses/gram	27.5	27.8	27.6	32.0	30.4	31.5	16.2	9.6	14.1
Gur and sugar	14.9	16.3	15.3	17.0	18.0	17.3	13.9	10.9	12.9
Milk and milk products	15.6	21.1	17.3	22.8	22.0	22.5	45.6	4.5	30.1
Edible oils	25.3	27.6	26.0	30.5	35.3	32.0	20.4	27.9	22.8
Eggs, meat and fish	31.1	34.2	32.1	29.0	33.8	30.4	-6.9	-1.0	-5.0
Fruits and vegetables	37.3	39.0	37.8	39.4	44.6	41.0	5.8	14.3	8.4
Other food	24.4	27.9	25.5	21.8	24.8	22.7	-10.5	-11.2	-10.8
All non-cereal food	176.1	193.8	181.6	192.4	209.0	197.5	9.2	7.8	8.7
All food	265.4	284.2	271.3	286.4	306.4	292.5	7.9	7.8	7.8

Table 7.10

Average Per Capita Consumption of Food Items in All Districts

(Rs/month)

Commodity	FUS-I			FUS-II			Percentage Change		
	Participants	Non-Participants	All	Participants	Non-Participants	All	Participants	Non-Participants	All
Rice	79.9	87.1	83.0	78.4	84.7	81.0	-2.0	-2.8	-2.3
Wheat	3.9	3.2	3.6	5.7	5.1	5.5	45.8	57.1	50.1
Bajra/jowar	9.5	7.3	8.6	9.5	6.5	8.3	0.4	-10.8	-3.5
Maize	0.4	0.3	0.4	0.3	0.3	0.3	-22.7	6.4	-12.6
Other cereals	3.2	4.7	3.8	3.4	3.9	3.6	7.8	-17.1	-5.2
All cereals	96.9	102.6	99.3	97.4	100.5	98.7	0.4	-2.1	-0.7
Pulses/gram	20.1	17.6	19.1	24.0	21.4	22.9	19.6	21.3	20.3
Gur and sugar	12.3	12.7	12.5	17.3	17.5	17.4	40.5	38.0	39.4
Milk and milk products	18.0	20.3	19.0	22.3	22.7	22.4	23.7	11.7	18.3
Edible oils	22.1	22.1	22.1	26.9	27.9	27.3	22.1	26.0	23.7
Eggs, meat and fish	27.9	28.6	28.2	32.7	35.9	34.1	17.5	25.4	20.8
Fruits and vegetables	29.5	28.1	28.9	40.1	41.7	40.8	36.1	48.3	41.1
Other foods	19.8	18.7	19.4	20.6	22.5	21.4	4.0	19.9	10.5
All non-cereal food	149.6	148.3	149.1	184.0	189.6	186.4	23.0	27.9	25.0
All food	246.6	250.9	248.4	281.3	290.1	285.0	14.1	15.6	14.7

Table 7.11

Changes in Consumption Pattern

(Rs per household/annum)

Commodity Group	Round	All Households				Srikakulam			Anantapur			Adilabad			Districts			Poverty Status			
		All	Participants	Non-Participants	Sig	Participants	Non-Participants	Sig	Participants	Non-Participants	Sig	Participants	Non-Participants	Sig	SKLM	ANTP	ADB	PoP	Poor	NSP	NP
Avg. no. of milch animals	FUS-II	1.40	1.45	1.35		1.76	1.55		1.53	1.38		1.10	1.14		1.66	1.46	1.12	1.32	1.48	1.41	1.51
	FUS-I	1.32	1.40	1.22		1.35	1.47		1.73	1.23		1.10	0.97		1.41	1.51	1.04	1.23	1.42	1.27	1.52
	Diff.	0.09	0.04	0.14		0.41	0.08		-0.20	0.16		0.01	0.16		0.26	-0.04	0.08	0.10	0.06	0.14	-0.02
Non-food	FUS-II	6729	6430	6864		7569	6473		6856	6907	**	7354	6162		6997	6885	6710	7472	7744	7019	6871
	FUS-I	4868	4455	4922		5346	4205		5535	5253		4775	4564		4727	5372	4658	5524	5686	5144	4799
	Diff.	1861	1975	1942		2223	2268		1321	1654		2579	1598		2270	1513	2052	1948	2058	1875	2072
Total expenditure	FUS-II	32686	30573	33809		35581	31573		34361	32326		37112	32705		33490	33216	34732	37290	36846	34950	33957
	FUS-I	30583	24750	26652		28243	22565		32641	25474		26405	26099		25166	28494	26235	28966	29804	25989	25423
	Diff.	2103	5823	7157		7338	9008		1720	6852		10707	6606		8324	4722	8497	8324	7042	8961	8534
Per capita expenditure	FUS-II	8471	7540	8473	*	8355	8465		7643	8786		8908	8566		8412	8286	8723	8529	8604	8719	8409
	FUS-I	6920	5949	6425		6365	5840		6856	6764		6226	6497		6080	6803	6377	6379	6668	6500	6131
	Diff.	1551	1591	2048		1990	2625		787	2022		2682	2069		2332	1483	2346	2150	1936	2219	2278
Budget share on food (%)	FUS-II	46.80	45.20	46.30		46.50	45.20		46.10	45.90		46.90	47.20		45.80	45.90	47.10	45.70	47.10	45.90	46.80
	FUS-I	49.30	49.30	48.60		52.70	47.60		49.20	48.00	*	49.30	45.90		49.90	48.50	47.50	50.70	49.60	48.40	48.20
	Diff.	-2.50	-4.10	-2.30		-6.20	-2.40		-3.10	-2.10	*	-2.40	1.30		-4.10	-2.60	-0.40	-5.00	-2.50	-2.50	-1.40
Budget share on alcohol and tobacco (%)	FUS-II	4.10	4.30	3.80		3.40	3.90		3.60	3.60		4.40	3.80		3.70	3.60	4.10	4.00	4.00	3.60	3.60
	FUS-I	4.70	4.60	4.20		3.60	4.60		4.60	3.70	**	4.60	4.20		4.10	4.10	4.40	4.10	4.90	4.00	4.10
	Diff.	-0.60	-0.30	-0.40		-0.20	-0.70		-1.00	-0.10		-0.20	-0.40		-0.40	-0.50	-0.30	-0.10	-0.90	-0.40	-0.50
Budget share on non-food items (%)	FUS-II	21.80	22.30	21.90		22.20	21.20		21.90	23.30		21.40	21.40		21.70	22.70	21.40	21.60	22.10	22.10	21.70
	FUS-I	19.00	18.20	18.90	***	19.80	18.40		19.10	18.70		18.60	19.10	**	19.00	18.90	18.90	20.10	19.70	19.00	19.00
	Diff.	2.80	4.10	3.00	*	2.40	2.80		2.80	4.60		2.80	2.30	*	2.70	3.80	2.50	1.50	2.40	3.10	2.70
Budget share on education (%)	FUS-II	2.20	2.50	2.50		3.00	2.70		2.30	1.80		2.90	2.40		2.80	2.00	2.60	2.60	2.80	2.70	2.50
	FUS-I	2.20	1.80	2.10	**	2.50	1.70		2.40	1.90		2.50	1.70		2.10	2.10	2.00	2.10	2.40	2.00	2.20
	Diff.	0.00	0.70	0.40	*	0.50	1.00		-0.10	-0.10		0.40	0.70		0.70	-0.10	0.60	0.50	0.40	0.70	0.30
Budget share on health (%)	FUS-II	8.40	8.50	8.20		7.90	7.90		7.70	8.60		7.80	9.00		7.90	8.20	8.40	8.60	7.60	7.80	8.50
	FUS-I	7.20	7.30	6.90		7.30	6.30		7.90	6.40	*	7.30	6.80		6.80	7.00	7.00	7.00	7.70	6.70	6.90
	Diff.	1.20	1.20	1.30		0.60	1.60		-0.20	2.20		0.50	2.20		1.10	1.20	1.40	1.60	-0.10	1.10	1.60

Table 7.12

Food Insecurity

Distress Events	*Round*	*All*				*Districts*			*Poverty Status*			
		All	*Partici-pants*	*Non-Participants*	*Sig.*	*SKLM*	*ANTP*	*ADB*	*PoP*	*Poor*	*NSP*	*NP*
% of HHs experienced any food insecurity in last 12 months	FUS-II	0.04	0.03	0.05	*	0.04	0.06	0.02	0.04	0.04	0.05	0.05
	FUS-I	0.17	0.18	0.17		0.40	0.05	0.05	0.17	0.16	0.20	0.17
	Diff.	0.12	0.10	0.14		0.05	0.30	0.17	0.12	0.12	0.13	0.13

Table 7.13

Improved Food Security

Expenditure	Round	Total	Participants	Non-Participants	Sig.	Srikakulam	Anantapur	Adilabad	PoP	Poor	NSP	NP
Spending on cereals & pulses (Rs/year)	FUS-II	6330	7013	5655	***	5840	6064	7591	6538	6336	6032	6310
	FUS-I	7957	8044	7871		5964	10484	7398	7207	8452	9138	6519
	Diff.	-1627	-1031	-2215		-124	-4420	193	-669	-2115	-3107	-210
Spending on sugar & *gur* (Rs/year)	FUS-II	926	1043	810	***	919	821	1040	970	977	866	748
	FUS-I	756	829	684		510	818	967	786	844	641	608
	Diff.	170	215	126		409	3	73	184	133	225	141
Spending on milk & milk products (Rs/year)	FUS-II	1157	1262	1053	***	1007	1253	1349	1184	1120	1195	1109
	FUS-I	1079	1083	1074		1286	864	1110	1172	1027	1016	1015
	Diff.	78	179	-21		-279	390	239	12	93	179	95
Spending on edible oil (Rs/year)	FUS-II	1433	1561	1307	***	1244	1219	1918	1448	1458	1421	1290
	FUS-I	1360	1287	1432		1205	1286	1644	1519	1255	1317	1081
	Diff.	73	273	-125	*	38	-66	275	-71	203	104	209
Spending on egg, chicken, meat and fish (Rs/year)	FUS-II	1790	1897	1685	***	1892	1738	1829	1756	1776	1929	1711
	FUS-I	1587	1640	1534	**	1534	1282	2045	1585	1604	1687	1352
	Diff.	204	257	151		358	456	-216	170	171	242	359
Spending on egg, fruits and vegetables (Rs/year)	FUS-II	5418	5896	4947	***	5992	5279	4788	5519	5499	5393	5267
	FUS-I	4053	4250	3858		3646	3629	4899	4039	4076	4035	3971
	Diff.	1365	1645	1089	**	2346	1650	-111	1480	1423	1358	1296
Spending on other foods (Rs/year)	FUS-II	1393	1392	1393		1174	1350	1664	1303	1395	1627	1295
	FUS-I	2004	2110	1899		1679	1610	2890	1875	1937	2481	1618
	Diff.	-611	-717	-506		-505	-260	-1226	-572	-542	-854	-323

contd...

...contd...

Expenditure	*Round*	*Total*	*Participants*	*Non-Participants*	*Sig.*	*Srikakulam*	*Anantapur*	*Adilabad*	*PoP*	*Poor*	*NSP*	*NP*
Spending on other non-food (Rs/year)	FUS-II	2264	2559	1972	***	2314	2086	2348	2309	2313	2133	2182
	FUS-I	2192	2385	2002	*	2060	1704	2918	2409	2141	2027	2041
	Diff.	71	173	-30		254	382	-572	-100	172	106	141
Budget share of cereals and pulses	FUS-II	0.1528	0.1558	0.1494		0.1565	0.1461	0.1597	0.1545	0.1513	0.1514	0.1526
	FUS-I	0.1638	0.1570	0.1705	***	0.1640	0.1888	0.1400	0.1607	0.1660	0.1636	0.1704
	Diff.	-0.0110	-0.0012	-0.0211		-0.0075	-0.0427	0.0197	-0.0062	-0.0146	-0.0122	-0.0178
Budget share of sugar and *gur*	FUS-II	0.0210	0.0219	0.0201	**	0.0209	0.0196	0.0220	0.0216	0.0217	0.0201	0.0185
	FUS-I	0.0169	0.0167	0.0171		0.0136	0.0187	0.0187	0.0171	0.0174	0.0158	0.0156
	Diff.	0.0042	0.0052	0.0031		0.0072	0.0009	0.0033	0.0044	0.0043	0.0043	0.0028
Budget share of milk and milk products	FUS-II	0.0247	0.0250	0.0243		0.0216	0.0281	0.0248	0.0245	0.0242	0.0252	0.0259
	FUS-I	0.0236	0.0226	0.0246		0.0293	0.0220	0.0194	0.0241	0.0229	0.0230	0.0248
	Diff.	0.0011	0.0024	-0.0003		-0.0077	0.0061	0.0055	0.0003	0.0014	0.0022	0.0011
Budget share of edible oil	FUS-II	0.0352	0.0354	0.0350		0.0345	0.0291	0.0426	0.0354	0.0350	0.0359	0.0319
	FUS-I	0.0310	0.0296	0.0323	***	0.0339	0.0272	0.0325	0.0300	0.0310	0.0331	0.0293
	Diff.	0.0042	0.0057	0.0028	*	0.0006	0.0019	0.0101	0.0054	0.0039	0.0028	0.0026
Budget share of eggs, chicken, meat and fish	FUS-II	0.0423	0.0411	0.0435		0.0477	0.0410	0.0386	0.0415	0.0419	0.0448	0.0403
	FUS-I	0.0377	0.0367	0.0388		0.0400	0.0353	0.0398	0.0375	0.0374	0.0398	0.0359
	Diff.	0.0045	0.0044	0.0047		0.0077	0.0058	-0.0012	0.0040	0.0045	0.0050	0.0044
Budget share of fruits and vegetables	FUS-II	0.1148	0.1119	0.1180	*	0.1271	0.1150	0.0978	0.1184	0.1104	0.1176	0.1136
	FUS-I	0.0937	0.0934	0.0940		0.0962	0.0937	0.0895	0.0924	0.0931	0.0958	0.0970
	Diff.	0.0211	0.0185	0.0241	**	0.0309	0.0213	0.0083	0.0260	0.0173	0.0218	0.0166
Budget share of other food item	FUS-II	0.0309	0.0302	0.0317		0.0258	0.0313	0.0349	0.0302	0.0316	0.0309	0.0319
	FUS-I	0.0432	0.0432	0.0432		0.0423	0.0401	0.0496	0.0413	0.0426	0.0496	0.0394
	Diff.	-0.0123	-0.0130	-0.0115		-0.0166	-0.0088	-0.0147	-0.0110	-0.0110	-0.0187	-0.0075
Budget share of PDS quantities	FUS-II	0.0303	0.0306	0.0300		0.0372	0.0264	0.0255	0.0303	0.0321	0.0288	0.0276
	FUS-I	0.0302	0.0285	0.0319		0.0313	0.0341	0.0252	0.0289	0.0321	0.0309	0.0275
	Diff.	0.0001	0.0021	-0.0019		0.0059	-0.0077	0.0003	0.0014	-0.0001	-0.0021	0.0001

contd...

...contd...

Expenditure	*Round*	*Total*	*Participants*	*Non-Participants*	*Sig.*	*Srikakulam*	*Anantapur*	*Adilabad*	*PoP*	*Poor*	*NSP*	*NP*
Budget share of fuel and lightning	FUS-II	0.0832	0.0843	0.0819		0.1056	0.0700	0.0689	0.0825	0.0806	0.0872	0.0831
	FUS-I	0.0642	0.0610	0.0674	***	0.0798	0.0596	0.0537	0.0650	0.0639	0.0634	0.0627
	Diff.	0.0190	0.0233	0.0145	***	0.0258	0.0104	0.0152	0.0175	0.0166	0.0238	0.0204
Budget share of other non-food items	FUS-II	0.0489	0.0501	0.0474		0.0512	0.0472	0.0467	0.0489	0.0487	0.0486	0.0490
	FUS-I	0.0468	0.0470	0.0466		0.0557	0.0382	0.0461	0.0476	0.0470	0.0462	0.0477
	Diff.	0.0021	0.0031	0.0009		-0.0045	0.0090	0.0005	0.0013	0.0017	0.0023	0.0014
Total per capita spending (Rs/year)	FUS-II	12601	12365	12861		13566	12373	11837	12707	13194	12098	11856
	FUS-I	12348	12268	12428		11825	12137	12852	12974	12672	11661	10347
	Diff.	-53	138	-265		1265	-19	-1230	-623	231	200	1278
Total household spending	FUS-II	51544	56830	46316	***	53179	49780	53033	50989	55688	48992	47099
	FUS-I	52989	56019	49992	**	49831	50957	59668	54824	55479	49427	44065
	Diff.	-1445	811	-3676	**	3348	-1177	-6635	-3835	209	-435	3035
Any access to PDS	FUS-II	0.8144	0.8831	0.7464	***	0.8445	0.8077	0.8002	0.7982	0.8448	0.7981	0.8309
	FUS-I	0.8232	0.8331	0.8134	**	0.8377	0.8179	0.8333	0.8269	0.8398	0.8000	0.8116
	Diff.	-0.0088	0.0500	-0.0670	***	0.0068	-0.0102	-0.0331	-0.0287	0.0050	-0.0019	0.0193
Spending on food (Rs/year)	FUS-II	18447	20063	16849	***	18067	17725	20179	18717	18561	18462	17730
	FUS-I	18794	19243	18351		15824	19973	20952	18182	19196	20315	16163
	Diff.	-347	821	-1501	*	2243	-2248	-774	535	-635	-1853	1567
Spending on PDS (Rs/year)	FUS-II	1183	1299	1068	***	1411	962	1135	1215	1311	1033	983
	FUS-I	2155	2255	2055		930	4091	1261	1008	2914	3617	858
	Diff.	-972	-956	-987		481	-3130	-125	207	-1603	-2585	125
Total spending on alcohol/tobacco	FUS-II	5283	5523	5045		5631	3979	6640	4597	5810	6547	4004
	FUS-I	7322	8089	6563	***	7404	4073	10864	7732	7450	7081	5571
	Diff.	-2039	-2566	-1518		-1773	-94	-4224	-3135	-1641	-535	-1567
Spending on non-food items (Rs/year)	FUS-II	9075	9934	8226	***	8730	9620	8781	8900	9137	9186	9530
	FUS-I	8586	7966	9199		6693	9186	10100	10350	7636	7325	7163
	Diff.	489	1968	-974	*	2037	433	-1321	-1452	1501	1862	2367

contd...

...contd...

Expenditure	Round	Total	Participants	Non-Participants	Sig.	Srikakulam	Anantapur	Adilabad	PoP	Poor	NSP	NP
Spending on miscellaneous (Rs/year)	FUS-II	11487	13369	9626	**	14165	11499	9001	11023	15147	7783	9191
	FUS-I	11487	13369	9626	**	14165	11499	9001	11023	15147	7783	9191
	Diff.	0	0	0		0	0	0	0	0	0	0
Spending on education (Rs/year)	FUS-II	1179	1223	1136		1185	770	1691	1316	1142	1029	950
	FUS-I	1034	1098	971		705	795	1682	1212	771	1176	668
	Diff.	146	125	166		480	-26	9	104	371	-147	282
Spending on health (Rs/year)	FUS-II	2892	3226	2561	**	2625	2811	3272	3362	2613	2743	2546
	FUS-I	2892	3226	2561	**	2625	2811	3272	3362	2613	2743	2546
	Diff.	0.0000	0.0000	0.0000		0.0000	0.0000	0.0000	0.0000	0.0000	0.0000	0.0000
Budget share of food	FUS-II	0.4217	0.4213	0.4221		0.4340	0.4102	0.4204	0.4261	0.4160	0.4259	0.4146
	FUS-I	0.4099	0.3993	0.4204	***	0.4194	0.4258	0.3895	0.4032	0.4104	0.4207	0.4124
	Diff.	0.0118	0.0220	0.0017	*	0.0147	-0.0156	0.0309	0.0229	0.0056	0.0052	0.0023
Budget share of alcohol & tobacco	FUS-II	0.0828	0.0857	0.0796		0.0932	0.0546	0.1089	0.0796	0.0902	0.0845	0.0712
	FUS-I	0.1364	0.1435	0.1295	**	0.1546	0.0876	0.1710	0.1366	0.1437	0.1331	0.1126
	Diff.	-0.0537	-0.0578	-0.0498		-0.0614	-0.0330	-0.0621	-0.0570	-0.0534	-0.0486	-0.0414
Budget share of non-food	FUS-II	0.2131	0.2138	0.2124		0.2187	0.2252	0.1890	0.2080	0.2108	0.2199	0.2236
	FUS-I	0.1729	0.1712	0.1747		0.1823	0.1591	0.1809	0.1711	0.1738	0.1756	0.1777
	Diff.	0.0402	0.0426	0.0377	*	0.0364	0.0660	0.0081	0.0368	0.0370	0.0444	0.0459
Budget share of education	FUS-II	0.0192	0.0192	0.0192		0.0192	0.0155	0.0233	0.0191	0.0197	0.0180	0.0193
	FUS-I	0.0170	0.0176	0.0164		0.0132	0.0165	0.0223	0.0192	0.0143	0.0177	0.0135
	Diff.	0.0022	0.0016	0.0028		0.0060	-0.0010	0.0009	0.0000	0.0055	0.0003	0.0058
Budget share of health	FUS-II	0.0582	0.0573	0.0591		0.0526	0.0596	0.0602	0.0603	0.0560	0.0581	0.0595
	FUS-I	0.0620	0.0639	0.0601		0.0548	0.0661	0.0552	0.0649	0.0599	0.0609	0.0635
	Diff.	0.0000	0.0000	0.0000		0.0000	0.0000	0.0000	0.0000	0.0000	0.0000	0.0000
	FUS-I	0.1365	0.1400	0.1331	*	0.1158	0.1753	0.1128	0.1383	0.1369	0.1252	0.1551
	Diff.	0.0000	0.0000	0.0000		0.0000	0.0000	0.0000	0.0000	0.0000	0.0000	0.0000

Table 7.14

Shocks

Distress Events	Round	All	Participants	Non-Participants	Sig.	SKLM	ANTP	ADB	PoP	Poor	NSP	NP
% household	FUS-II	0.27	0.28	0.25	*	0.24	0.61	0.04	0.26	0.27	0.27	0.30
affected by	FUS-I	0.46	0.45	0.46		0.47	0.77	0.12	0.44	0.46	0.45	0.56
drought	Diff.	-0.19	-0.17	-0.21		-0.23	-0.16	-0.07	-0.17	-0.20	-0.18	-0.26
Total loss	FUS-II	5614.94	6644.19	4677.44		3721.71	7671.43	2199.38	5707.24	4760.61	7047.78	4820.51
associated	FUS-I	11263.48	12188.89	10372.53		3997.71	16844.42	13007.80	11623.32	9915.94	12661.75	11039.87
with drought	Diff.	-5648.54	-5544.70	-5695.09		-276.00	-9172.99	-10808.40	-5916.08	-5155.33	-5613.97	-6219.36
% household	FUS-II	0.04	0.04	0.05		0.04	0.07	0.04	0.05	0.03	0.05	0.07
affected by death of	FUS-I	0.06	0.05	0.07		0.08	0.05	0.04	0.07	0.06	0.06	0.05
family member	Diff.	-0.01	-0.01	-0.02		-0.04	0.01	0.00	-0.02	-0.03	-0.01	0.03
Total loss associated	FUS-II	567.23	798.04	368.65		928.57	504.63	379.07	632.47	301.42	781.25	851.06
with death of	FUS-I	5947.24	6389.10	5614.93		6936.43	3697.70	10934.51	5547.46	7413.85	6568.18	3625.00
family member	Diff.	-5380.01	-5591.06	-5246.27		-6007.86	-3193.07	-10555.40	-4914.99	-7112.43	-5786.93	-2773.94
% household	FUS-II	0.18	0.21	0.16	**	0.17	0.13	0.27	0.20	0.17	0.18	0.14
affected by flood	FUS-I	0.20	0.24	0.16	***	0.18	0.10	0.34	0.22	0.19	0.21	0.18
or pest	Diff.	-0.02	-0.03	-0.01		-0.01	0.01	-0.05	-0.02	-0.02	-0.02	-0.07
Total loss associated	FUS-II	2080.66	2620.91	1577.07	***	1774.36	974.33	4622.85	1807.75	2033.90	2487.55	2605.61
with flood or pest	FUS-I	8025.90	8476.95	7414.99		5755.01	6207.93	10557.73	7668.91	8413.33	8130.42	8240.93
	Diff.	-1268.84	-1601.44	-951.34		-887.48	-186.67	-2236.16	-1495.39	-1077.67	-1239.90	-1013.81
% household	FUS-II	0.07	0.06	0.07		0.06	0.09	0.07	0.08	0.06	0.05	0.07
affected by	FUS-I	0.13	0.12	0.14		0.15	0.06	0.17	0.13	0.13	0.11	0.13
health shock	Diff.	-0.06	-0.05	-0.07		-0.09	0.03	-0.10	-0.05	-0.07	-0.07	-0.07

contd...

...contd...

Distress Events	*Round*	*All*	*Partici-pants*	*Non-Participants*	*Sig.*	*SKLM*	*ANTP*	*ADB*	*PoP*	*Poor*	*NSP*	*NP*
Total loss associated with health shock	FUS-II	1122.48	941.26	1280.79		1358.69	929.15	1611.62	1470.77	1050.40	1021.13	660.64
	FUS-I	11090.27	8919.80	12930.00		7239.46	14825.62	13878.18	9968.68	14312.00	10319.21	5560.00
	Diff.	-9967.79	-7978.54	-11649.20		-5880.77	-13896.50	-12266.60	-8497.91	-13261.60	-9298.08	-4899.36
% household affected by other shocks	FUS-II	0.29	0.33	0.25	***	0.29	0.34	0.24	0.29	0.27	0.31	0.30
	FUS-I	0.66	0.69	0.64	***	0.67	0.82	0.53	0.65	0.67	0.66	0.73
	Diff.	-0.38	-0.36	-0.39		-0.37	-0.48	-0.28	-0.36	-0.40	-0.36	-0.43
Avg. no of events per household	FUS-II	0.76	0.88	0.65	***	0.55	1.21	0.54	0.77	0.72	0.77	0.84
	FUS-I	1.20	1.26	1.15	*	1.14	1.70	0.86	1.19	1.20	1.18	1.33
	Diff.	-0.44	-0.38	-0.50		-0.58	-0.49	-0.32	-0.42	-0.48	-0.40	-0.50
% household having no events	FUS-II	0.55	0.50	0.59	***	0.64	0.32	0.67	0.54	0.56	0.55	0.53
	FUS-I	0.33	0.30	0.35	***	0.32	0.18	0.46	0.34	0.32	0.33	0.25
	Diff.	0.22	0.20	0.24		0.32	0.15	0.20	0.20	0.24	0.22	0.28
% household having one event	FUS-II	0.35	0.38	0.32	***	0.25	0.55	0.25	0.35	0.34	0.34	0.37
	FUS-I	0.45	0.47	0.44	*	0.44	0.60	0.34	0.43	0.46	0.46	0.51
	Diff.	-0.10	-0.09	-0.12		-0.19	-0.05	-0.09	-0.09	-0.12	-0.12	-0.14
% household having two events	FUS-II	0.07	0.08	0.06	**	0.09	0.07	0.06	0.08	0.07	0.08	0.06
	FUS-I	0.14	0.14	0.14		0.16	0.13	0.13	0.14	0.14	0.13	0.16
	Diff.	-0.07	-0.06	-0.07		-0.07	-0.06	-0.07	-0.07	-0.07	-0.05	-0.11
	FUS-II	0.01	0.01	0.01	*	0.01	0.01	0.01	0.01	0.01	0.00	0.01
% household	FUS-I	0.04	0.05	0.04		0.06	0.03	0.04	0.04	0.04	0.05	0.04
having	Diff.	-0.03	-0.04	-0.03		-0.05	-0.01	-0.03	-0.03	-0.03	-0.04	-0.02
three events	FUS-I	0.04	0.04	0.04		0.02	0.07	0.03	0.04	0.04	0.03	0.04
	Diff.	-0.01	-0.01	-0.02		-0.01	-0.03	-0.01	-0.01	-0.02	-0.01	-0.01

Table 7.15

Coping Mechanism

Distress Events	Round	All	Partici-pants	Non-Participants	Sig.	SKLM	ANTP	ADB	PoP	Poor	NSP	NP
% of HH drought	FUS-II	0.23	0.25	0.21	**	0.23	0.35	0.06	0.22	0.22	0.25	0.24
	FUS-I	0.59	0.56	0.63	***	0.58	0.81	0.31	0.58	0.60	0.59	0.65
	Diff.	-0.37	-0.32	-0.42	***	-0.35	-0.46	-0.25	-0.36	-0.38	-0.34	-0.41
% of HH natural events	FUS-II	0.15	0.17	0.13	***	0.17	0.06	0.24	0.16	0.14	0.16	0.12
	FUS-I	0.24	0.28	0.20	***	0.23	0.11	0.44	0.26	0.23	0.23	0.21
	Diff.	-0.09	-0.1[illegible]	-0.07		-0.05	-0.05	-0.19	-0.10	-0.09	-0.08	-0.10
% of HH death of family member	FUS-II	0.04	0.04	0.04		0.04	0.03	0.03	0.04	0.02	0.04	0.05
	FUS-I	0.06	0.05	0.07		0.09	0.05	0.04	0.07	0.06	0.05	0.05
	Diff.	-0.02	-0.02	-0.03		-0.04	-0.02	-0.01	-0.03	-0.04	0.00	0.01
% of HH health problems	FUS-II	0.05	0.05	0.05		0.05	0.04	0.06	0.07	0.05	0.04	0.05
	FUS-I	0.15	0.14	0.17		0.17	0.07	0.23	0.17	0.16	0.13	0.13
	Diff.	-0.10	-0.09	-0.11		-0.12	-0.03	-0.17	-0.10	-0.11	-0.09	-0.09
% of HH mortgage/sell assets	FUS-II	0.04	0.05	0.03	*	0.05	0.04	0.03	0.05	0.04	0.04	0.05
	FUS-I	-0.14	-0.14	-0.15		-0.18	-0.07	-0.20	-0.15	-0.15	-0.13	-0.13
	Diff.	0.00	0.0[illegible]	-0.01		0.04	-0.01	-0.03	0.01	-0.02	-0.02	0.04
% of HH use savings	FUS-II	0.09	0.09	0.09		0.09	0.09	0.09	0.09	0.08	0.11	0.06
	FUS-I	0.13	0.15	0.11	**	0.17	0.07	0.18	0.14	0.12	0.14	0.12
	Diff.	-0.04	-0.06	-0.03		-0.09	0.02	-0.09	-0.05	-0.04	-0.03	-0.05
% of HH withdraw children from school	FUS-II	0.00	0.00	0.00		0.00	0.01	0.00	0.00	0.00	0.00	0.01
	FUS-I	0.00	0.01	0.00		0.00	0.00	0.01	0.01	0.00	0.00	0.00
	Diff.	0.00	0.00	0.00		0.00	0.01	-0.01	0.00	0.00	0.00	0.01
% of HH migration	FUS-II	0.01	0.01	0.01		0.02	0.01	0.01	0.01	0.01	0.01	0.02
	FUS-I	0.01	0.01	0.01		0.01	0.01	0.01	0.01	0.01	0.00	0.02
	Diff.	0.00	0.00	0.00		0.00	0.00	0.00	0.00	0.00	0.00	0.00
% of HH attached labour	FUS-II	0.00	0.00	0.00		0.00	0.00	0.01	0.00	0.00	0.00	0.00
	FUS-I	0.01	0.01	0.01		0.00	0.00	0.01	0.01	0.00	0.01	0.00
	Diff.	0.00	0.00	0.00		0.00	0.00	0.00	-0.01	0.00	0.00	0.00

contd...

...contd...

Distress Events	Round	All	Partici-pants	Non-Participants	Sig.	SKLM	ANTP	ADB	PoP	Poor	NSP	NP
% of HH borrowings	FUS-II	0.30	0.31	0.29		0.26	0.37	0.25	0.30	0.31	0.28	0.28
	FUS-I	0.46	0.44	0.47		0.55	0.41	0.41	0.45	0.46	0.47	0.46
	Diff.	-0.16	-0.13	-0.19	*	-0.29	-0.05	-0.17	-0.15	-0.15	-0.18	-0.18
% of HH reduce consumption	FUS-II	0.06	0.06	0.06		0.05	0.11	0.01	0.07	0.05	0.06	0.08
	FUS-I	0.08	0.09	0.08		0.05	0.12	0.08	0.09	0.09	0.05	0.10
	Diff.	-0.02	-0.02	-0.03		0.00	-0.02	-0.06	-0.03	-0.04	0.01	-0.02
% of HH more wage rate	FUS-II	0.08	0.08	0.07		0.01	0.09	0.14	0.09	0.07	0.06	0.08
	FUS-I	0.10	0.10	0.10		0.01	0.18	0.09	0.10	0.10	0.09	0.16
	Diff.	-0.02	-0.02	-0.03		-0.01	-0.09	0.05	-0.01	-0.03	-0.02	-0.08
% of HH others	FUS-II	0.01	0.01	0.01		0.01	0.00	0.01	0.01	0.01	0.00	0.01
	FUS-I	0.06	0.06	0.06		0.06	0.06	0.06	0.06	0.06	0.06	0.07
	Diff.	-0.05	-0.04	-0.05		-0.05	-0.05	-0.05	-0.04	-0.05	-0.06	-0.06
% of HH mortgage/ sell assets	FUS-II	0.02	0.02	0.03		0.04	0.02	0.01	0.03	0.03	0.02	0.01
	FUS-I	0.03	0.03	0.03		0.02	0.04	0.03	0.04	0.03	0.03	0.03
	Diff.	-0.01	-0.01	0.00		0.02	-0.02	-0.02	-0.01	0.00	-0.01	-0.02
% of HH use savings	FUS-II	0.05	0.06	0.04		0.05	0.07	0.03	0.06	0.06	0.04	0.03
	FUS-I	0.05	0.06	0.04		0.07	0.03	0.07	0.05	0.05	0.05	0.05
	Diff.	0.00	0.01	0.00		-0.02	0.03	-0.04	0.01	0.01	0.00	-0.02
% of HH withdraw children from school	FUS-II	0.01	0.00	0.01		0.01	0.01	0.00	0.01	0.01	0.01	0.01
	FUS-I	0.01	0.01	0.01		0.01	0.01	0.02	0.01	0.01	0.01	0.01
	Diff.	0.00	-0.01	0.00		-0.01	0.00	-0.02	-0.01	-0.01	0.00	0.00
% of HH migration	FUS-II	0.00	0.00	0.01		0.01	0.00	0.01	0.00	0.01	0.00	0.01
	FUS-I	0.01	0.00	0.01		0.01	0.01	0.00	0.01	0.00	0.01	0.01
	Diff.	0.00	0.00	0.00		-0.01	0.00	0.01	-0.01	0.00	0.00	0.00
% of HH attached labour	FUS-II	0.00	0.00	0.00		0.00	0.00	0.00	0.00	0.00	0.00	0.00
	FUS-I	0.00	0.00	0.00		0.01	0.00	0.00	0.00	0.01	0.00	0.00
	Diff.	0.00	0.00	0.00		-0.01	0.00	0.00	0.00	0.00	0.00	0.00
% of HH borrowings	FUS-II	0.13	0.14	0.12		0.08	0.19	0.07	0.14	0.11	0.14	0.18
	FUS-I	0.27	0.27	0.27		0.17	0.31	0.35	0.26	0.25	0.32	0.29
	Diff.	-0.14	-0.13	-0.15		-0.09	-0.12	-0.28	-0.12	-0.14	-0.18	-0.10

contd...

...contd...

Distress Events	*Round*	*All*	*Partici-pants*	*Non-Participants*	*Sig.*	*SKLM*	*ANTP*	*ADB*	*PoP*	*Poor*	*NSP*	*NP*
% of HH	FUS-II	0.11	0.11	0.11		0.03	0.17	0.08	0.09	0.14	0.10	0.10
reduce	FUS-I	0.29	0.27	0.30		0.47	0.24	0.13	0.26	0.32	0.30	0.27
consumption	Diff.	-0.18	-0.17	-0.19		-0.44	-0.07	-0.05	-0.17	-0.18	-0.20	-0.17
% of HH more	FUS-II	0.07	0.08	0.07		0.00	0.10	0.12	0.08	0.07	0.09	0.04
wage rate	FUS-I	0.11	0.11	0.11		0.04	0.15	0.12	0.12	0.13	0.07	0.14
	Diff.	-0.04	-0.03	-0.05		-0.04	-0.05	0.00	-0.04	-0.06	0.02	-0.10
% of HH	FUS-II	0.02	0.02	0.01		0.01	0.03	0.00	0.02	0.02	0.02	0.02
others	FUS-I	0.08	0.08	0.07		0.12	0.05	0.09	0.09	0.07	0.06	0.06
	Diff.	-0.06	-0.06	-0.06		-0.11	-0.02	-0.08	-0.08	-0.06	-0.04	-0.03
% of HH	FUS-II	0.06	0.07	0.06		0.13	0.05	0.03	0.08	0.06	0.04	0.04
mortgage/	FUS-I	0.04	0.03	0.05		0.03	0.04	0.09	0.03	0.04	0.05	0.04
sell assets	Diff.	0.02	0.03	0.01		0.10	0.01	-0.06	0.05	0.03	-0.01	0.00
% of HH	FUS-II	0.02	0.03	0.01		0.01	0.02	0.03	0.03	0.01	0.02	0.04
use savings	FUS-I	0.05	0.06	0.03		0.10	0.04	0.03	0.08	0.00	0.04	0.07
	Diff.	-0.02	-0.02	-0.02		-0.08	-0.01	0.00	-0.05	0.01	-0.01	-0.02
% of HH	FUS-II	0.01	0.00	0.01		0.00	0.00	0.03	0.00	0.02	0.00	0.00
withdraw children	FUS-I	0.02	0.01	0.03		0.00	0.02	0.06	0.01	0.03	0.01	0.04
from school	Diff.	-0.02	-0.01	-0.02		0.00	-0.02	-0.03	-0.01	-0.01	-0.01	-0.04
% of HH	FUS-II	0.01	0.01	0.01		0.03	0.01	0.00	0.01	0.01	0.02	0.00
migration	FUS-I	0.03	0.02	0.03		0.04	0.02	0.00	0.03	0.03	0.05	0.00
	Diff.	-0.02	0.00	-0.03		-0.01	-0.02	0.00	-0.03	-0.02	-0.02	0.00
% of HH	FUS-II	0.00	0.00	0.00		0.00	0.00	0.00	0.00	0.00	0.00	0.00
attached labour	FUS-I	0.00	0.00	0.00		0.00	0.00	0.03	0.00	0.01	0.00	0.00
	Diff.	0.00	0.00	0.00		0.00	0.00	-0.03	0.00	-0.01	0.00	0.00
% of HH	FUS-II	0.05	0.03	0.06		0.07	0.04	0.09	0.05	0.07	0.06	0.02
borrowings	FUS-I	0.18	0.23	0.12	***	0.04	0.20	0.29	0.19	0.18	0.13	0.20
	Diff.	-0.13	-0.19	-0.06	***	0.03	-0.16	-0.20	-0.14	-0.11	-0.07	-0.17
% of HH	FUS-II	0.06	0.07	0.06		0.10	0.06	0.06	0.05	0.04	0.10	0.11
reduce	FUS-I	0.19	0.15	0.24	**	0.31	0.17	0.09	0.20	0.19	0.15	0.15
consumption	Diff.	-0.12	-0.08	-0.18	**	-0.21	-0.11	-0.03	-0.15	-0.15	-0.06	-0.04
% of HH	FUS-II	0.05	0.07	0.03		0.03	0.06	0.06	0.05	0.05	0.05	0.09
more wage rate	FUS-I	0.20	0.15	0.25	**	0.04	0.25	0.11	0.16	0.24	0.26	0.13
	Diff.	-0.14	-0.08	-0.21	***	-0.01	-0.19	-0.06	-0.11	-0.19	-0.21	-0.04
% of HH others	FUS-II	0.04	0.05	0.03		0.03	0.04	0.03	0.04	0.04	0.04	0.04
	FUS-I	0.09	0.08	0.10		0.11	0.09	0.03	0.07	0.09	0.11	0.07
	Diff.	-0.05	-0.03	-0.07		-0.08	-0.04	0.00	-0.03	-0.05	-0.07	-0.02

References

Blaikie, P., T. Cannon, J. Davis and B. Wisner (1994). *At Risk. Natural Hazards, People's Vulnerability and Disasters*. London and New York: Routledge.

Cohen, D. (2005). "Achieving Food Security in Vulnerable Populations", *British Medical Journal* 331: 775-777.

Dahl, S.L. (1993). "Sustainable Livelihood Security", *The Indian Geographical Journal* 68(1): 21-32.

Dev, Mahendra, K.P. Kannan, Nira Ramachandran (2003). "Introduction", in Mahendra Dev, K.P. Kannan and Nira Ramachandran (eds.), *Towards a Food Secure India: Issues and Policies*. New Delhi: Institute for Human Development.

Government of India (2000). *Expenditure Reforms Commission*, Ministry of Finance, Government of India.

Vyas, Vijay S. (2003). "Economic Policies for Ensuring Food Security", Introduction in Mahendra Dev, K.P. Kannan and Nira Ramachandran (eds.), *Towards a Food Secure India: Issues and Policies*. New Delhi: Institute for Human Development.

Section III

Organisational Assessment and Improvement

8 Emerging Self-Help Group Federations and Challenges

C.S. Reddy, N. Tirupathaiah and S. Ramalakshmi

Evolution of Self-Help Group (SHG) Federations

Overview of SHG Movement

The SHG model is the dominant form of microfinance in India. SHGs have grown explosively in recent years. It is reported that by March 2008, three million SHGs were reaching about 38 million women members. Such outreach appears to represent a major breakthrough in a country where 50 million households live in poverty, with very limited access to financial services.

Although the term SHG is used in different countries to describe a variety of financial and non-financial associations; in India SHGs are small groups that deliver small loans to their members. SHGs are run by their members, who choose their own leaders. They decide on compulsory savings amounts, interest rates, lending norms and distribution of surpluses. Accounts are maintained by literate members, hired book-keepers, or staff of promoting institutions. Most groups have 10 to 20 members. Members typically are low-income women (or men) who have similar socioeconomic backgrounds and who are from the same locality. SHGs collect periodic savings and provide loans to their members.

SHGs are formed with the assistance of self-help promotion institutions (SHPIs), which include non-governmental organisations (NGOs), government agencies, banks, cooperatives and microfinance institutions (MFIs). In addition to helping with group formation, SHPIs provide training, monitoring, and other support services. Occasionally, promoters give SHGs initial seed capital to lend, but more typically, groups begin by saving and lending out their members' own resources. Most, but by no means all, SHGs eventually borrow from an external source, usually a bank. This bank linkage is the most distinctive characteristic of the Indian SHG model achieving significant scale and has shown exponential growth and quantum of loan to SHGs. The need of the hour after the empowerment of the SHGs for years now is to scale them up to a stage where the tertiary body has the competency providing the services of larger magnitude at a larger scale with efficiency. And for the same the SHGs need to be federated.

Piloting of SHG Federations

Federation is a network of several SHGs, a structure or a body evolved by SHGs themselves consisting of representatives from all member-SHGs, with a motive of supporting member-SHGs attain the goals of economic and social empowerment of women members and their capacity building. In other words, a federation is a democratic body formed with certain number of SHGs functioning in a specific geographical area with the objective of uniting such SHGs for common cause and for achieving those causes which an individual SHG would not be able to do. In short, the SHG federation has to be necessarily of SHGs, by SHGs and for SHGs. Networking of SHGs was inspired by the felt need of the SHGs that are not able to deal with issues that are beyond their reach. SHGs are too small and informal to deal with larger issues to realise the needs and aspirations of women members. Inter-group lending, ability to negotiate with higher level structures and to gain greater bargaining power, were the reasons as to why informal SHG networking was initiated by NGOs. The unique feature of the SHG federations is that the primaries i.e., the SHGs, are not legal entities and do not have body corporate status. However, SHGs are recognised as per the RBI guidelines to engage in financial transactions with banks. The SHG federations function as per the subsidiarity principle—undertake those roles that cannot be performed by member-SHGs. SHG federations have been promoted by the NGOs and the Government from mid-1990s to address the issues of ensuring quality while upscaling, ensure that costs of promotion are low, and create sustainable institutions to facilitate withdrawal of the promoting organisation, from some of its functions and roles.

Professional Assistance for Development Action (PRADAN) and Mysore Resettlement and Development Agency (MYRADA) were the two NGOs, which pioneered the concept of SHG federations. PRADAN in 1992 promoted the Sri Padmavathi Mahila Abhyudaya Sangham (SPMS) in Tirupati. Development of Humane Action (DHAN) Foundation that was evolved from PRADAN has formed several SHG federations across South India. These are registered under the Societies Registration Act, 1860.

Credit Analysis and Research Limited (CARE) initiated its microfinance activity in early 1990s in Chevella and nearby *mandals* of Rangareddy district of Andhra Pradesh, and has established a three-tier federation structure of SHG-Cluster-Federation. Later on CARE's Credit and Savings for Household Enterprise (CASHE) project partner NGOs promoted large of number of cluster and block level federations in three states of India: Andhra Pradesh, Orissa and West Bengal.

United Nations Development Programme (UNDP), South Asia Poverty Alleviation Project (SAPAP) started in 1994 in Andhra Pradesh and was implemented in 20 *mandals* spread across three districts. SHGs in each *mandal* are federated into a *mandal samakhya* (MS) as a three-tier structure of SHG-village organisation (VO)—*mandal samakhya*, and are registered under the Andhra Pradesh Mutually Aided Cooperative Societies (APMACS) Act, 1995. This model has been scaled up under the World Bank funded Poverty Reduction Program in Andhra Pradesh covering all the rural areas in the state.

A large number of NGOs promoted SHG federations as a two-tier structure to facilitate sustainable institutions of the poor. While SHGs are informal, the federations often become formal institutions adopting appropriate legal forms. NGOs either directly access funds for on-lending to federations or facilitate the SHG federations accessing bulk loans from a variety of financial institutions including banks. In most of these cases, the SHG federations perform both financial and non-financial functions. Some of the promoting organisations have ensured that the SHG federations perform the functions of a financial institution, others having facilitating the federations taking a more holistic role including marketing activities.

Need for Federation

There are a variety of reasons for federating the SHGs, one which could assist the promoting institutions and others which are for the direct benefit of the members. The reasons are:

- To scale up the present level of activities and support for weaker and default SHGs.
- It is necessary to build people's institutions that can eventually and independently carry forward the social and economic empowerment agenda so as to provide sustainability to SHG activity initiated and nurtured by the promoter even after its withdrawal.
- To take up community action programmes, mobilise and lead collective action to resolve the social issues.
- Lobbying with the government and other institutions.
- To establish sustainable linkages with financial and non-financial institutions to access greater funds and benefits.
- To provide marketing linkages and supplementary bargaining power.
- To provide value added and supervisory services to strengthen SHGs.

Disadvantages of Promoting SHG Federations

As has been explained before, there are several benefits in promoting SHG federations. However, there are several disadvantages or dangers if federations are promoted. The promoters must be fully aware of these and follow a process by which many of these could be mitigated. The following are the limitations of SHG federations:

1. Majority of the well-functioning SHGs have bank linkage. SHG federation is not required to play the financial intermediary role as SHG-bank linkage is a sustainable relationship.
2. Some federations are themselves federating and aim to create new financial institutions. India already has commercial banks, regional rural banks, primary agricultural credit societies (PACSs) and district central cooperative bank (DCCB) branches; some are not functioning properly but the way to improve these federations is to reform them, not to create yet another set of institutions.

3. The existing financial institutions are not properly regulated or supervised and there are frequent failures and frauds. There is no way by which the authorities can take on yet another type of institution; SHG federations will need supervision but will not receive it.
4. The better of among the poor may capture all the benefits of the SHG federation.
5. The process of promoting an SHG is not easy but bankers and new SHG members themselves are increasingly taking over the task, thus reducing the need for dependence on NGOs and subsidy. Promoting a federation is much more difficult and requires much longer 'hand-holding'.
6. A single SHG does not contain enough voters to be worth 'hijacking' by political interests but a federation is a very attractive target.
7. The day-to-day operations of a federation cost money. This may come in the form of contributions or interest spreads paid by member-SHGs or from individual members' voluntary work. Federations will make these burdens worse.
8. One of the most 'empowering' aspects of SHG membership is the way it allows members to pick and choose between financial service providers.
9. Lastly, banks, PACS and MFIs are obliged to compete for SHG members' business. Federations can demand 'loyalty', which is essentially a loss of freedom.

Promotion of SHG Federations

Initial piloting of SHG federation promotion in the early nineties evolved the institutional model and the step-by-step approach in promoting SHG federations. Also, a large number of NGOs and externally funded projects of the Government began SHG federation promotion in late nineties. Table 8.1 gives estimates of number of SHG federations in those states that have been engaged in promoting SHG federations in a big way.

Over the past few years, the concept of SHG federation has been incorporated in the initial design of many multilateral and bilateral funded projects. In fact, almost all the large-scale projects that have SHGs as part of the strategy for poverty reduction and women empowerment also have taken up the federation promotion. As majority of these externally aided projects are implemented by the Government, either through NGOs or directly, target-oriented approach is followed in promoting SHG federations. In some cases, the federations are promoted even before the SHGs are promoted. The International Fund for Agriculture Development

Table 8.1

Major Promoters of SHG Federations in Select Few States

State	*Major Promoters***	*No. of SHG Federations**
Andhra Pradesh	Society for Elimination of Rural Poverty (SERP), UNDP, NGO partners of CASHE project of CARE India, Ankuram Sangamam Poram (ASP), GRAM, Calvary Educational and Economic Development Trust (CEED), Confederation of Voluntary Associations (COVA), MYRADA, DHAN Foundation, Young India Project (YIP), Outreach etc.	29265
Tamil Nadu	Tamil Nadu Corporation for Women Development Ltd. (TNCDW) (Govt.), PRADAN, Outreach, DHAN, MYRADA	14104
Karnataka	MYRADA, Outreach	220
Maharashtra	Mahila Arthik Vikas Mahamandal (MAVIM), NGO Network Support by Chaitanya	120
Kerala	Kudumbashree (Govt.)	15153
Orissa	Mission Shakti, Bharat Integrated Social Welfare Agency (BISWA), Swayamshree, Gramodbhav, Friends' Association for Rural Reconstruction (FARR)	5429
West Bengal	CARE, Rural Development Consortium	300
Gujarat	Gujarat Rajya Rachanatmak Karyakar Sangh Janani, International Centre for Entrepreneurship and Career Development	63
Uttar Pradesh	People's Action for National Integration (PANI), NEED	92
Other federations under Swashakti and Swayamsidha Projects (Govt.)		1826
	Total	66572

Note and Source:

* The number of SHG federations in a given state is a best guess only.

** Above information is collected through websites and telephones.

(IFAD) funded large-scale projects—Tamil Nadu Women's Development Project (TNWDP), Maharashtra Rural Credit Programme implemented by MAVIM and Swashakti project implemented in Bihar, Gujarat, Haryana, Karnataka, Madhya Pradesh and Uttar Pradesh—promoted SHG federations at the cluster level. The IFAD funded projects together have contributed to the introduction of the SHG federation concept in eight Indian states. At present there are a large number of projects funded by the World Bank and Government of India being implemented in several Indian states that promote SHG federations. Department for International Development (DFID) funded projects have supported the SHG federation promotion in Andhra Pradesh, Orissa and West Bengal. On the whole, the SHG federation concept has been promoted in almost all parts of India including the Northeast, though it is widely in practice in South India with more than 66,000 SHG federations—majority of them being at the village/cluster level.

In Kerala the federations are promoted under the Kudumbashree programme with more than 14,000 area development societies (ADS) and 1,050 community development societies (CDS). In Tamil Nadu, more than 12,000 *panchayat* level SHG federations are functioning under the TNCWD and a large number of NGOs. In Karnataka there are a large number of federations promoted by NGOs—prominent among them being MYRADA (340 federations) and Outreach (120 federations). It is to be noted that MYRADA promotes federations for social intermediation and promotes community managed resource centres (CMRCs) to provide a variety of support services to the SHGs on a fee-for-service basis. In Andhra Pradesh there are more than 30,000 SHG federations promoted by Indira Kranthi Patham (IKP) programme funded by World Bank and several NGOs.

In the rest of the country, majority of the federations are promoted by NGOs with limited number of federations promoted under the government supported programmes. Women and Child Development (WCD) department of Government of India promoting several cluster level federations through its programmes called Swashakti and Swayamsidha. The DFID funded Poorest Areas Civil Society (PACS) which is being implemented in several northern states is in the process of promoting village/cluster level federations for social intermediation. In addition, World

Bank is funding several poverty reduction projects through the state governments. Many of these projects incorporate SHGs and SHG federations as the institutional mechanism for poverty reduction.

Status of SHG Federation Based on APMAS Rating Findings

Andhra Pradesh Mahila Abhivruddhi Society (APMAS) emerged from the felt need to have a resource organisation that provides high quality technical and managerial support for strengthening the SHG movement in India, more specifically in Andhra Pradesh. One of the mandates of APMAS is to establish standards for the SHG federations based on practice. To enable the promoters of SHG federations in adopting the standards, APMAS provides capacity building through a series of training of trainers' programmes. To facilitate an independent third party assessment of the quality of the SHG federations, APMAS developed a quality assessment (QA) system for rating SHG federation, called GRADES, which is developed in collaboration with Micro Credit Ratings International Limited (M-CRIL), New Delhi. GRADES, represents the key assessment areas of the federation assessment—governance and strategy, resources, asset quality, design of systems and implementation, efficiency and profitability, services to SHGs in addition to the SHG performance. QA is revised every year and GRADES version 2.0 is used currently. The rating of SHG federations would aid the promoters to understand the performance of the federations. The rating could also facilitate financial flows to the federations from banks and other financial institutions. The GRADES tool has been successfully utilised for the assessment of over 400 SHG federations promoted by International funded (World Bank) projects and NGOs, District Rural Development Agency (DRDA), NGOs and MFIs.

Performance of Federations

The findings of the SHG federation rating done by APMAS are presented here to give an overview of the present status of SHG federations in India. While analysing the data, only the data of comparable SHG federations is taken. The purpose of presenting the findings of our ratings is to clearly bring out the key issues and challenges in promoting sustainable SHG federations. The analysis included 83 SHG federations rated by APMAS during 2003-2005. The SHG federations' overall performance is moderate that converted into a letter grade 'B-'. Federations have performed reasonably good at resource, moderate in the areas *viz.*, governance, design of system federations and its implementations, services to SHGs and overall SHG performance and poor in the areas of asset quality and efficiency and profitability.

Good governance contributed to higher grades. However, where regularity of meetings (one unit of good governance) contributed clearly to higher grades, quality boards (another unit of good governance) did not. One explanation for this could be that good governance is a result of SHPI role in governance. There is a marked absence of second line leadership at the federation level to take on leadership role when the first set of leaders step down. Added to this, majority of federations' are not performing legal compliance except for external audit. The human resource in federations is qualified, competent and has reasonably good field experience and are recruited, oriented and paid by the promoting organisation. Majority of Federations are heavily dependent on the promoter for their resources which might dominate autonomy of these institutions. Most SHPIs invest considerably in human resource development, and this appears to have paid dividend. It is not enough to invest in staff capacity building. Investment in boards, too, is required, especially by user-owned, democratically structured organisations.

The funds available per member-SHG increased in federations with age. But the fund availability at federations per SHGs is not sufficient to meet member-SHG demands and accessing external borrowings by SHGs directly and federation as well. The quality of assets appeared to improve at first with age, only to deteriorate again with more passage of time. While 75 per cent of the federations had an external repayment rate of over 95 per cent, only 22 per cent of them had an internal repayment rate of over 95 per cent. Several federations that appeared to be performing well, were in fact repaying to creditors from either member savings or profits earned, or grant funds, as their member-SHGs had not repaid their loans to the federation. The average internal recovery rate in the federations is 66 per cent (ranges from 20 per cent-100 per cent).

Accounting systems in federations appeared to be improving with age. However, much more effort is needed to be put into management information systems and internal controls. Good accounting systems by themselves, and without effective monitoring systems and internal controls, cannot contribute to sound portfolio management. Despite the generous support that many federations had received over a period of time, 138 per cent of the federations were operationally self-sufficient and 73 per cent were financially self-sufficient. Lack of financial self-sufficiency indicates a life span related to the rate at which funds at the disposal of the federation will be used up. But the staff efficiency reasonable in terms of managing of number of SHGs per staff is 75, outstanding loan per staff is Rs 5 lakh and the average operating cost ratio is 12.5 per cent. The financial services being provided comprise of only loans and compulsory savings and few federations are offering insurance services. The non-financial services include bank linkage to member-SHGs, trainings, grading the performance of SHGs are provided to some extent (Table 8.2).

The meetings in member-SHGs were neither regular nor well attended, with over 60 per cent of SHGs faring badly on both counts. Book-keeping appeared to be of reasonable quality on the whole, and SHPIs appeared to have invested in improved accounting both at SHG and at federation levels. The low velocity of lending (73 per cent of SHGs lent less than 1 rupee for every rupee available), difference between what could have been lent (corpus = Rs 73,000) and what actually lay with members as loans (Rs 55,000), portfolio at risk (47 per cent of SHGs with over 25 per cent PAR), all indicated that funds were not well managed by SHGs. As in the case of federations, good book-keeping was not enough to assure good financial management.

Challenges

Design of the federation: In federations, their combined assessments indicated certain design features, which, if incorporated, could perhaps contribute to better performance. Their location *vis-à-vis* their member-SHGs and the form of organisation adopted appeared to affect their likelihood of success. Federations closer to their member-SHGs, such as those at village or cluster levels performed better than those at *mandal/*

Table 8.2

Summary of Quantitative Performance Indicators against Benchmark

S.No	Indicator	Average*	Benchmark**	Remark
1.	Regularity of meetings (%)	94.8	100.0	Regular meetings with less attendance
2.	Attendance in board meeting (%)	74.7	>90.0	
3.	Attendance in general body (GB) meeting (%)	41.4	>66.6	Some federations are conducting GB without minimum quorum
4.	Village coverage (%)	85.3	>95.0	
5.	Target beneficiaries coverage (%)	80.4	>90.0	
6.	Available funds per SHG (Rs)	9,776	At least Rs. 10,000	
7.	Idle fund to total assets (%)	17.4	<5.0	Federations have lot of idle funds
8.	Capital adequacy ratio (CAR) (%)	42.8	20.0	Majority of federations are running with donated capital so that CAR is high
9.	External repayment rate (%)	90.0	>95.0	
10.	Internal repayment rate (%)	65.8	>90.0	Very less repayment of internal loans
11.	Loan outstanding to SHGs (%)	55.5	>75.0	Half of the SHGs in federation have loans
12.	Portfolio at risk > 90 days (%)	23.7	<10.0	High risk portfolio
13.	Portfolio at risk >180 days (%)	17.4	<5.0	

contd...

...contd...

S.No	*Indicator*	*Average**	*Benchmark***	*Remark*
14.	Arrears rate > 90 days (%)	6.8	<3.0	
15.	SHGs per staff (no.)	75	At least 40 SHGs	
16.	Loan outstanding per staff (Rs)	4,96,552	At least Rs 8 Lakh	The earning on average loan outstanding is not sufficient to meet staff salaries
17.	Yield on portfolio (%)	13.0	Equal to interest rate	The average interest charging by federations is 18%, but federations are recovering only 13 (i.e., 72%)
18.	Operational cost ratio (OCR) (%)	12.5	<10.0	Majority of federations do not have external loans and are running with donated capital so that the OCR (12.5%) is high cost
19.	Operational self-sufficiency (%)	138.2	> 100.0	In majority federations the costs are born by the promoters
20.	Financial self-sufficiency (%)	73.4	>=100.0	
21.	Return on assets (%)	3.5	>6.0	Returns are not at expected level
22.	Return on equity (%)	8.6	>12.0	
23.	Loan outstanding *vs.* total assets (%)	78.0	>90.0	22% idle/invested in infrastructure

Note: * Average of 83 federations.

** Benchmarks (standard) according to APMAS.

block levels. This is not to say that there were no *mandal* level federations that performed well. However, on the whole, it appears that the closer a federation to its member-SHGs, the more likely it is to succeed. So, also the cooperative form of organisation appears to offer greater likelihood of good performance than the society form or the unregistered form.

Weak governance: The federation board does not feel true ownership of the federation. Most of these federations have socially-motivated members who tend to put a priority on the institution's achievement of social objectives. The board of directors of most such institutions is often ineffective in overseeing the institutions; frequently they are chosen because they are vocal and active with inadequate understanding of the financial management aspects of microfinance. Moreover, newly appointed board members are not aware of the vision and objectives of federation, even though they exhibit good commitment and interest to build the institution. The question that arises here is how to ensure that the vision of the federation is in fact driven by its members. The staff of the promoters has limited capacity to build the capacity of the boards. Many federations are not registered under an appropriate legal form. The board has limited understanding of the bye-laws of their own organisation. Many federations which are registered as cooperatives, do not get their accounts audited, and do not present their annual reports and accounts to their members.

Trained human resource: Most of the existing federations do not have skilled human resource which is not available for local level accounting. Dropout of trained staff is very high. In most of the federations, staff are recruited, trained and paid by promoting agency in initial period and later the persons become employees of the federations. So the staff are accountable (or committed) towards promoting institution rather than federation. At the same time, it is the staff members who occupy the position of board members on rotation. So it is difficult on the part of the federation to review the staff performance and make them accountable for their actions.

Recovery performance and portfolio quality: Increasing size of financial services to member-SHGs is often equated with good performance of a federation. Field reality, however, indicates that repayment to external creditors is made without internal loan recovery from member-SHGs. Thus there is a dire need of SHG loan recovery from its members.

Finalising and standardisation of systems and procedures: The systems and processes in federations are still evolving and are in the process of being formalised. SHPIs have spent considerable money and time designing systems and procedures. The manual accounting system in the federations is reasonably good but the quality information system is low across the federations. Though the records maintained at the SHG level are adequate, accuracy and timeliness in recording information is low. With federations handling multiple activities, and geared to play a major role in the social and economic empowerment of women, having strong systems would help in building institutions with long-term sustainability. Many federations do not have internal audit and control.

Cost of promotion: Encouraging SHG federations is a costly activity for a promoting institution (PI) to undertake. The two types of costs involved in promoting federations are promotional costs and operational costs. While estimating the cost of group formation is difficult and depends on the quality and quantity of support provided, the Ministry of Rural Development has established a norm of Rs 10,000 per SHG. If there is an average of 250 SHGs in one federation, the cost is an astonishingly high of Rs 2.5 million. In addition to the SHG promotion costs, there are considerable costs of promoting federations. It may cost Rs 2-5 lakh to promote a smaller federation and Rs 10-25 lakh to promote larger federation. Considering PIs estimate it takes anywhere from 5-10 years for a federation to become sustainable, promoting institutions must incur huge costs simply to promote one federation.

Institutional sustainability: While the management skills of federation members and leaders in changing environments was seen as important, their ability to contribute effectively was limited due to their low literacy levels and the limited exposure to the formal sector and with formal systems. As mentioned above, one of the rationale behind creating SHG federations is that they are more likely to become sustainable than individual SHGs. Although this might be the case, the current state of federations across the country demonstrates low financial sustainability. There is enough evidence to show the contribution of SHG federations for the sustainability of SHGs, it is by far the most significant challenge in the future. In this context, financial sustainability is whether the SHG federation is being held afloat using grant money or on its own accord.

Recommendations

1. While networking has distinct advantages, it also has several disadvantages. It is absolutely critical that these federations are built based on the felt need of the members through a process-oriented approach. The promoters need to have long-term vision on developing sustainable institutions for the poor. SHPIs need to understand the democratic form of organisation better, and take care not to fashion federations after charitable societies, which are promoter-chief executive driven. Federations must be member-driven for any chance of success, and chief executives must be fully accountable to their elected boards, unlike societies in which promoter-chief executives invite people to join their boards.
2. SHPIs need to invest more on elected boards, and not put all their energies into investing in full time staff. When boards change, new directors need to be endowed with more powers. The owners of federations are their members, and board members are the representatives of the owners. Staff cannot be expected to perform in an accountable manner, if owners' representatives do not understand the concern involved.
3. Much more effort needs to go into the provision of 'support services' to member-SHGs by federations. Current concentration on provision of financial services to member-SHGs and neglect of the closely linked 'support' services, has resulted in poor financial quality of member organisations, and poor quality of financial relationship with member organisations (SHGs). Support services appear to contribute to the improved quality of financial operations, and ought to be more central in the scheme of federation services.
4. Reporting systems must concentrate more on loans on demand and recovery of loans on demand, rather than on total loans disbursed. So, too, the current hype on good repayment rate of bank loans must give way to rewarding and encouraging loan recovery from members

to their SHG federations. SHPIs must encourage their own staff as well as federation boards to identify source of repayment of external loans. This must be debated on within SHPIs and federations, so that the risks to member's savings and to conscientious members, who repay loans regularly, are fully understood. So, too, the sustainability of current practices needs to be fully comprehended. The grading system and the monitoring of the SHGs have to be practiced from time to time for enabling good disbursement and effective recovery rate.

5. The federations are registered under various acts but they are not complying with the legal obligations. The federations should work towards complying with all legal obligations and requirements in time. Particularly, all federations, registered or unregistered, must ensure annual audit of their accounts by a qualified auditor, prepare their annual report and conduct annual general body meeting ensuring at least 50 per cent of their members' participation. The annual general body meeting (AGM) could be conducted as a business and social event to celebrate their success and to show their collective strength.
6. The changing complexities of member management, human resource development, and financial management have necessitated the availability of professional assistance to SHG federations through adequate trained and professional paid staff on appropriate terms working under the general guidance of a democratically elected body. Building large number of institutions of the poor requires adequate availability of professionals with adequate knowledge, skills, competencies and experience. The available human resources for facilitating emergence of SHG federations in the form of clusters, village organisations and higher level federations are limited. Hence, there is a need to make significant investments in developing professionals and para-professionals to escort the emerging SHG federations.
7. Across the organisations, there is a scope to improve the accounting, information system and internal controls, develop and establish system. For the financial institutions to run efficiently and effectively, accurate and up-to-date accounting and reporting is

necessary. The capacities of the board of directors of federations need to be built to interpret the financial statements such as balance sheet, receipts and payments and income and expenditure statement. There is a need for suitable software to meet the Management Information System (MIS) needs of the SHG federations.

In conclusion, SHG federation has been evolved as a model that promotes sustainability of the SHGs and provides the much needed institutional base for the women to realise their dreams and aspirations. The SHG federation model has achieved significant scale and considerable acceptance among all the major stakeholders. There is great potential for the SHG federation model to address issues of poverty. In many ways, the model is unique—the women are the owners, managers, users and controllers. This is here to stay. While there are many benefits of SHG federation model, it has several limitations. The promoters need to be aware of both. Within the SHG federation model there are several variations driven by the local considerations and the strategy of the promoting organisation.

References

Basu, Priya and Pradeep Srivastava (2004). "India Scaling-up Access to Finance for India's Rural Poor", *WPS* 3646, The World Bank, December.

Devaprakash, R. (2005). "Balancing Quality and Quantity in SHGs in India", *IBA Bulletin*, August.

Nair, Ajai (2005). *Sustainability of Microfinance Self Help Groups in India: Would Federating Help?*. World Bank, February.

APMAS (n.d.). *Promotion of Vibrant and Sustainable Federations of SHGs*. Unpublished report by APMAS.

Rajagopalan, Shashi (2003). "Designing Secondary Institutions of Self-Help Groups", *Discussion Paper*. APMAS, June.

Reddy, C.S. and L.B. Prakash (2003). *Status of SHG Federations in Andhra Pradesh- APMAS Assessment Findings*. APMAS, March.

Sa-Dhan (2004). *SHG Federations in India: Emerging Structures and Practices*. July.

———. (2005). *SHG-Federation-Emergence, Roles and Prospects: A Discussion Paper Series*. May.

Satyamurti, V. and S. Haokip (2002). *Microfinance Concept and Delivery Channels in India*. All India Association for Micro Enterprise Development (AIAMED).

Tankha, Ajay (2002). *Self Help Groups as Financial Intermediaries in India: Cost of Promotion, Sustainability and Impact*. Sa-Dhan, August.

Harper, Malcolm (2002). *Do We Really Need SHG Federations?*.

CARE (2000). *State Level Convention on Federations: A Report.*

Fernandez, A.P. (2001). *Putting Institutions First-Even in Micro Finance: MYRADA.*

Friends of Women's World Banking (FWWB, India) (1998). *India's Emerging Federations of Women's Savings and Credit Groups.*

Menon, G.A. and S. Gupta (1999). *From Margin to Mainstream: Building Stakes in the SHG-Bank Linkage Programme*. Swayam Shikshan Prayog.

MYRADA (2001). *The MYRADA Experience: A Manual for Capacity Building of Self-Help Affinity Groups.*

Rajasekhar, D. (1994). *Savings and Credit Systems of the Poor: Some Non-Governmental Organization (NGO) Experiences.* NOVIB and HIVOS.

Tamil Nadu Corporation for Development of Women Limited (1999). *A Guide to SHG Federations.*

Tiwari, Piyush and S.M. Fahad (1997). "Microfinance Institutions in India", *Concept Paper*, Mumbai: HDFC.

9 Self-Help Group: An Institutional Model

A Basix Experience

Rama Kandarpa

Background

BASIX, a new generation livelihood promotion institution was set up in 1996. The mission of BASIX is to promote a large number of sustainable livelihoods, including for the rural poor and women, through the provision of financial services and technical assistance in an integrated manner. BASIX will strive to yield a competitive return for its investors so as to be able to access mainstream capital and human resources on a continuous basis.

BASIX comprises a group of companies, of which one is a holding company and others are its subsidiaries. The holding company is called Bhartiya Samruddhi Investments and Consulting Services Ltd. (BASICS Ltd.). The financial arm of the group comprises a non-banking financial company (NBFC), Bhartiya Samruddhi Finance Ltd. (Samruddhi) and a bank, Krishna Bhima Samruddhi Local Area Bank Ltd. Apart from these, Indian Grameen Services is a non-profit subsidiary company, which provides technical assistance and support services to the entire clientele of the BASIX group. BASIX employs a strategy known as 'The Livelihood Triad', through which three types of services believed to be essential for livelihood promotion especially for poorer people in backward regions, are provided in an integrated fashion. They are: (i) livelihood financial services (including savings, credit, insurance, remittances etc.), (ii) agri/business development services (including productivity enhancement, local value addition, market linkages, risk mitigation etc.) and (iii) institutional development services (formation and strengthening of self-help groups (SHGs), federations, producer groups, formal institutions like cooperatives, non-government organisations (NGOs), microfinance institutions (MFIs), policy analysis and sector work etc.

Realising that any one institution is not in a position to provide the three types of services required for livelihood promotion, BASIX adopts a collaborative strategy wherein other institutions with the requisite expertise are roped in and sustainable partnerships are facilitated. BASIX also promotes livelihoods by influencing the thinking of other agencies working in livelihood promotion (government agencies, NGOs, large projects) through institutional development and consulting services.

BASIX and SHGs

BASIX works with the entire cross-section of the rural economy, that comprises small enterprises, commercial farmers, small farmers, subsistence workers and marginal farmers, who are in turn interlinked. BASIX believes that these different segments of borrowers in the rural economy cannot be reached by the same mode of operation. To effectively cater to the entire rural populace, BASIX evolved methodologies and loan mechanisms to suit different segments of the economy. The segmentation is as follows:

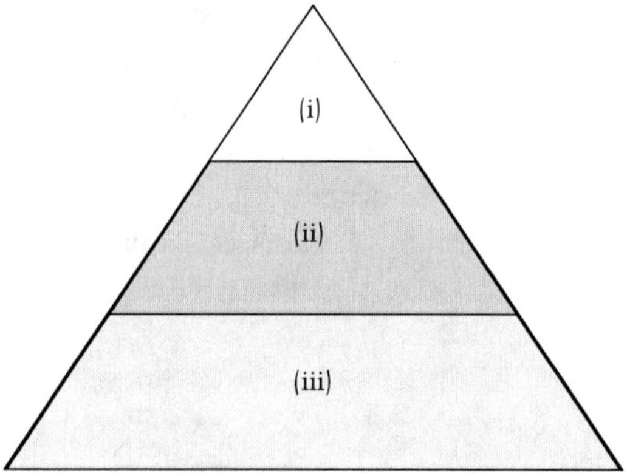

(i) Small enterprises/commercial farmers—direct loans with collateral security;

(ii) Microenterprises/small farmers—through joint liability groups/ through on-lenders;

(iii) Subsistence workers/marginal farmers—through self-help groups.

BASIX reaches a broad range of clientele, ranging from the not so poor entrepreneurs to the poor and the middle level clientele. BASIX abiding engagement with SHGs can be traced to the determining work on savings and credit groups that was done in Professional Assistance for Development Action (Pradan) and Mysore Resettlement and Development Agency (MYRADA) and other NGOs during the eighties, with whom the promoters of BASIX were intensely involved with and deeply influenced by. In 1994-95, the Reserve Bank of India (RBI) set up a Working Group on credit to the rural poor through SHGs and NGOs. The group established the SHG-bank linkage guidelines and National Bank for Agriculture and Rural Development (NABARD) adopted a target of one million SHGs by 2008.

The Formative Years

BASIX started its operations in 1996 with the offering of micro-credit and incidentally the very first loan disbursed by BASIX was to eight SHGs supported by an NGO called Prerana in Koppar village of Raichur district of Karnataka. In the first year of operations, BASIX extended loans to 51 SHGs with total membership of more than 1,000 women, which were promoted and supported by NGOs like Prerana (Raichur), Star Youth Association (Kurnool) and ACTIVE (Khammam). In 1998, a very useful collaboration was established with the UNDP's South Asia Poverty Alleviation Project (SAPAP), which was working for the social and economic empowerment of rural poor women in Mahabubnagar, Kurnool and Anantapur districts of Andhra Pradesh. While BASIX had extended credit to the women members of SHGs of this project, it also worked closely with the UNDP-SAPAP staff to improve the capacity of SHGs and their federations in accounting, financial management and adoption of new livelihood ideas. Similar efforts were also on with the federations and groups supported by CARE in Chevella, Rangareddy district of Andhra Pradesh.

Thus, in the first 3-4 years of setting up its operations, BASIX's engagement with SHGs and/or their federations (used interchangeably with village organisations) was more in the nature of promotion,[1] capacity

1. More often than not, promotion included digging out the 1991 NABARD circular regarding opening of bank accounts for SHGs, in order to convince the bank manager.

building towards creditworthiness, assessment and lending. This work was highly acclaimed inasmuch it was setting the norms of quality and successful objective assessment based lending, and was the cornerstone for all future institutional development efforts of BASIX. From 2000 onwards, while continuing the work with SHGs and federations in BASIX area of operations, there was demand from other NGOs/MFIs to help with their own microfinance programmes, a very significant part of which was SHG based. Similarly, there was an increasing demand from various government and apex agencies to provide direction to and support their own SHG programmes. BASIX actively involved itself in this sector work, building upon its own experiences, while building the capabilities of the human resources of those organisations and providing specific inputs on vision building, systems, legal and capital structures, among others. All throughout, BASIX therefore has been dealing with the development of SHGs as institutions, in the context of its social mission of sustainable 'livelihoods' promotion.

Conscious of the world around that deals with SHGs with an overarching 'empowerment' paradigm, BASIX chose to deal with them with a 'market' paradigm. In this endeavour, we focussed on building capacities of the group, rather than that of the individuals forming the group, believing that the former would naturally lead to the latter. Individuals within the collective and their needs were given importance in so far as it related to the group dynamics, no more. BASIX set upon itself the task of systematically building the linkages to instill in the groups strong dynamics coupled with a keen commercial sense and later on linking them with the markets.

The Rolf Lynton model of institution building is based on the understanding of the term 'institution' as used for systems created to change their environments—prevailing norms, range of concerns, and ways of being in the world. Institutions also set out to achieve concrete goals within their contemporary setting and society; in that they are like organisations in general. (Organisations too may influence norms but they do not aim to do that.) He further goes on to enunciate the various kinds of internal and external components in an institutional development (ID) framework (see Annexure A-9.1 for details).

Enabling Linkages

Developing a Methodology for the Promotion of SHGs: The MFA Programme

In 1998, BASIX developed a methodology promoting SHGs with the help of agents who are paid based on their performance. BASIX provides support in terms of training of agents and SHGs promoted by them. The agents involved in promotion of SHGs are called microfinance agents (MFAs) and it is called the MFA programme. The methodology was developed in response to the fact that though various government and non-government agencies have been involved in formation of SHGs, not many of them had been of very good quality. The cost involved in organising the poor women into their SHGs through these institutions was also fairly high. Various steps involved in promotion of SHGs using MFAs include identification, and training of MFAs, pre-group formation processes at village level, group formation, SHG training (three phases), regular meetings, graduation test and post-linkage monitoring.

BASIX started implementing this programme in Bhadrachalam area of Khammam unit in 1998. Different attempts were made to appoint non-government development agencies as well as individual rural youth as MFAs. The experimental phase of the programme was managed by Indian Grameen Services (IGS). After conclusion of this phase, the developed methodology was handed over to Bhartiya Samruddhi Finance Limited who took charge of the management of SHGs promoted using MFAs and have continued to use a similar methodology to promote SHGs in other areas. This experiment demonstrated that SHG promotion can be a business proposition both for the promoting institution and the MFAs. It has been a good method of developing a channel to lend to the landless and poor and that too in a forested tribal area where credit discipline is acknowledged to be weak. The portfolio quality has been very high, even better than SHGs promoted by NGOs. This is because there has been intensive monitoring of the groups by BASIX and the MFAs. Our experience showed that individual rural youth fare better over small NGOs as MFAs, both in terms of number of groups organised and their quality.

However SHG promotion is also very time consuming and the initial costs are very high. It takes time to build up business volumes and substantial lending to the SHG happens only in the third loan cycle. Thus, break-even time is much longer in comparison to direct lending. The cost of promotion of these groups would be close to Rs 9,000. One of the difficulties faced was competition from the banks. After the groups were organised, banks often started lending to them without paying for the promotional cost, at a lower rate of interest which led to some depletion. However, experiences of the groups which were weaned away too early in their life have not been positive. This programme was also used in Bhokar and Nalgonda to form over 315 groups, of which 179 graduated and 130 were linked with financial institutions. These groups were provided various training inputs which included training for leaders and book-keepers. Subsequently, 700 SHGs have been promoted in different unit locations of BASIX and provided with various training inputs.

Quality Improvement of SHGs

The SHG Quality Improvement Programme (SHGQIP) was one of the initial ID offerings where various capacity building inputs are provided to SHGs. The model was simple: under this programme, the development organisation (both government and non-government) provided group management inputs, while income generating scheme (IGS) provided book-keeping, record maintenance, commercial inputs, which are their relative areas of strength. With the help of IGS and with the above mentioned inputs, the SHGs improved their performance in economic activities also. Recognising that the SHGQIP was very effective in improving and sustaining the quality of the groups, the SHGQIP soon became an integral part of BASIX ID work. So much so, today, the loan product to SHGs is bundled with SHGQIP, free of cost. More than 1,800 SHGs and 100 SHG federations in Andhra Pradesh, Karnataka, Orissa, Maharashtra, Jharkhand, Bihar and Madhya Pradesh and over 1,000 common interest groups (CIGs) in Rajasthan, have been trained in conducting meetings, book-keeping and livelihood promotion. As the SHGs slowly evolved into their federations/mutually aided cooperative thrift and credit societies (MACTSs), a similar, yet much more intensive hand-holding programme was designed keeping in view the growing and varied requirements of the federations. This gained popularity not only in Andhra Pradesh, but more so in other states like Jharkhand, Madhya Pradesh, Orissa, Bihar, Karnataka etc.

Technology Innovations for SHGs

A strong believer in the power of information systems, BASIX encouraged the use of software developed by Safal Solutions—SafalFin MIS package for SHGs. This helps in monitoring member loans and member savings. The software is designed mainly to keep track of:

- SHG internal lending and bank linkage.
- Loan outstanding and overdue of members.
- Savings and repayment details through the digitised demand information (DIDI) sheet.
- All account books and to produce accounting reports.

Apart from the financial information of SHGs the software also helps to keep a track of the area of operations of the SHG, the details of groups and members through various modules of the software such as the masters, transactions, accounts, corrections, reports, opening balance, system tools. Simple accounting package has been integrated with SafalFin to create accounts, enter transactions, generate reports and print books of account separately for each group and these can be consolidated to federation, village and block level. One can get detailed information regarding payments, receipts, deposit/withdrawal, journal voucher, transfer to bad debts and withdrawal of member savings through various reports the software generates. BASIX facilitated the installation of FAMIS PLUS an in-house developed software for use by the 15 MACTS promoted by GRAM, an NGO in Nizamabad. Both member accounts and financial accounts are fully online and the board of the Indur Intideepam MACTS Federation (IIMF) Ltd. bases its management decisions on the reports generated. It is very 'empowering' to hear the women, *albeit* with low levels of literacy, speak of portfolio at risk (PAR) and loan losses with as much or more clarity and understanding that one would expect from a educated board! This success prompted a regular stream of visitors to the federation and as on March 31, 2009 the operations of Samruddhi extended to almost 12,574 villages in 77 districts across 13 states.

Functional Linkages

Paving a Way for Access to Financial Institutions

BASIX commenced its operations with a loan to SHGs in Raichur district. SHG lending has always been an integral part of its operations, and BASIX has very often been the first lender; especially when no financial institution (including banks) was willing to take the risk, as SHGs promoted by GRAM will vouch for. In the early days of the SHG-bank linkage programme, despite the guidelines issued by RBI and NABARD on SHG lending, banks had their own apprehensions to finance SHGs. In 1997, BASIX took a lot of initiatives to finance SHGs in Andhra Pradesh and won the 'state level award for best performance under SHG-Bank linkage programme', a performance that did an encore in the year 2000-01. This initiative and the record repayment rates of the SHGs encouraged banks to commence lending to SHGs in a big way.

Similarly, the process of lending involving a rigorous appraisal was developed for federations as well. The lending model was intricately linked to the quality of the federation—thus if the federation was of A grade it would obtain a loan at cheaper rate, while that in the C grade would obtain it at a percentage 6 per cent higher. This strict quality based lending made the federations acutely aware of the benefits of quality. As on March 31, 2009, in financial inclusion services, BASIX has disbursed over Rs 5,864 million in microcredit, had over 574, 293 clients and disbursed a cumulative amount of Rs 105 million to SHGs and Rs 61 million to SHG federations/MACTS in several states. Very often the first loan given by BASIX to the group or to the federation and its subsequent successful repayment has led to a procession of lenders at the federation's doorsteps. The Indur Intideepam MACTS Federation Ltd. is a case in point. BASIX lent Rs 5 million to the federation in 2005-06. This loan boosted the confidence of a host of banks, who subsequently lent to them and as on March 31, 2007, IIMF had an outstanding liability (lenders) of Rs 134 million!

Formation of a Fund

Recognising the non-risk taking ability of formal financial institutions, while accepting its own inherent skill of handholding institutions, IGS started a 'Livelihood and Microfinance Promotion Fund' (LAMP Fund) in the year 2001. Armed with a contribution of Rs 2 million to support and strengthen many small and emerging MFIs, linking many more poor people to the formal banking sector, this fund has been capitalised to the extent of Rs 56 million recently. The fund is used to extend financial support to MFIs and community based organisations (CBOs), helping them building their capital base, to access mainstream capital, along with building their capacities, with appropriate incentives for performance. It is helpful to have this fund to provide ID support to small and start-up MFIs but also influence them to broaden their offering from micro-credit to include livelihood promotion services. Till date Rs 20 million has been disbursed in loans and Rs 7 million in grants.

Towards Livelihood Promotion

Inter-Borrower Expertise Exchange Programme (IBEX): In the experience of BASIX, sometimes it is the rural entrepreneurs themselves who are the best counsellors for others involved in the same activity. They could inform each other about the best practices suitable for the local area, or about the sources of raw material or market. To facilitate such inter-borrower advisory process, IGS started IBEX programme. The idea of such a programme is to disseminate the knowledge about efficient practices either in agriculture or any enterprise using local expertise. Under the IBEX programme, women SHG members from IIMF and officials of Kamareddy Chilling Plant visited Wanaparthy to see the functioning of dairy cooperatives and the tripartite linkage among dairy farmers, Andhra Pradesh Dairy Development Cooperation Federation Limited (APDDCF) and BASIX. The exposure provided the direction to the MACTS and subsequently a livelihood finance project for the promotion of a dairy for the women in IIMF was drawn up with an approximate project outlay of Rs 14 crore.

Experiments with the Market

Vegetable retailing: Recognising the significant margins in the retail trading of vegetables, attempts were also made to establish a retail network in Hyderabad in collaboration with Confederation of Voluntary Associations (COVA), an NGO and their SHGs. Though these experiences of marketing did not succeed, they indeed taught BASIX valuable lessons and confirmed that the vegetable markets had become quite competitive and were operating efficiently. The return that the farmers were getting from cultivation of vegetables could not be substantially increased unless some new breakthrough was achieved. Substantial investments need to be made in infrastructure and technology for the farmers to benefit from this sub-sector. Efforts at Virudhunagar with the SHGs of Association for Sarva Seva Farms (ASSEFA) in linking SHGs to the market in the vegetables sector, linking the SHGs of Chevella to the Taj Group of Hotels for supply of vegetables are other examples of our work, where we were able to derive some measure of success.

Dairy: Twenty-five women of Moosapet village of Mahabubnagar, organised in the form of SHG associated with NGO Adarsh Welfare Society (AWS), raised a demand for dairy loans. The NGO agreed to organise the dairy farmer women and ensure minimum volume. Loan was given to individual dairy farmers and linked to Andhra Pradesh Dairy Development Corporation (APDDC). Similarly more than 100 women in Kottala, Aspari, Nagardona and Mugati villages (Kurnool District) also took up dairy activities with the support of BASIX. They have been linked to Vanavasi Dairy, a private firm. BASIX was similarly involved with the SHGs/MACTS of AWS at Mahabubnagar, where efforts were made to help them set up a highway restaurant (*dhaba*) and a supermarket. Intensive efforts went in to building the market negotiation skills of these women.

Rural retailing: For effective utilisation of the savings that the SHGs had built over the last few years and enhancing livelihoods by reducing their effective cost of living (instead of increasing income), IGS initiated action research in rural retailing. It worked with Navipet, Nandipet, Jakranpally and Dichpally Mutually Aided Cooperative Society (MACS) promoted by GRAM to set up a system for using their own network of SHGs to make good quality domestic requirements of consumables available, at a reasonable price, at their doorstep, while using the trade margins for their own SHGs. This action research quickly drew attention of the state government, which decided to replicate the same using the Apna Bazar network. The retail work was tied up to the Apna Bazar network, but the programme fell through in succeeding months due to problems and constraints in the operational model.

This setback however did not deter BASIX, and it designed a new retailing model to be piloted in Jabalpur in Madhya Pradesh and Ranchi in Jharkhand in 2002-03 through a project supported by the Ministry of Rural Development. The objective of this research was to explore the models for enhancing livelihoods (of rural women) by way of reducing their cost on retail purchases, while ensuring availability of good quality products. This also utilised the institutional mechanism existing in the form of women SHGs and the latent ownership of demand with these institutions. The experiments are being conducted in collaboration with local NGOs, Nav Bharat Jagriti Kendra (NBJK) in Jharkhand. As on March 2007, in Ranchi, 1,200 Tribal Women SHG members have been registered under a cooperative structure. The cooperative body is linked with retailing activity on a business mode. There are two wholesale shops cum warehouses, with a chain of 34 franchises. The whole set up is organised under the brand name of 'Suvidha' and have collectively done a business turnover of Rs 2.6 million in 2006-07. Systems of purchase, stock management, accounts and audit have been developed for these institutions.

Aggregation

Several NGOs, such as AWS in Mahabubnagar, GRAM in Nizamabad, NBJK in Hazaribagh, Jharkhand, Rashtriya Grameen Vikas Nidhi (RGVN) in Ganjam, Orissa and Oxfam Intermon supported NGOs in Marathwada have formed hundreds of SHGs in a contiguous area and encouraged them to establish a federation and in most cases, register the federation as a mutually aided cooperative society (or equivalent). BASIX helped build the capacity of these for self-management, through training and accounting systems. This work covered over 100 SHG federations, supported by over 98 NGOs and the work is supported variously by ICICI Bank, Small Industries Development Bank of India (SIDBI), Credit Analysis and Research Limited (CARE) and Oxfam Intermon. See Annexure A-9.2 for details.

New Models for Legal Form of SHG Federation

When BASIX was working with ASSEFA promoted SHGs, which were located in Tamil Nadu, Rajasthan and Bihar, the need for a legal structural model emerged. This model was to enable the current services that SHGs were providing to their members and also arrange for borrowings for on-lending purposes. After a great deal of deliberation, the SHGs were brought together into Sarvodaya Mutual Benefit Trusts (SMBTs), profit-making trusts under the Indian Trusts Act (1882), and then these together have subscribed to the share capital of a company called Sarvodaya Nano Finance Ltd. (SNFL), Chennai. Thus was born the world's first 100 per cent SHG women-owned non-banking financial company (NBFC). This entity, which got five years of sustained institutional development services from BASIX, serves over 373.811 women organised into over 23,102 SHGs which are federated in 94 mutual benefit trusts, with cumulative disbursements of over Rs 2,776 million and outstanding of nearly Rs 644 million.

This model caught the attention of many institutions and today is a model for states where the model cooperative laws have not been enacted. BASIX itself has used it to work with SHG federations formed in four districts of Maharashtra.

Normative Linkages

Development of Tools

Recognising the enormity of the task involved in supporting SHGs, in 1996-97, when we started working with them, we realised that less than one per cent of the poor women had been organised into their SHGs. Even if half of the 50 million poor households organise themselves, there would be more than a million SHGs. Though most SHGs started their work with savings, the money saved by them was often not adequate for taking up economic activities. Hence, after establishing a system of regular savings and internal lending from that they had to access external funds. For them to be sustainable, these funds had to be loan funds and not grant funds, to which they already had some access. But extending a loan necessitates a more rigorous assessment of the receiver group than for extending a grant. Assessment of a SHG involved not only looking into some of their quantitative performance indicators (such as total savings), but also many qualitative parameters (such as whether the group was controlled by one person). With the need to assess some qualitative parameters, subjectivity in the assessment creeps in. Such subjectivity also brings in individual differences, and the need to involve more experienced people for using their judgment. This in turn increases the cost of assessment.

We realised that we have to use an assessment:

- which looks into not only the quantitative performance parameters,
- which can be used to assess a large number of groups,
- which can be used by large number of people with limited experience,
- with minimum scope of variation arising out of personal judgment errors, without loosing the quality of information.

SHGs being a group of individuals, conducting financial transactions while interacting on social aspects, we designed an objective SHG assessment and rating tool that could cater to these special aspects. Thus, the assessment tool was formulated and used, not only by BASIX but adopted by several agencies and eventually NABARD developed a modified version for nationwide use in 1999. A similar tool was designed to assess SHGs federations. The information required to assess the federation is divided into different categories looking at essential information about the federation, internal non-financial, internal financial, external non-financial and external financial information about the federation.

The last category gives supplementary information to allow the assessor to sharpen his judgment about the federation. The tool requires that one or two federation meetings are attended, in addition to discussions with the promoter of the federation.

Development of ID Processes

The conceptualisation of the intensive handholding work with different NGOs/MFIs across the country was a normative influence in itself. The efforts put in by BASIX to develop the processes involved, the entire change management process have been innovative in themselves. BASIX has thus played a key role in developing the HR capabilities in the sector, propagating the values of performance based action, objective assessment, strong focus on operating, human relations (HR) and information systems and quality has today led to a proliferation of service providers in virtually every small town and city offering ID services.

Diffuse Linkages

At a forum on 'Building India's Leadership in Microfinance' in November 1998, the Reserve Bank of India (RBI) Governor appointed a Task Force through NABARD for suggesting a supportive regulatory framework for microfinance, led by the then chairman of NABARD. This Microfinance Task Force report of 1999 was a breakthrough and it gave impetus to both the SHG-bank linkage model, as well as bank lending through MFIs. In 1999, BASIX successfully raised a loan of Rs 20 million from the Global Trust Bank. This deal had many firsts: the first loan by a private commercial bank to an MFI; the first loan to an MFI which is a for-profit NBFC; the first such loan to be refinanced by NABARD, in which it notably imposed no on-lending rate by the MFI to SHGs. In other states like Orissa, Bihar, Jharkhand and Chhattisgarh, where SHGs and their federations are being actively promoted, BASIX provides consulting services to the state governments on shaping the state strategy for SHG and microfinance promotion.

Collegial Linkages

In September 1998, after two years of preparatory work, BASIX helped establish Sa-Dhan, an association of major microfinance organisations in the country. Sa-Dhan's endeavour has been to develop the field of community development finance and help members and associate institutions engaged in propagating different models of microfinance, render better services to low-income households, particularly in both rural and urban India, and establish stable livelihoods to improve their quality of life. Mr Mahajan was Co-Chair of the Board for five years and Dr Sankar Datta headed the Capacity Building group for three years. Several other BASIX colleagues gave inputs to Sa-Dhan. One important initiative BASIX was involved in during 1998-99 was the study of the women's savings and credit movement in Andhra Pradesh. This study was initiated at the behest of the Andhra Pradesh government and was supported by the Department for International Development (DFID), UK. Its main purpose was to evolve a strategy for strengthening and systematic growth of over 150,000 women savings and credit groups which had been formed in Andhra Pradesh. In 2001, after two years of preparatory work including a feasibility study, BASIX helped establish the Andhra Pradesh Mahila Abhivruddhi Society

(APMAS) as an independent, public-private partnership (PPP), focussed on building the capacity of women's savings and credit groups in the state. BASIX continues to play a supportive role to APMAS and subsumed its work related to SHG support in the state of Andhra Pradesh to this body.

Reflections and Learning

Focus on Individuals within the Groups

The needs of the individuals within the groups have not given as much a focussed attention. While products are offered to SHGs, these are more in the nature of 'general purpose loan' as we believe that the choice of the ultimate loan lies with the group itself. However, if we are working with a market paradigm we should also view it from that angle. Given that the majority of the groups are women's groups, the whole gender issue comes in. The individuals in question are themselves 'gendered beings', the subjugated 'other' within the gender relations, be it at home, society or the market place. And so even market paradigm-led SHG work should look at the aspects of gender.

A Livelihood Intervention for women Enterprise (ALIWE) is a project currently being piloted in Wardha unit of BASIX operations. This project examines the role of individual women livelihood promotion both in the context of the household as well as the market. The project is expected to generate gender sensitive processes and products and services that recognise and acknowledge women as actors in livelihood promotion.

Annexure A-9.1

ID Framework

The ID framework has five internal and six external components. The five internal components are:

- doctrine (mission, policies, norms),
- leadership,
- programme,
- resources,
- internal structure.

The six external components—linkages to the I-'s environment(s) are:

- enabling (to assure communal, e.g. legal acceptance),
- normative (to tune into and out of current standards),
- functional (to deal with, e.g., clients, suppliers *et al.*),
- diffuse (to build and maintain widespread good will),
- collegial (to stay in touch with individual and I- expertise),
- supportive personal (to access personal counselling , coaching),

The linkage variables as articulated by Rolf Lynton.

Enabling linkages provide the institution with legitimate authority to start and to operate, and to give it access to the funds and other support it needs.

Functional	Functional linkages provide for substantive exchanges with the environment.
Normative	Normative linkages deal with the establishment of standards in the institution and with its attempts to influence norms in the environment.
Diffuse	Diffuse linkages are for building widespread understanding and support for the institution.
Collegial	A fifth type of (collegial) linkage provides at the institutional level what colleagueship does at the individual level, through exchanging experimental information and developing common strategies and common resources.
Supportive personal	Linkage provided at a personal level to access personal counselling, coaching etc.

He also indicates that classic imbalances occur between:

- internal and external components,
- functional and enabling linkages,
- normative and diffuse linkages (most neglected),
- overload and conflict (through making easiest linkages serve many purposes).

Annexure A-9.2

Institutional Development Services Volume and Outreach of the Organisations (which are Availing ID Services from BASIX)

State	*No. of Organisations*	*Type of Service*	*No. of Blocks*	*No. of Villages*	*No. of Institutions*	*Total No. of Members*	*Outstanding Amount (in '000s)*
Andhra Pradesh	2	IT	14	112	380	8400	2568
Bihar	4	ITID	36	458	3293	48538	2432
Jharkhand	6	ITID	71	2512	4178	52286	61431
Uttar Pradesh	1	IT	21	258	1306	20430	18341
Karnataka	3	ITID	30	268	1696	23999	110492
Tamil Nadu	2	IT	110	15139	23722	380666	655067
Madhya Pradesh	8	ITID	19	423	983	14455	9487
Maharashtra	5	ITID	18	214	708	4298	10392
Rajasthan	1		-	-	995	10945	-
Orissa	10	ITID	47	1912	5934	70526	170234
Total reach of partner organisations			366	21296	43195	634543	1040444

Source: Annual Report, various issues, BASIX.

10 Microfinance Organisations for Women

The Cooperative Model

Nandita Ray

Introduction

The last two decades have seen a major growth in the formation of new microfinance institutions (MFIs) in the country, notably in Andhra Pradesh (AP). It is not easy to fully categorise the various types of MFIs because most of them grew up as 'informal' organisations largely in response to the failure of 'formal' financial institutions to cater to the needs of the poor and many continue not to have a legal shape. However, there are certain basic models that have become popular, of which two have acquired a legal shape while a third may shortly acquire one when a bill, currently in Parliament, becomes a law. These basic models are as follows:

- The non-government organisation (NGO) promoted MFI.
- The government promoted MFI.
- The savings and credit cooperative.
- The corporate MFI, both for-profit and not-for-profit.

Of these, the two latter categories are legally registered under the Cooperative Act and the Companies Act, respectively. When one refers to the cooperative act in this context, one means the mutually aided cooperative society acts which have been enacted in some states, starting with Andhra Pradesh, in 1995. This law was enacted with the specific idea of making it easier for cooperative institutions to function as autonomous bodies as the existing laws had, over the years, resulted in severe erosion of cooperative independence. The company MFI is normally a non-banking finance company (NBFC) and is regulated by the Reserve Bank of India (RBI) as with other banking organisations. Not many of these MFIs are happy with this legal format for the pursuit of their objectives but they have been unable to find a suitable alternative, so far. It is estimated that there are around 1,000 NGO-MFIs, over 3,000 cooperative MFIs and about 20 corporate MFIs (Sarkar, 2007). The government-promoted MFIs were, till very recently, almost entirely in the state of Andhra Pradesh though several other states have recently followed suite. The government-promoted MFI are normally tied up with the banking system through the SHG-bank linkage programme of National Bank for Agriculture and Rural Development (NABARD) and today, the state makes up approximately, one-third of the SHG-bank linkage in monetary terms. Some NGO-promoted MFIs are also linked to the banks as financial intermediaries in this way. However, to date, the MFI following the cooperative model are generally not (not even with cooperative banks that continue to be registered under the earlier cooperative acts) and work almost entirely with self-generated funds, mobilised through member savings.

Objectives and Methodology

The purpose of this paper is to examine in some depth the cooperative model because it is perhaps the oldest of the institutionalised MFIs and to examine the role it has played in the development of alternative banking for the poor and in the empowerment of poor women.

The methodology used for the purpose consists of:

- Examination of the material produced by the Cooperative Development Foundation (CDF), the NGO that has played the lead role in the promotion of this model, including its regular annual and performance reports and studies conducted from time to time.
- Examination of the secondary data which is very limited.
- Examination of a recent study for a PhD thesis that has sought to compare in some detail different models of NGO and state-promoted MFIs including the cooperative model.

The selected sample for the third purpose is one of the older CDF-promoted cooperatives located in the village of Ratnagiri in Karimnagar district of Andhra Pradesh, having around 350 households. A participatory rural appraisal (PRA) was conducted to determine the household characteristics for the whole village followed by a detailed questionnaire being administered to 50 households (40 members and 10 non-members). The parameters used for the analysis of the data were:

1. The levels of participation by poor women achieved by the different organisations.
2. The extent of the increase in income and asset formation.
3. The levels of economic empowerment achieved by the members.
4. The level of empowerment in other related areas.

The CDF (previously known as Samakhya), is a registered society started in 1982, at Hyderabad, to specifically set up and promote the development of cooperative institutions. So significant has been its role in the promotion of cooperatives, in particular thrift and credit cooperatives for rural women, that when one speaks of the cooperative model of MFI, one associates them with CDF. The thrift and credit cooperatives are located mainly in the districts of Karimnagar and Warangal in Andhra Pradesh. To ensure the 'visibility' of the membership, their presence and activities are concentrated in a limited geographical area in order to maximise impact and to help ensure the continuity and independence of the organisation. Today there are around 1.2 lakh members (both men and women) in a geographical area roughly covering a little over 100 kilometre radius around Warangal town.

The cooperatives are democratically governed by a set of bye-laws and business rules decided upon by the members at the time of formation. The boundaries of a cooperative are roughly the boundaries of a village and normally consists of around 200-500 members. Members meet on a fixed day each month with monthly savings that is the same for each member. Currently, the monthly thrift amount is Rs 20 in most of the women's cooperatives. Borrowers bring loan repayments and interest also to the meetings. With the pooled thrift, loan installments and interest received, fresh loans are made to eligible members based on need up to three times the member's thrift. Loans are made for production or consumption but wasteful expenditure is discouraged. Members' passbooks and accounts are also updated at the meeting. Interest used to be charged at 24 per cent, 21 per cent, or 18 per cent depending on total member thrift in the cooperative and 12 per cent is paid on member savings. After 2002, it was decided to lower interest rates even further to 18 per cent, 15 per cent and

12 per cent respectively. An additional 3 per cent is paid to members at the year-end as bonus if there is a surplus. Since 1999 most CDF cooperatives have added new voluntary savings products such as fixed deposits and recurring deposits but these do not, however, alter a member's loan entitlement. At the end of December 2006, these totalled, approximately, Rs 8 million. But it is hoped that these savings instruments will augment the total fund over time (*Annual Report 2006*).

For organisation purposes, the village cooperatives are divided into '*grameen*' type 'peer' groups of five, in which members stand surety for each other's loans. All individual members together form the general body of the cooperatives. They, in turn, elect a committee to implement their policy decisions on a day-to-day basis. Every month, the elected committee reviews the progress of the thrift cooperative and takes relevant decisions. At the end of the year, the committee prepares the annual statements, gets them audited both internally by its network and externally by a chartered accountant. The annual general meeting is held where members are presented with the annual report of the activities and the audited financial statements. The general body has the right to take policy decisions on the growth of the cooperative.

Individual cooperatives are, in their turn, members of an association, which provides such services as its member thrift cooperatives cannot organise by themselves or when these are too expensive for them to provide. Services generally provided are:

- Regular review of performance.
- Provision of stationery.
- Organisation of training to management and staff of member cooperatives.
- Assist in the submission of returns to the department of cooperation.
- Organise the Debt Relief Assurance Scheme (DRAS) under which, when a member with a loan dies, the family does not suffer.
- Organise optimum utilisation of surplus funds through providing loans to its needy member cooperatives.

- Provide a platform to share experiences, learn from each other, develop strategies to overcome obstacle, develop internal control systems, provide audit services etc.

There is also an apex organisation for all CDF promoted cooperatives in Warangal and Karimnagar districts but this, unlike the Association of Women's Thrift Cooperative (AWTC), is not a registered body.

The direct role of CDF in the thrift and credit cooperatives, in whose formation it has been involved, has been diminishing over the years. They are financially self-sufficient and depend entirely on self-generated funds for day-to-day operation costs. CDF operates a Cooperative Revolving Fund (CRF) from which cooperatives have taken loans for buildings and office equipment. However, no external grants or borrowings have been made for on-lending to members, a feature of CDF-promoted thrift cooperatives which sets it apart from almost all other alternative banking organisations. The reason as per CDF's own definition is as follows:

> Cooperatives...if dependent on high levels of member participation, behaved responsibly and elected persons of competence and integrity to their managements. Where, however, they were not dependent on member participation for survival and had access to soft funding in any form, they and their members tended to be irresponsible and the need to be in control of the funds became of greater concern than the servicing of members.

Theoretically, CDF does not rule out the possibility of these cooperatives taking loans from mainstream institutions sometime in the future, so long as these are on their own terms and as per their own requirements, not as a part of poverty directed soft loan programme or 'priority sector' lending. CDF believes that its own function is to play 'the role of an enabler and facilitator for the emergence of mutually aided cooperatives that function as democratically controlled autonomous business enterprises'. CDF as we have seen does provide some assistance for development of infrastructure and ensure that their own funds earn them a better return.

Other than the fact that CDF-promoted thrift cooperatives do not access external funds for on-lending to members, a second distinctive feature of its governance is the absence of 'targeting'. Membership, unlike in many similar poverty alleviation programmes, is not restricted by income criteria but based on the ideology that whoever has the need for the services offered by the cooperative is entitled to be a member. The situation of the poor requires that they be linked to the village and area economy. Hence, the issue of poverty is not treated in isolation and CDF promotes a homogeneous concept of development. 'The relatively low amount of share capital per member (Rs 10-20) as well as monthly required thrift (typically Rs 20) allows women from across the spectrum of the village to participate' (Galab *et al.,* 2003). Loan entitlements are limited to three times the compulsory thrift and 75 per cent of voluntary savings. Periodic surveys have shown that leadership and participation in the thrift cooperatives by and large represent all castes and classes in the rural community. An internal study revealed that a little over 55 per cent of the members were landless, while another 32 per cent held less than three acres of land. A little less than 49 per cent of the leadership came from the landless sections, while another 38 per cent came from those with less than 3 acres of land. A little over 86 per cent of the borrowers during the year were those with no land or with less than 3 acres of land. Together they accessed 83 per cent of the loans disbursed during the year and accounted for 89 per cent of delinquency in repayment. This shows that the landless were able to access, proportionately, a higher number of the loans notwithstanding a marginally higher level of non-repayment. Of 420 elected leaders, only 18 came from families with 5 to 10 acres of land, while 4 came from more than 10 acres of land (CDF, 1997).

The attitude of the CDF promoted thrift cooperatives to government promoted Development of Women and Children in Rural Areas (DWCRA) groups within its geographical area of operations is ambivalent. It does not restrict dual membership but has not in any way compromised on its own membership rules and regulations. This does not appear to have affected restricted membership in any way.

CDF is as strict about transparency and financial discipline in its own operations as it expects its member cooperatives to be. At the time of its 25th anniversary in year 2000, it estimated that it had spent no more than Rs 2.6 crore for its recurring expenses from its donors and in return for that, the members of the cooperatives have received several times that amount in terms of economic benefits. Much of this amount is spent on its promotional expenses, support services to the cooperatives and cooperative advocacy, while a large part of its running expenses is raised through its service fees from the cooperatives and external consultancy work. Further CDF raises a considerable portion of its income through its own activities, which by the end of December 2006 was 45 per cent of total income, the remaining being from grants-in-aid.

CDF has made a significant strategic policy departure in recently promoting a dairy cooperative union for women only, in collaboration with the National Dairy Development Board (NDDB). While promotion of paddy cooperatives had been the main part of CDF activity since inception, its policy with regard to thrift cooperatives has been largely 'minimalist'. Generally speaking, a pattern among the members has been observed (and documented by the organisation), whereby they have graduated on their own from borrowing for 'consumption' purposes to more 'productive' activities over a period of time. More recently, however, with the growth in the size of the women's funds and corresponding increase in loan entitlements there has been some change in member perceptions. Loan sanctions are being scrutinised more thoroughly to ensure that the chosen activity yields sufficient returns to ensure repayment and more attention is being paid to the productivity of the chosen loan purpose than hitherto. Another reason is the absence of suitable and adequate avenues for productive investment, as a result of which it has been noticed that there are considerable idle funds lying with the thrift cooperatives. This has led CDF to try and increase avenues of investment for the women members. Since dairy is a widespread activity among them and many have taken loans for the purchase of milch animals, infrastructure for a new dairy, it was felt, would make an important economic contribution. The dairy was constructed at a distance of 2 km from Mulukanoor with a capacity of 25,000 litres of milk per day (expandable to 50,000 LPD) and having a catchment area of 72 villages in the area for collection of milk and commissioned on 17 August 2002. It exclusively serves a membership from the women's thrift cooperatives. There were 68 such cooperatives with a membership of 8,000 women as on 31 March 2002 with an average daily procurement for the year of 12,000 litres (*CDF Annual Report 2002-03*). A study was also undertaken to try and identify other profitable economic activities in the area. A second women's cooperative dairy was started in Wardhannapet, which as on 31 March 2006, had 84 women development cooperatives (WDCs) with 2,040 members.

CDF has always put a great deal of emphasis on training and awareness generation and today has a full-fledged cooperative training centre on the outskirts of Warangal. In this respect it concentrates on two primary areas *viz*., training for those outside CDF as part of its cooperative advocacy work and leadership training for its own office bearers, for elected and appointed functionaries. The training is extremely detailed and covers more than 20 different topics relating to cooperative principles, laws, administration, management and accounts and to specific schemes offered by the cooperatives in question. However, CDF does not offer such intensive training to the membership at large and taken in conjunction with the fact that the cooperatives do not rotate the posts of its office-bearers; there is a noticeable gap in the quality and level of awareness between the leadership and membership at large. Recently, however, CDF has provided skill training to the members of the new dairy cooperative.

CDF has found the lack of literacy among the bulk of the women members to be a limitation on the growth, the autonomy and sustainability of the cooperatives in particular among the leadership. It had attempted, though not very successfully, to remedy this situation from time to time.

Impact of the Model

In the last decade and a half, the success of the women's thrift and credit groups in this region, recently expanded to Medak district also, has exceeded CDF's expectations. They have developed into full-scale cooperative organisations and with their geographically consolidated networks, most of whom are individually and as associations, now registered under the Andhra Pradesh Mutually Aided Cooperative Societies (APMACS) Act of 1995, a piece of legislation that CDF itself influenced and have overtaken agricultural cooperatives as CDF's primary field of activity. They had over 79,238 women members with Rs 19.51 crore of entirely self-generated funds as on 31 December 2006 in 269 cooperatives associated with 22 networks. The corresponding figures for membership in the men's thrift and credit cooperatives were 43,677 members in 176 cooperatives associated with 15 networks, with a total fund of Rs 19.84 crore, the relatively higher amount in the men's cooperatives, started much later, being due to the higher level of savings. It is a measure of CDF's success with women's thrift and credit cooperatives that men have sought to form their own thrift and credit societies in the same geographical area. The same is true of the fact that eight other states in India have followed the pioneering work in Andhra Pradesh to enact similar legislation to the APMACS Act. At the end of 31 December 2006 with CDF's active help in their promotion, there were over 10,500 MACS registered in Andhra Pradesh.

CDF has influenced many other NGOs in the promotion of thrift and credit groups and now has a specific programme to do so through partner NGOs such as Peoples Rural Education Development Society (PREDS) with a membership of 7,600 at the end of December 2003. The influence of CDF on the growth and development of the cooperative model of microfinance has been profound even on some organisations which may not yet have legally registered as cooperatives, so far. It has been helped in its efforts by the Cooperative Initiative Panel, set up by the NDDB at Anand in Gujarat, the promoter of a major network of milk producer cooperatives in parts of the country. In May 2002, the Multi-State Cooperative Societies Act, relating to cooperatives that cross state boundaries, was also amended and the Union Minister for Agriculture has announced a package of Rs 8,000 crore to help states that adopt similar laws (The Link, 2002).

Notwithstanding this apparent success, the cooperative model has been taken up by few organisations outside the influence of CDF. It is possible that this is because of the emphasis that the latter places on autonomy both financial and otherwise. The MFIs that have registered as corporate NBFCs have borrowed heavily from the banks and function primarily as lending rather than savings organisations, being restricted from taking deposits from the public under the current laws. The other major promoters of savings and credit groups are the AP government and more recently other state governments, who have tended to treat these as another anti-poverty programme rather than an instrument for building autonomous and financially viable people's community organisations, notwithstanding statements to the contrary. The continued attempts at subsidisation of interest rates and the use of women SHGs as political vote banks run directly in contradiction to the CDF ideology on what cooperative organisations ought to be. Hence, although CDF did influence the early evolution of the DWCRA groups into the SHGs and their federations of today these have, in practice, deviated from the CDF model.

Participation in Thrift and Credit Cooperatives Promoted by CDF

In a recent study, it was found that at the Pragati Thrift and Credit Cooperative of Ratnagiri village in Karimnagar district, participation levels were higher than in other models studied, such as the *Grameen* model-corporate MFI, the UNDP/SAPAP model or the NGO-Outreach-NRM model. With a total of 385 members and part of the Kothapalli Association of Women's Thrift Cooperatives (AWTC) with 4,196 members, it is one of the oldest CDF women's cooperatives and among the first to be registered under the APMACS Act in 1995. All women in the village between the ages of 18 and 65 were eligible for membership, including more than one woman from a single household, no distinction being made on the basis of caste or class, as with all cooperatives under the CDF model.

It was observed that more than two-thirds of village households were members of the WTC in December 1996. The landholding characteristics of members in relation to non-member households were analysed carefully. This is particularly important in the case of CDF, which does not target any particular group for membership in its thrift cooperatives, to determine the extent of participation by poor women.

Table 10.1

Rate of Participating Households in CDF by Landholding Size

Sl. No.	*Description of the Category*	*Number of Households*	*Number of Participating Households*	*Percentage of Participating Households*
1	2	3	4	5
1.	Landless	68	40	58.8
2.	Marginal farmers	224	165	73.7
3.	Small farmers	56	39	59.6
4.	Medium farmers	8	8	100.0
5.	Large farmers	-	-	
6.	All	356	252	70.2

Source: Sample Survey.

Table 10.1 shows that the participation of landless households was found to be 12 percentage points lower than the overall participation rate and that of small farmers is 17 percentage points lower. The participation of marginal farmers who form the largest number of households was, however, almost 4 percentage points higher. All the medium farmer households had cooperative members, there being no large farmers in the village. There were altogether 252 participating households but the number of members is actually larger, because the rules of the cooperative permit more than one member from the same household, unlike the other models studied. In fact there were several women below the age of 18 who were members, though those below 16 were not permitted to take loans. Subsequent to the registration of the cooperative, the bye-laws were changed and the membership of these girls and women over 65 were deleted in the year 2000, though they may save in their name if they wish. A member who has withdrawn once is not eligible for re-admission. Notwithstanding this fact the membership had grown over the years and stabilised around the year 2000.

It was found that there were more than 80 members belonging to some 54 households which included households with more than one member, besides the single women members living in other people's houses. Only five women-headed households lived in their own house and these were all members of the cooperative. At present, the cooperative has around 20 members from women-headed households but their proportion to the overall village population could not be ascertained. It is possible that households with more than one member have an advantage with regard to the quantum of loans for which they are eligible.

The thrift-based financing system of the 'cooperative' MFI makes sure that the financial sustainability of the institution is high. Further, 'the savings of members in the WTC are more in the nature of capital' because they cannot be withdrawn except when the member withdraws from the cooperative itself (Biswas and Mahajan, 1997). Combined with the fact that the CDF cooperatives cannot borrow more than 80 per cent of their total thrift from within the system *viz.*, its association, also ensures capital adequacy for against loan default. Since member involvement and control is also high and by using human resources mostly what is available locally and thus low cost, add to the factors make for a sustainable organisation.

The absence of any external loans for on-lending makes the cooperatives financially ultra-conservative but CDF justifies this on the grounds of the environment that is inimical to financial discipline. The recent moves by the state government of Andhra Pradesh in bringing back interest subsidies to SHGs, lends support to this point of view. However, it has been observed that the economic impact of the cooperative, judged by the parameters of income and asset increases, were lower in the cooperatives than in the other models studied. The *Grameen* model in particular caters to members' credit needs the most, notwithstanding its low emphasis on savings. The proportion of loans taken from outside the MFIs was found to be much higher in the CDF cooperatives than with the other models, though this was compensated to some extent by the Mulukanoor Cooperative Rural Bank which caters to agriculture loans, at least in Karimnagar district. Many members, however, appear to rate their ability to save with the cooperative just as highly as access to credit and the fact that their membership has greatly improved their 'creditworthiness' in general. The following case studies illustrate better the different ways in which the cooperative helps its members.

Case study-1 illustrates how a member has found CDF loans helpful in improving her economic status but this has been possible in conjunction with other loans, in this instance from the Mulukanoor Cooperative Rural Bank (and not private moneylenders) of which her husband is a member. CDF follows a deliberate strategy of promoting women's thrift cooperatives in the same geographical area as agriculture cooperatives in order to help both men and women and concentrate development efforts in a single area.

The case study-2 shows how a member has taken very large loans from a moneylender but it is the thrift cooperative which proved to be the family's mainstay when attempts to expand the business failed. The effect was to reduce its vulnerability but not to significantly improve its income levels.

Case Study–1

Slow and Steady Progress to the Top

Urmila is a resident of Ratnagiri village who has been a member of the Pragathi Thrift and Credit Cooperative in 1992, a year after its commencement, when it was still an unregistered organisation consisting of informal thrift and credit groups. Her family consists of her husband Sammaiah, who is a member of the Mulukanoor cooperative rural bank, two daughters aged 14 and 19 and two sons aged 12 and 8 years.

Prior to their membership of these organisations the family was dependent entirely on agricultural labour wages although they did inherit a little land. This was because 16 years previously when the joint family broke up only one bullock came as part of their share. They were obliged to send their daughters for wage labour as well. The first break came when her husband was able to get a loan from the Mulukanoor Rural Cooperative Bank for a pair of bullocks with which they were able to cultivate their land. However, they were still obliged to take loans from moneylenders from time to time at 36 per cent interest per annum, which they had to repay in single installments and their income from agriculture was exhausted with loan repayments. This situation changed after Urmila became a member of the women's thrift cooperative as she was able to obtain loans whenever the need arose and repay in easy installments.

All in all, Urmila has taken five loans to the tune of Rs 21,000 of which Rs 13,000 has been spent on agriculture. In the course of time the family has succeeded in buying some more land, 1 acre wet and 2 acres dry. Her husband has obtained further loans to dig a well and purchase a pump-set. Earlier, the family had been unable to send their girls to school and they remained illiterate. She says that had they been young now she would have sent them to school but the elder daughter is now married. Her boys are going to school for the past six years. Impressed by her way of managing credit—she has always repaid her loans regularly—, the members elected her to the Managing Committee three months prior to the second study visit. The couple has future plans to develop their agriculture further by taking up commercial crops and to make their *'kutcha'* house a *'pucca'* one.

Case Study–2

The Cooperative: A True Safety Net

Laxmi is a resident of Ratnagiri, who joined the thrift and credit cooperative in 1992. She and her husband Sappaiah live with a married son who owns just one acre of dry land. The family also has a fruit and vegetable vending business in which the whole family is engaged.

She has taken altogether Rs 28,000 worth of loans from the cooperative, most of which has gone into the family business that yields a monthly income of Rs 2,000. They tried to increase the size of the business by leasing a fruit garden with the help of a large loan from moneylenders at an interest of 36 per cent per annum. However, due to rains during flowering time, they incurred losses of Rs 1 lakh and the whole family had to work in a nearby market for three years to repay it. She faced a similar situation again in 1999-2000, when the family again tried to grow cotton on two acres of land with a loan from moneylenders, from which they incurred a loss of Rs 20,000.

While the above household does not appear to have been very successful, Laxmi's membership in fact saved the family from starvation, as they were at least able to continue their fruit and vegetable vending business with the help of loans from the cooperative.

Observing the purpose for which loans are taken in the cooperatives, it showed that 'consumption' loans continue to dominate usage. Table 10.2 shows the number of loans, in order of priority, that have been taken for various purposes.

Table 10.2

Purpose of Loans: CDF

Sl.No.	*Purpose of Loans*	*No. of Loans*	*Percentage of Total*
1.	Health	27	22.31
2.	Agriculture	21	17.36
3.	Repayment of other loans	18	14.88
4.	Consumption	14	11.57
5.	Business	10	8.27
6.	Education	9	7.44
7.	Cattle	8	6.66
8.	Marriage	6	4.96
9.	Land	4	3.30
10.	Bore well	2	1.65
11.	House	1	0.83
12.	Others	1	0.82

Source: Sample Survey.

The largest number of loans from the cooperative was for health, agriculture, repayment of other loans and consumption. Enterprise loans were in fifth place. However, if animal husbandry is included in the same category, then the combined total takes third place at 18 per cent. Repayment of other loans is a significant item in that it demonstrates members' preference for cooperative loans to loans from other sources. Health and education taken together would be far the most important category of loans from the cooperative, proportionately, amounting to almost 30 per cent of the total number of loans taken. It is interesting that a few members have used loans for land purchase. The contrast with the *Grameen* MFI model with its emphasis on 'productive' loans for small enterprise is strong. Unlike the cooperatives the latter does not allow loans for 'consumption'.

CDF argues that over the years the amounts used for 'productive' purposes increase and this has been found to be the case in other NGO MFIs as well. In fact, it was found in the study as a whole that the main restricting factor for the above was the lack of livelihood opportunities rather than shortage of credit. In CDF, after 1996, the loan turnover ratio fell steadily not for lack of demand which is always high among poor families but because of lack of productive avenues of investment that enhances their repayment capacities. As the loan entitlement of members increased, the cooperatives have become more careful about giving large loans to members who they feel may be unable to repay them. With regard to loans from external sources, it was found that by far the largest number, at about 28 per cent of the total, have been taken for consumption, followed by land and marriage at 11 per cent each, with agriculture and health at 10 per cent each. Other purposes for external loans were found to be bore wells, business and house construction. There appear to be an overlap in the categories of internal and external loans, confirming the fact that thrift cooperative loans are not sufficient at all times for member requirements. However whether this is because the money is not available or whether the cooperative is unwilling to advance risky loans requires further investigation.

Class-wise analysis with regard to type and quantum of loans shows no significant pattern. Women-headed households, however, have proportionately taken a larger number of loans at an average of 2.8 loans per person against 2.1 loans for others. While male-headed households had taken a significantly higher number of loans for agriculture, women-headed households have taken more loans for health and consumption. It was found that although in general male-headed households benefitted more across the models in terms of total quantum of loans, but proportionately speaking women-headed households had a larger share of their overall credit needs being catered to by the respective MFI, thus proving the usefulness of women's MFIs for single women, who frequently have few other sources for credit.

Changes in Levels of Income and Asset Formation

Of the various models that made up the selected sample of the study, CDF cooperatives showed the lowest income increase and asset formation among the members. Taken as a whole, 20 per cent of the members reported an increase in income of 0-10 per cent, 22.2 per cent said that their income had gone up by 10-20 per cent, slightly more than 11 per cent reported an increase of between 20-30 per cent and just 4.4 per cent of the sampled members reported an increase of 40-50 per cent. Over 42 per cent of the members reported no increase in income. This is substantially lower than the other models studied. In contrast, among non-participants only 20 per cent reported an increase in income of between 0-10 per cent, while the 80 per cent reported no improvement. Overall improvements in income of over half of the sampled members appear to be real but modest in comparison to non-members.

The largest number of households reporting no increase in income was landless. Given the fact that loans have by and large been fairly given, this shows that these poor households, while reducing their 'vulnerability' with access to consumption loans, had not been able to invest in income-enhancing activities. However two households reporting the highest increase were, interestingly, landless. The self-employed have shown higher increases in income than the wage-employed which confirms the above conclusion that these members have been in a position to utilise loans better. With reference to asset formation, most sampled households who had acquired assets had done so in connection with their business and the survey did not collect information on long-term and working capital, separately. However, it is assumed that those members of the cooperative, who have mentioned their business as a part of asset formation, have in fact acquired some long-term assets in connection with it. The most popular asset acquired by members were milch animals and four women had bought buffaloes and two of them, cows. Another woman had purchased pigs and one woman had used her loan for a poultry farm. Four other women reported putting money into a provision shop, two bangle stores and a vegetable business, respectively. Two women significantly used their loans for land acquisition, one on a house and one on purchase of jewellery. One woman reported buying a year's supply of food grains under this heading. Altogether, a third of the sample reported any asset formation. This is substantially less than in the *Grameen* model with a reported increase of 87 per cent of the sample and in the UNDP model of 83 per cent having acquired assets and some more than one.

The extent to which women succeeded in running viable economic activities, was considered a major indicator of their economic empowerment as also the fact of the extent to which women have control on the enterprise in question. The indicators selected to gauge the level of this empowerment were as follows:

Of the number of members in the selected sample who had taken loans for economic activities, including agriculture:

- The extent to which the above consisted of earlier ongoing activities as opposed to new enterprises.
- The extent to which these were found to be run independently by the women concerned.
- The control that women members felt that they had over the loans taken by them.

Table 10.3 summarises the responses of the participants in the sample survey with regard to the level of women's economic empowerment, on the basis of the above indicators in the four selected alternative banking organisations.

Table 10.3

Responses of the Participants with Regard to Level of Women's Economic Empowerment

Name of the Organisation	*Per cent of Women with Loans for Economic Activity*	*Old Economic Activity (Per cent)*	*New Economy Activity (Per cent)*	*Independent Activity (Per cent of Women)*	*Control on Loan (Per cent of Women)*
CDF/cooperative	53.33	48.88	4.44	15.56	42.86
SHARE/*Grameen*	100.00	11.90	88.10	4.76	28.57
UNDP/SAPAP	95.24	19.05	76.19	4.76	40.48
Outreach/NRM	100.00	72.09	27.91	Nil	25.58

Source: Sample Survey.

The summary shows that the number of households in the selected sample whose women members had taken loans for economic activity (including agriculture), is 100 per cent in the *Grameen* model ('productive' loans are obligatory for *Grameen* clients), 100 per cent in NGO/NRM model and 95 per cent in UNDP/SAPAP model. It is substantially lower in CDF at 53.33 per cent; presumably more loans have been taken for other purposes such as consumption, health and education, repayment of loans and so on as revealed earlier. In relation to new economic activity, the highest number was members of the *Grameen* model at 88 per cent, followed by UNDP/SAPAP model at 76 per cent. At Outreach, the number of households having started new activities is slightly more than 27 per cent with only 4.4 per cent members of CDF doing likewise. As far as strengthening of existing economic activities were concerned, however, the highest number were from Outreach at 72 per cent, followed by just under 50 per cent from CDF, 19 per cent at UNDP and a low of just under 12 per cent at SHARE.

A very different pattern emerged when it came to the degree of independent economic activity undertaken by the women and the extent of control they have over their loans. At CDF, 15.56 per cent of the selected sample of respondents were found to be pursuing independent economic activity with the help of cooperative loans, while among SHARE and UNDP, 4.76 per cent of members only were pursuing independent enterprises. At the Outreach project, there were no such members among the selected sample. Hence, although the number of independent economic activities pursued by women across all organisations is low, it is substantially higher at CDF. When we examine the extent of control that women members have over loans, the members of CDF have the highest level of control at almost 43 per cent of the sample, followed closely by those of UNDP at 40.5 per cent. At SHARE, this level of control was found to be 28.57 per cent and at Outreach, it was 25.58 per cent. The quantum of loans taken for business activity as well as the substantially higher increases in income revealed by the study for these two latter organisations, raises questions as to the reasons for the low level of control over loans exercised by the women members. A few women at SHARE even stated that some of the men from their households, had withdrawn from wage labour and were spending more time in the new economic activity, exercising greater control on its decisions while putting in far less time and effort into its working. Thus, CDF shows the highest women economic empowerment, in spite of a low level of new economic activity resulting from cooperative loans and the lowest loan utilisation for income generation. This is in sharp contrast to the *Grameen* model where notwithstanding substantial economic gains mentioned earlier and new business activity, the gains for women's economic empowerment are comparatively low.

Women's Empowerment in Related Areas

For economic empowerment to be truly effective there is a need for women to progress in certain related areas also. Most alternative banking organisations working with poor women recognise this, though the nature, degree and priority of the different organisations given to these related areas, vary. Table 10.4 gives the relative development of the women in certain selected areas across the four selected villages, considered to be of relevance for the purpose of the study referred to.

The table shows the results of the sample survey in the selected indicators of progress considered relevant for poor rural women. The figures represent the percentage of women in the sample who reported improvement in these areas.

Table 10.4

Indicators of Empowerment Relevant for Poor Rural Women

Empowerment Indicator	*CDF*	*SHARE*	*UNDP/ SAPAP*	*Outreach*
Greater market access	20	80.94	24	14
Skill development	11	-	-	-
Improved mobility/individual autonomy	90.5	6	9.5	51
Higher social status	54.4	95.2	95	42
Education development	2.2	4.76	4.76	4.65
Increased confidence levels	88.9	100	93	44
Better health	46.6	52.3	16.67	28
Group solidarity	9.9	11.9	7	46.5
Training & exposure	13.3	97.6	92.86	97.96

Note: The above figures represent the percentage of women in the sample.
Source: Sample Survey.

The parameters on which the cooperative model unequivocally scores the highest are on increased mobility and confidence. They also do well on improved skills and better health. The low rating on training and exposure may be due to the fact that although CDF does a great deal of training, it tends to be more for the leaders rather than the rank and file members.

Conclusion

Institutional development has been a major achievement of the thrift and credit cooperatives, in keeping with its objectives of building up an alternative banking institution for rural women. Starting from small, informal beginnings, there is today a well-defined structure of women's (and men's) thrift and credit cooperatives with a highly visible membership in a concentrated geographical area. CDF, by being instrumental in bringing about effective change in the cooperative law, not just in the state of Andhra Pradesh but elsewhere in India, has made major strides in creating an environment where cooperatives can flourish as democratically functioning member-controlled organisations. The thrift and credit cooperatives for women are cost-effective, have developed sound internal administrative and financial practices and continue to gradually develop their membership and networks. More than other models of microfinance organisations, the cooperatives offer a valuable opportunity for providing an opportunity for the poor to save, which they value as much as access to credit, a fact not acknowledged often enough. That the cooperatives rely on internal savings mobilisation, recently expanded to include more voluntary savings products, have served to increase their independence. They are thus on the road to becoming sustainable institutions, capable for the most part in functioning without the promoting organisation.

Participation rates are high and in keeping with the holistic and inclusive model promoted by CDF, membership cutting across all classes. This demonstrates that it is not always necessary to have to target only the poorest in order to enlist their participation, provided the services and structures of the organisation are right. However, notwithstanding this promising picture with respect to two of the major areas examined, the results were more mixed with regard to the actual impact of the cooperatives, financial and otherwise. It has already been mentioned that the cooperative model has not found favour outside the CDF-promoted organisations. Study findings have further shown that the women's thrift and credit cooperatives cater only partially to the credit requirements of its members. In this respect they are less effective than other models that provide larger and more varied loan products as with the 'grameen-corporate' model. While this is not surprising in view of the fact that all funds in CDF cooperatives are internally generated, it is more surprising that even these limited funds are not currently being fully utilised.

It was found that turnover of funds had actually been going down for the organisation as a whole. CDF has been increasingly concerned about idle funds across several cooperatives, in spite of the facility through the network for cooperatives to borrow from each other to avail of surplus funds within the system. At a meeting held to discuss this problem on 27 January 2002, two main conclusions were reached. First, that the thrift cooperatives were being increasingly favoured more as a safe haven for savings rather than a source of credit, a fact detrimental in the long run for the sustainability of the cooperatives. With savings doubling in less than 12 years at current rates of interest (and some of the older cooperatives have a very low interest spread), if lending levels failed to increase sufficiently, the financial viability of the institution, it was felt, could suffer. That the lower off-take of loans was not due to lack of a need for credit was apparent from the extent of loans taken from outside the cooperative but these loans were not necessarily for productive purposes. In fact second conclusion was that the limited loan off-take was the result of a lack of adequate opportunities for productive investment. In fact the practice of members simply recycling their loans or using one loan to repay another and other forms of malpractices, difficult to check with growing size and numbers, was also found by CDF to be growing and made easier, no doubt by members' increasing creditworthiness. However, the practice of borrowing from one MFI to repay another was found to be more widespread in the 'grameen-corporate' model as observed during the microfinance crisis in Andhra Pradesh in March 2006 in the districts of Krishna and Guntur, which revealed the extent of the over-exposure of women to multiple loans which they were unable to repay. These are probably symptoms of systemic bottlenecks in the rural economy. Unfortunately, the government policies have emphasised 'financial inclusion' alone as a primary driver for growth. While financial inclusion is a necessary condition, it is not sufficient for economic growth. The larger constraints include infrastructure and policy framework that are generally too large for MFIs to handle, though CDF has worked hard to change the cooperative environment and been a major instrument in changing the law. CDF is currently attempting to deal with some of the other factors such as livelihood opportunities by promoting dairy, lowering interest rates and there have also been suggestions not yet implemented, that members may from time to time be permitted to withdraw savings for asset formation.

Other worrying factors revealed in the study of impact of the thrift and credit on its members is the low level of increase in their incomes and although levels of economic empowerment are higher in this than in the other selected samples, it is nonetheless low. The major economic benefit to the members from the thrift and credit cooperatives has been the access to consumption credit and a ready source for health and education expenditure. They have given more room for the member household to manouevre its loan portfolio (increased creditworthiness and use of loans from one source to repay another) and as mentioned earlier, providing members with a safe place to keep their savings and they have seen a steady growth of those savings. There are also major advances in women's self-confidence, mobility and a visibly growing membership (both in terms of depth within the village and expansion into adjoining areas) in a sustainable institution. These are no mean achievements but stagnation in the economic arena may erode these gains in the long run and affect the sustainability of the cooperative itself. While CDF has sought to increase livelihood opportunities in recent years for its members, the capacity of any single MFI to create these on any scale is necessarily limited.

References

Biswas, Arun and Vijay Mahajan (1997). *Sustainable Banking with the Poor: A Case Study on the Women's Thrift Cooperative System in Warangal and Karimnagar Districts of Andhra Pradesh.*

Chakravarty, Saswati (2006). "Crackdown on MFIs in Andhra", *Econmic Times,* 14 March. Miscellaneous published reports of CDF and other MFI models.

Cooperative Development Foundation (1997). Annual Report.

———. (2006). 31st Annual Report.

Galab, S. and N. Chandrashekhara Rao (2003). "Women's Self-Help Groups, Poverty Alleviation and Employment", *Economic and Political Weekly* 12 and 13, March 22-April 14.

Ghosh, Jayati (1998). *Cooperatives Under the Andhra Pradesh Mutually Aided Cooperative Societies' Act, 1995*. New Delhi: Centre for Economic Studies and Planning School of Social Sciences, Jawaharlal Nehru University.

Kabeer, Naila (2005). "Is Microfinance a 'Magic Bullet' for Women's Empowerment?: Analysis of Findings from South Asia", *Economic and Political Weekly* 44 and 45, October.

Mahajan, Vijay (2005). "From Microcredit to Livelihood Finance", *Economic and Political Weekly* 41, October.

Rajagopalan, Shashi (2000). *25 Years of Learning 1975-2000*. Cooperative Development Publications.

Ray, Nandita and D.P. Vasundhara (1996). "Like My Mother's House: Women's Thrift and Credit Cooperatives in South India", in Carr *et al.* (eds.), *Speaking Out: Women's Economic Empowerment in South India*. London: IT Publications.

Ray, Nandita (2005). "Alternative Banking for Rural Women, The NGO Experience: Some Issues of Upscaling", PhD Dissertation.

Sarkar, Keya (2007). "A Bill That Leaves a Lot to be Desired", *Business Standard,* 24 January.

The Link (2002). *CIP Newsletter*, May-June.

11 What have the Women and the Poor Taught us?

P.V. Satheesh

A Disagreement

It is not normal to start an article with a disagreement. But I am compelled to start on a discordant note because the entire premise of my study is a rejection of the notion of self-help groups (SHGs) and empowerment. As the feminist movement has repeatedly asserted since 1960s, naming is at the heart of all discourses. If you named something wrongly or dubiously, you have already misled the discourse. Therefore I start with my personal problem with two words that form this paper's core discussion. SHG and Empowerment.

The civil society work in most of South India for more than four decades has concentrated on building grassroot people's organisations. Most of them were called *sanghams*. It was not just a translation of the word collective. It was much more than a collective. The word *sangham* has a far deeper connotation. The Sanskrit saying *Sanghe Shaktih Kalau yuge* (In *Kali Yuga, sangha* is the power) echoes the Buddhist tenet in which *sangham* coexists in the same plain as Buddha *and Dhammam (Buddham Sharanam Gachhami), Dhammam Sharanam Gachhami, Sangham Sharanam Gachhami]*. Islam recognises the power of *Jamaat*, the collective while Christian saying 'Wherever the Ten of you, there I am' denotes that God will be present with the collectives. All these provide the concept of *sangham* a profoundly spiritual connotation. *Sanghams* also denote strength and bonding among social groups. Therefore they are more than self-help.

In contrast, the term and concept of SHG is extremely limiting. It suggests a sense of mundane practicality. Let alone profoundness, the name does not provide even a mild inspiration. In recent times, led by microfinance operators and government programmes, the terminology has been so restricted to monetary activities, that it is not even self-help any more. It is so much dependent on outside support and dictation that it has lost much of its identity. The other word that makes me squirm is empowerment. I feel that this word lets people play God. It connotes that some people have the power to empower others and therefore smacks of a quiet arrogance. Empowerment is a two-way street. In development if two or more set of actors are engaged, such an engagement empowers everyone, not just one set of actors. What is currently happening in the name of women's empowerment is a mime of empowerment defined by a culture of monetisation of women's concerns that makes it all the more disempowering and degrading. The current discourse of empowerment overrides all values that women have cherished: independent decision-making, taking control of their lives, saving their environment, about working toward social justice. It has been reduced to a monetary balance sheet no matter what you sell: from maize to chemical fertilisers and of course mass transportation to meetings of the political masters of the day.

Thus, given the task of writing about empowerment and SHGs, I find myself disagreeing with both the terms. My disagreement is neither theoretical nor academic. It emanates from my two decades of engagement with groups of low income Dalit women whose capacity to design their own lives and goals has fascinated me no end.

A Bit of Background

I work with the Deccan Development Society [DDS], a network of nearly 75 *sanghams*. The society works in 70 villages. Each village has a *sangham*—a village level women's group. It has nearly 5,000 women from low income families as its members. The women primarily come from the Dalit caste—socially the most marginalised groups in India. All the *sanghams* are in the Zaheerabad region of Medak District in Andhra Pradesh, which is situated in the semi-arid tract. Semi-arid belt is home to the poorest in the world. Thus the women of DDS *sanghams* suffer from multiple jeopardies: jeopardy of habitat (being rural), of economy (poverty), of caste (as Dalits) and gender (as women). Added to these is the harsh physical environment in which the people of the Zaheerabad region live.

Andhra Pradesh is the fifth largest state both in area and population. Its area is 275,068 sq.km and has a population of 66,508,008 (2001 Census). Andhra Pradesh has 23 districts and the state is divided into three regions namely, Rayalaseema, Coastal Andhra Pradesh and Telangana. Rayalaseema and Telangana are rain deficit areas. Medak district is one of the 10 districts of the Telangana region, which has an area of 9,699 sq.km (3.5 per cent of the total area of the state). Medak district has 1,265 villages and 10 towns with a population of 2,269,800 (2001 Census). It is located on the tableland of Deccan Plateau. Hot summers when temperatures soar to 43-45 °C characterise the climate of the district. The average rainfall in the district ranges between 550-600 mm. Manjira, a tributary of the river Godavari flows for 90 kms in the district but supplies water to Hyderabad city, the state capital. Not even a hectare of the land in the district is under river canal irrigation.

Zaheerabad region is endowed with red laterite soil. A few patches of black soil too exist. It is remarkable that these soils are used by farmers to grow a bouquet of crops ranging from 10-22 different crop varieties per acre without irrigated water. Most farms survive just on rainwater. On black and deep red soils farmers also grow a second crop in winter which they evocately call *satyam pantalu* (crops of truth) because they grow without even the support of rain. The red soil host sorghum, millets, pulses and oilseeds. Nearly 50 varieties are routinely planted on these soils. About 35 varieties of crops form the *satyam pantalu* consisting of winter sorghum, chickpea, safflower, mustard, linseed, peas and assorted food crops grow completely under rainfed condition. Knowledge of farming on these soils and their capability rests in the community and is passed on from generation to generation through oral tradition and practical apprenticeship on the farm. The eroded natural resource base on which they live and their own marginalisation in terms of caste, gender and income has always stared at the women of DDS communities. However, this has not put down their spirit. On the contrary, they have demonstrated an extraordinary capacity to regenerate their lives and their communities. This vibrant hope that the women brought with them has laid the foundation of the DDS's effort to consolidate the village groups into vital organs of primary local governance, and federate them into a strong pressure lobby for women, the poor and Dalits. A host of continuing dialogues, debates, educational and other activities with the people, facilitated by the society, are working towards translating this vision into a reality.

Over the years, the programmes of the society have evolved from meeting the simple sustenance needs of the *sangham* members to create an enabling environment for the community to address the larger issues of food sovereignty, natural resource enhancement, education and health needs of the region. The integration of various activities of the society is intended to retrieve women's natural leadership positions in their communities, and to negate the lack of access and control over their own resources. These activities have been able to offer the women a new-found dignity and profile in their village communities.

Theoretical Framework

The DDS was started by a group of professionals, which picked up the rural development initiatives left unfinished by a chemical company, as it had to wind up its rural development work because of its own compulsions. The initial objectives of the society were to blend the ecological and employment parameters to regenerate livelihoods in the area utilising people-oriented technology. It also targeted its work at the least privileged in these village communities. This translated into working with Dalit communities who were condemned to live with poverty and hunger as their permanent companions. In its early years, DDS, to guide its initiatives, constructed a theoretical framework that combined the Gandhian vision of community self-sufficiency with Maoist strategy of creation of barefoot cadres.

Though these were noble intentions, they were clouded by a thinking that outsider solutions could work for the poor. Poverty alleviation was the mission and it did not matter how this was accomplished. As a consequence, it was the technology of the outsiders which was implemented in the early years. Community housing was done with urban architects, eucalyptus plantations were undertaken for village woodlots with no consultation with the local communities, wells were dug for the poor without a thought whether in a semi-arid tract such wells will work to their advantage or disadvantage. All activities were focussed on men and taken up in response to their demands. A number of such mistakes were made. The mistakes did not multiply because DDS had a healthy tradition of subjecting all its field actions to a series of continuing debate within the group. This helped us to confront the consequences of our action and develop a critical discourse about our own understanding of development.

As the vibrancy of these debates grew, a new theoretical framework started emerging. Over a decade or so was spent in arriving at this framework, which would now refocus our work towards three vital principles:

- Gender justice,
- Environmental soundness,
- People's knowledge.

Of these, I consider the 'people's knowledge' as the most critical of the DDS articulations. A significant number of NGOs work towards gender and environment. But there are very few who combine this with a deep respect for people's knowledge. Within DDS, this recognition, though it came belatedly, completely transformed the way we work. It forced us to move away from a 'think tank' approach to using intense participatory processes with the communities. It made us concede that insider solutions were better than outsider prescriptions, however educated the outsiders were and whatever their expertise was.

But more excitingly it ushered in perspectives of rural Dalit women into the centre of our thinking. We developed deep respect for these perspectives and changed the way we think and work. This meant the following:

- The Board of DDS consisting of professors, academicians, management experts and veterans of development used to take all the decisions in the '80s and early '90s. Today almost all the decisions are taken by the *sanghams* and the staff council of DDS 95 per cent of which is composed of Dalits from the region and 60 per cent of which are women.
- The concept of core management team, which in the beginning was a sub-committee of the Board of DDS and later a combined team of the members from the Board and senior management of the staff, which reviewed and planned the DDS programmes on a regular basis, have been completely dispensed with.

- Currently the function of the Community Media Trust (CMT) has been taken over by a group that is drawn from all the sections of the staff, vertically and horizontally.
- Overseeing all these is a Policy Group of senior women of DDS *sanghams* who are Dalits, rural and non-literate.

Since 2005, DDS has begun the process of creating autonomous trusts to manage different initiatives of the society. These trusts are 100 per cent composed of women from the DDS *sanghams*. They include:

a. Food Sovereignty Trust (FST),

b. Natural Resources Trust (NRT),

c. Healers Trust (HT),

d. Community Media Trust (CMT),

e. Market Trust (MT).

Of these, the CMT is a five-year old reality fully self-managed and autonomous while the FST was formed on March 30, 2006. While at one level, all these new bodies came into existence as a result of the participatory processes that became the hallmark of the society, at another level it also marks the new theoretical framework constructed by it. The overarching principle of this new construct is the creation of autonomous communities.

Autonomous Communities

At the heart of this thinking and action is the fundamental principle of access and control that leads to the issue of autonomy of local communities. The autonomy becomes far more important in a globalising world, shrinking national boundaries, and disappearing national sovereignties. In this context, it has become crucial for local communities to give themselves certain spheres of autonomies to protect themselves from being walked over by the unseen globalising forces. It is in this scenario that the women of the DDS *sanghams* have worked towards a cycle of autonomies:

- autonomy over food production,
- autonomy over seeds,
- autonomy over natural resources and their management,

- autonomous health care systems,
- autonomous market,
- autonomous media,
- accepting with respect the subsistence vision which they embodied,
- enhancing the ecological sustainability of the region and
- developing a new vibrant articulation on non-irrigated crops.

Box 11.1

Food Sovereignty Trust: Preamble

Deccan Development Society (DDS), a non-profit developmental organisation was registered under AP (Telangana Area) Public Societies Registration Act 1350 Fasli on 2 September 1983. The main objective of the society is to work with women's *sanghams*, the members of which are the poorest of the poor in their village communities. Most of them are Dalits, the lowest group in the Indian social hierarchy.

Currently the DDS has been working in 75 villages around Zaheerabad in Medak district. The society's work has transformed the local communities into vibrant organisations of civil society creating conditions to achieve local autonomies in food production, seeds, natural resources, health care, market and media. Evolution of such conditions has led the DDS to believe that this evolving autonomy must be institutionalised in order to strengthen the self-reliant character of DDS *sanghams*. Such an institutionalisation could manifest itself through establishment of four independent Trusts with definite objectives that could systematically rearrange their different fields of work.

The DDS Food Sovereignty Trust (FST) is the first among these four Trusts and will start functioning with effect from April 1, 2006. The DDS-FST has the basic aim of restoring the dignity of the poor by helping them to establish total autonomy over their food production, storage and distribution systems at the community levels.

Such work of the DDS-FST should lead to the following achievements:

1. Over a period of five years, hunger in all its manifestations shall vanish from all the communities where the FST is engaged in.
2. In order to achieve this profound goal, the DDS-FST shall work to establish a priority for cultivation of food crops over non-food crops in their communities.

contd...

...contd...

3. The eradication of hunger shall come through the enhancement of biodiverse farming systems in their communities. Such enhancement shall be visible on the farms of the poor in particular and all farmers in general. These farms shall sport more than 10 crops at the same time and space.
4. The DDS-FST shall ensure that every community with which it is engaged shall have more than 50 varieties of traditional seeds that are time tested, vibrant and therefore can simultaneously guarantee diverse yields and ecological security.
5. In this process the DDS-FST shall make sure that the leadership of women and Dalits over their food and seed systems shall be irrevocably established.
6. Through such enhancement of biodiverse farming systems, the DDS-FST shall also ensure that the landless and the poorer farmers shall get year round employment within the village itself and do not have to migrate out of their communities.
7. The DDS-FST shall strive to achieve this goal by repeating the successful model set up by their *sanghams* of retrieving every acre of cultivable fallow land in their villages under plough and putting it under food production.
8. The DDS-FST shall further cause dryland farming by promoting crops such as millets and pulses that do not need any irrigation. *satyam pantalu*, the 'crops of truth' as they have evocatively termed, it can be the only answer to food and nutritional security in the world. Therefore the promotion of this farming shall be the principal aim of the DDS-FST.
9. The DDS-FST shall never lose sight of the fact that such a food system ensures multiple securities to the community such as food, fodder, fibre, health, nutritional, livelihood and ecological.
10. The DDS-FST shall strongly articulate in the local, state, national and international fora the need to acknowledge the unique role played by dryland crops in conservation farming in terms of their capacity to save precious global resources such as water, providing ecological security by being totally organic in production, enhancing nutritional security of the poor by providing them safe and nutritionally superior food.
11. The DDS-FST shall ensure that such articulation invariably includes the issues of community sovereignty, leadership and control of women and Dalits over their food and natural resources.

Thus over a decade or so, DDS which came into existence with an objective to uplift the rural poor with initiatives such as digging irrigation well and planting eucalyptus had been turned on its head to accept the primacy of rainfed crops and the traditional knowledge systems that surround them. It had passed on the management of the society to the local people, especially the most marginalised. The entire theoretical framework had thus been changed beyond recognition. From one that tried to lead people into being led by the people. Such learning was possible for DDS, once we started listening to the poor as against the normal NGO burden of educating the people.

Listening to the Poor and the Women

When DDS started its work, as stated earlier, it was engaged in a couple of traditional NGO activities such as digging irrigational wells for farmers, creating 'productive assets' for the poor, building houses by becoming an 'honest broker' between the government and the poor. Above all we had begun with men by starting their *sanghams*.

Around 1986, something significant happened which compelled us to listen to women and the poor. In the government-housing programme that we had undertaken, women who were participating as labourers started getting into a dialogue with us. The dialogues turned into questions about our actions. Of the many questions they asked us, two were very significant:

- Why are you working exclusively with men and excluding women?
- How come your house construction programme is so dependent upon outside technology that excludes women and their local knowledge?

This set us thinking very seriously about the path we were pursuing. By this time we had also started understanding that the development vision of men was feeble. They were incorrigible dreamers, ambitious and rearing to make a quantum leap into nowhere. They wanted their poverty to be erased in a jiffy. In contrast we had come to understand that women had a far more realistic assessment of their situation and had the will, determination, resilience and patience to improve it in slow but firm steps. As we started understanding and appreciating this, a gendered vision of development started enveloping our work and our thinking. Our response to this situation was to start women's *sanghams* in about five villages. The starting point for the *sanghams* was 'saving and credit'. The use of the money saved by each *sangham* was democratically decided by the groups themselves. Within a couple of years the five *sanghams* grew into 29 *sanghams* that further expanded to 40 in a span of five years. This spontaneous growth of the Society was driven by the passion of the women leaders of the *sanghams*. As they started seeing *sanghams* as their own vehicle out of their cutting edge poverty, their desire to enlarge the circle of *sanghams* grew. This desire was fuelled by the utter deprivation they were suffering from.

Stories of many women vividly recollect the poverty, the misery they suffered in their pre-*sangham* lives.

Rojamma, 65, fom Mamidigi village of Nyalkal *mandal*, Medak district:

> At the harvest time we used to receive foxtail millet as wages. We could not even afford to wait for sun drying it [since we would have no food at home to eat]. We would heat it on a pan, grind it into flour and cook. When the harvests were over, there would be nothing to eat. We had to go and serve the landlord... There was this Tenugu Lachamma. She called me to coat her [mud] walls with fresh mud. I had nothing to eat. Nor did my children. When Lachamma called me, I thought that if I go and worked for her, she would give me some rotis. I could eat and feed my children. I went, completed her work, brought the rotis and fed my children. That was how I lived. The days were full of struggle... Only after I came to this Sangham [things became better]. [Rojamma weeps] I sometimes think that this Sangham is my mother and father.

Adds Fatima Bee, 55, from Kalbemal village in Nyalkal *mandal*:

> What poverty have we faced! My tummy was this small then [indicates with her hands]. So hollow. Nothing to eat no! Had to walk to Mannelli forest [about ten kms away] to scour for neem fruits. And sell it at five rupees a measure [of five kgs]. If unwashed. To wash it, we had to walk to that pond. The washed fruits sold at Six rupees a measure. With that money we would come back, buy some broken rice and cook for the night. Even that rice would be full of sand. And then nothing to eat the next morning.

Mamidigi Saremma, a 35-year old woman has this to add:

> My mother in law tells me, she would wear half a part of her saree and wash the other half. And then wear the washed half and wash the other half. In this fashion, she went through her life with one saree.

Mamidigi Rojamma comes back with this recollection of her situation:

> I had no cloth to wear. No mat to spread. No blanket to cover. If I came home drenched, I had no second saree to wear. I would hold it to fire, half dry it, spread the same on the floor, hold on to my baby and breast feed him. In the same half dry saree on the floor. There was no one in Mamidigi [her village] who saw as much troubles as I did.

Agrees Betamma of Mamidigi:

> ... The same apathy [struggle] for everyone. There was neither food to eat nor clothes to wear. If you went to fields for wage work, you could eat otherwise nothing. The Kaapus [landlords] would be afraid of giving us loans. With our eight anna [half a cent] wage, how could we repay their two rupee [two cents] loan? Even if we borrowed two rupees, it would see us through only for a day or two. Then again we would go hungry. Therefore for their eight anna wage, whether we liked it or not, we worked for them....

Since this was the situation, it was natural that the *sanghams* were initiated as saving and credit groups. The need for the credit was acute. And the availability of the credit had to be fashioned in such a manner that it not only saved the women from the grip of moneylenders who were often the upper caste oppressors also. The poverty they were facing was horrendous. If they had one meal in the morning, they could never be sure when and where their next meal would come from. Hunger constantly knocked at their door. Sometimes their only meal would consist of a gruel made out of the leaves of *amaranthus* plant, which they would drink in order to forget, not quell, their hunger.

> We couldn't even access rotis [unleavened bread which is the staple food of the area] regularly. We used to break the rice into small particles, almost like flour. Then cook it like porridge. Make the children drink a bit of this and the rest for the adults. Then I had to go for a four anna coolie [a day's wage work used to earn her 25 paise (half a cent). My husband would go for a daylong work like bunching sugarcane or making irrigation channels which would earn him eight annas [fifty paise=one cent] wage.

> Then we had untold difficulties. The morning porridge had to take care of us until the evening. Then we would go to the shop and buy broken rice and cook. If we had salt, we had no chillies. If we had chillies, we had no pulses. That was our situation.
>
> Nothing to wear. Nothing to spread. If we came home drenched in rain, we had no fuel wood even to warm ourselves. We would come home and sleep on the bare floor. We have seen untold difficulties. [Mamidigi Balamma]

The alleviation of this utter misery was the early goal of the women. But unlike men, who wanted their poverty to vanish like an early morning mist, the women were far more clear-headed, patient and ready to traverse a long road out of their poverty. Their immediate goal therefore was to address their immediate, most pressing needs.

Bidakanne Sammamma, a Dalit woman leader from the village Bidakanne who has been with the *sanghams* for nearly 20 years, recalls the early days and underlines the fact that when the women came together, they were not looking for big assets like bullocks or carts or land. They had small, achievable goals, a product of their realistic understanding of their situations and contexts.

> As soon as we came to the [Sangham] meeting, what were we talking?
>
> "What is your pressing problem?"
>
> When we spoke like that, someone would talk about her illness, another would say I have no land even while the third would say…
>
> [In spite of this] In the beginning, no one asked us [to help her purchase] for bullock and cart. Nor for land. First when we started sanghams, people saved five rupees [a week] and thought: "up to what extent should we save and how will it help us?". We started our sangham just on this.
>
> When we started in this fashion, we looked at each person's situation. "This one has four children, this one cannot access even one kilo of rice, she has even pawned her ration card. Her husband either drinks too much or has many problems, or has some disease and therefore she should get preference". Those of us who have some jowar [sorghum] at home to eat should not get loans for rice or for jowar. [We decided] that this woman [whose difficulties are severe] should be selected for our support and gave her several kinds of help, primarily for her food. Gradually we gave her jowar, gave her money to buy rice. Only then we entered into the issue of land [development].

Though their *sanghams* addressed such needs it is remarkable that, unlike the later day government and microfinance-sponsored SHGs, the DDS *sanghams* did not put money at the centre of their agenda. Instead, they concentrated on building up a sisterhood network of their own. For this to happen, bonding with each other was the most essential prerequisite. The women who had formed their *sanghams* had no previous history of coming and sitting together and discuss their issues. This was the first time ever that they were coming together. When they did, they ensured that money would not climb to the top of their consciousness. What characterised their *sangham* meetings was talking to each other, singing together, building a sense of camaraderie. In other words, this act of coming together started building a new community of women.

> Before [we started] Sangham, did we ever have the practice of sitting together? Talking to each other, to understand your situation—we never had this practice, did we? What did we use to do? You worked at your home and went to your field. I worked at my home and went to my field. Now what happened was that we sat in a group, we understood about each other, how many are in your family, how is your situation?
>
> We did not start with Rs 5 did we? Rather we first started sharing each other's difficulties as a group. First sitting as a group, talking about each other, singing a song, sharing our happiness...there was no talk of Rs 5. was it? You saved whatever money you had. As low as one rupee, two rupees. [Chinna Narsamma]

Money therefore was just a token. It did not matter whether a woman saved five rupees or one rupee. By contributing to the group kitty, she was expressing her solidarity with the group and not particularly her interest to get a loan or assistance. They did come by, but the initial intention was to be together, to share, to understand, to build solidarity. But even these simple steps were not easy. Even singing together was difficult.

> In the beginning, even to sing [in sangham meetings], we had to face a lot of hardships. We used to be harassed [by our men who would say] "why should we sing?" Men at home used to say "these women go there to sing, to dance. Why should they go the sanghams?" You know what explanation we gave? "There is always unhappiness at home. Problems galore. We are tied down by the family burden. When women come together for 5, 10 minutes in a group, they should be able to forget all this. Their intention is to come together as sisters. In order to get them together, we have this practice of singing. Some women might even be

sleeping at home. In order to make some noise, to wake them up and get them to the meeting, we sing in our sangham". [Sammamma]

A Gendered Vision of Development

For the women, confronting such extreme handicaps was not through a couple of monetised actions. But in their *sanghams*, they started building solidarity of the women and the poor. Simultaneously, they were also developing a gendered vision of development. Not through big dramatic actions but by taking a few small steps, one at a time. Over time, these small steps would become giant leaps for the DDS. Let us illustrate a few:

- The acute poverty of the people had condemned them to even pawn their ration cards to borrow small money for their emergencies. This meant that inexpensive food ration could not be accessed by them properly. Therefore they decided to use their savings and credit to help the poorest in the group to redeem their ration cards from the moneylenders. This ensured a level of food security for their families. A vision of 'food security' at a time when the term was not fashionable in the development community.
- As an extension of this, the groups started pooling their *sangham* corpus to purchase food grains such as sorghum, household essentials such as chillies etc., in bulk from the producers at the harvest time when they would be 30 per cent cheaper than the retail market. The members would then distribute these items among themselves and pay back the amount in small weekly installments. Thus, using a democratic financing system they had ensured their community food security much before the rest of the world started thinking in this fashion.
- When asked to build their own houses, they would rather use mud than stones. Like the famed Egyptial architect Hassan Fathy, they knew that mud was the best bet for their environment and would be amenable to their skills.

Gradually through such actions, the women started infusing a strong sense of people's knowledge-based direction into the DDS. From the simple act of reclaiming their ration cards and assuring their food security the women moved within a decade into a seminal territory of reclaiming their fallows and announcing their food sovereignty.

Autonomous Food and Farming

For the past two decades the DDS *sanghams* have been ensuring that their farming becomes autonomous and their household and community food security is ensured. Some of the highlights in their march from food 'security' to food 'sovereignty' are:

- Around 1987, the first step in this process began. All members of DDS who were owners of lands assigned by the government entered into an initiative through which they would create 100 days of employment for every member. These employment days would be utilised to improve the quality of their degraded lands through bunding, trenching, destoning and topsoil addition. This initiative which ran for more than a decade enabled the women of DDS *sanghams* to use among them about 1.2 million eco-employment days to bring back under active cultivation over 10,000 acres of degraded agricultural lands. Consequently, they have been able to raise over three million kilos of grain every year, which is six times more than half a million kilos of grains per year they used to produce earlier.
- Around the same time, the *sanghams* started leasing in land from bigger farmers and working on it as agro collectives. The women's groups in each *sangham* would identify the land that they want to lease, negotiate with landowners, work out a good lease amount and pay it with the help of DDS. Later the group would completely take on the management of these lands, grow primarily food crops on it. After harvest, they would calculate the annual installment of money that they had borrowed from DDS to be returned and pay it back. The rest of the harvested crops would be shared equally between the women in the lease group.

  Over last 10 years, 2,386 women, participating in this programme, had leased in close to 5,500 acre/years of land [number of acres x number of years). For e.g. 10 acres of land leased for five years constitutes 50 acre/years] and had produced an incredible 2.5 millions kgs of food grains on it apart from 2.8 lakh bundles of fodder, uncultivated greens, and at least 50,000 person days of employment. Every season, each woman participant had earned food grains sufficient for three months, fodder worth four months and greens worth one month.

Besides these, the intangible advantage they had gained was their new ability to work as a farming collective, managing large tracts of land [some groups had leased 100 acres of land], enhancing their capacity of farming operations in terms of seed ratio, calculating and managing inputs, scheduling labour etc.

- Both the eco-employment and the land lease programmes had enhanced individual household food security. Primarily they had addressed *sangham* members both as individuals and as groups. But the initiative they took in 1996 called Alternative Public Distribution System (APDS) through community grain banks addressed a very large issue. It also focussed on the entire village community whether the person was a *sangham* member or not. More importantly this created a new model of PDS for the country. A model whose main elements were local production, local storage and local distribution and the total control by women and the marginalised.

The programme was started in 1996 with objectives such as:

- Bring under plough all cultivable fallows in the village and produce millet crops to sustain a PDS in which production, procurement, storage and management are all local.
- Generate extra livelihoods through this initiative.
- Promote ecological agriculture.
- Reduce the overhead costs of PDS.
- Provide more nutritious traditional millets under PDS instead of rice.
- Enhance the self-esteem among the project partner women in order to manage the food security system on their own.

In the very first season, through the programme the women brought in 30 villages over 2,600 acres of fallows under the plough. They produced an extra 800,000 kilogram of sorghum in their villages. This meant that they were able to produce nearly three million extra meals in 30 villages, or 1,000 extra meals per family. The fodder provided by the newly cultivated fields sustained over 6,000 heads of cattle in 30 villages at the rate of 200 cattle per village. Currently, running in 77 villages, the APDS programme has regenerated 4,862 acres of fallows, produces two million kgs of grain every year on the poor lands owned by the poor, creates 10,000,000 extra meals for the communities, generates close to 250,000 person days of employment every season. Through the *jowar* ration card, the programme distributes 6,00,000 kgs of grains [worth about Rs 3,000,000] to about 50,000 poor belonging to 8,500 families every year.

Table 11.1

Some Highlights of the Alternative PDS

	Quantity	*Value in Rs*
Number of villages covered	79	
Number of acres brought under cultivation	4,832	
Number of farmer participants	3,758	
Annual production of grains [approx] in kgs	2,000,000	7000000
Number of employment days generated/year	2,41,600	8456000
Grain distributed per year, in kgs	6,00,000	2100000
Number of ration cards issued	8532	
Direct support rupees	16,396,900	1,75,56,000
Seed banks	27,000 kgs of seeds that can plant about 5,000 acres/year	
Fodder generated	Serving 10,000 heads of cattle per year in 79 villages	

- But most importantly, the entire management of this programme has rested with village level committees of women, primarily Dalits giving them total control over the food security of their communities.

Seed Sovereignty

Under another initiative, the women of DDS *sanghams* have taken complete control of their community seed needs by starting banks of traditional seeds in nearly 100 villages. Called community gene banks, these seed banks managed by one or two women in every village, store and supply nearly 60+ unavailable seed varieties to anyone who needs them in their community. In recent years, every woman in the DDS *sangham* has become a veritable seed bank herself. This is an enormous political and agrarian power restored to women. All these initiatives led to the practical realisation of the principle of 'community food sovereignty', a global ideology of activist groups and culminating in the setting up of the Food Sovereignty Trust of DDS which has set the following goals for itself.

In order to secure our food, health and nutrition, we shall ensure that:

- No family that is landless and have many dependent children, the destitute and the very old will suffer from hunger.
- Every landless person in the *sangham* will be helped with some livelihood avenue or the other so that every single day of the year s/he will be engaged in productive employment.
- Every landed family will be supported to procure adequate quantity of seeds and manure within the village.
- Each member of our communities will have access to ordinary farmyard manure, enriched compost, vermicompost and biomass, a combination of which will greatly enhance the soil fertility of our lands.
- We cover all the landless with ownership of livestock and/or eco-enterprises.

The Trust has already initiated a number of steps in pursuit of its objectives.

Capacitating Themselves

The women who constitute FST are from very low income families and are non-literate. Therefore the members of FST have started capacitating themselves to deal with the tasks in front of them. In order to do so they have started:

a. Holding extensive discussions among themselves.
b. Acquainting themselves with various governmental schemes.
c. Familiarise themselves with the process and rules of lending by banking and other financial institutions.

Soon they will also hold consultations with development researchers, bureaucrats and scientists to understand the overall situation from other perspectives. In order to bring their dead lands alive and breathe life into half dead lands, the members of the FST have:

- Completed a series of participatory rural appraisals (PRAs) to map the lands of the DDS communities and identify the fallows.
- Held detailed discussions with the members of the community to plan ecological food production over the next five years.
- Approached and negotiated with the government agencies, banks and other financial institutions to raise fund/offer credit for the above tasks.

Alongside food sovereignty, the FST will make sure that every member of the DDS *sanghams* herself becomes an individual gene bank, realising the ultimate aim of seed sovereignty at the household level.

Abolishing Hunger

In order to see that any residual hunger in the villages they are working in is eliminated the members of the FST have taken up a number of measures:

- A series of hunger maps have been done in all the villages of DDS *sanghams* and people who are destitutes, very old and incapable of producing food for themselves have been identified.
- In discussion with the *sanghams*, they have opened nearly 15 community kitchens in the *sangham* villages and have started offering two meals to the identified destitutes and the very poor.
- They have identified the families with silent hunger, families that cannot afford to have adequate nutritious meals for three times a day. Now they are planning out how they could be assisted with the programmes from within the DDS project and/or through government's development initiatives.

Assisting the Landless

- Through the PRAs the FST has identified the landless in the *sangham* villages and have begun measures to help them access government programmes.

- They have listed them as priority families that will be assisted through the DDS eco-enterprises.
- It will see that all livelihood opportunities that emerge as a result of DDS programmes will be utilised by these families.

Natural Resources Trust (NRT)

Apart from their autonomous food and farming, DDS *sanghams* have also been creating neighbourhood forests by planting close to a million plants in the wastelands close to their villages for over 20 years. This has resulted in the greening of over 1,000 acres in about 28 villages. This process has created a cadre of skilled rural women foresters who can raise plant nurseries, graft saplings and protect them. These are rare skills among the rural women. Almost 50 per cent of these plantations have got official *pattas* from the government indicating that the right over trees and produces from these lands will belong to the women who have raised these plantations.

Dalit Watersheds

The women of DDS communities have also designed and implemented a set of eight unique watersheds called Dalit Watersheds. In these watersheds, the women have bunded and trenched their lands for soil moisture conservation, carefully bringing it under cultivation and used ecological production methods to grow food crops. In order to consolidate this process, DDS is in the final stages of setting up an NRM trust in the footsteps of the FST. The NRMT is made up of women from each of the following sectors:

- plantation raisers,
- nursery raisers,
- medicinal plantation caretakers and
- watershed managers.

Democratising Health Care

DDS has been running a local knowledge and practice based folk health care programme since 1986. About 50 health workers, one from each of the 50 villages under the programme are working for this system. In one of our recent evaluations of the programme we came across the following amazing facts:

- Since 2002, these women had attended and cured over 45,000 illnesses of their community members at nearly no cost to the community.
- They had treated over 7,000 animals.
- They had attended to nearly 500 births and an equal number of cases of reproductive health needs.
- They had helped more than 50 women to access surgical care for their gynae problems.
- They had also got nearly 15,000 children immunised against polio in their villages.
- They had got close to 40,000 cattle vaccinated in their neighbourhood.

A cumulative effect of this was that the DDS health workers had saved nearly Rs 15 million from being spent on health care by their communities. This amounts to a per capita saving of Rs 5,000, equivalent to almost a half year's earning by an individual person. Apart from this cold monetisation, what the health group of DDS had achieved was to liberate the Dalit and the poor of their communities from the trauma that they go through every time they have to access any medicare. Saved them from the insults and harassment they have to undergo every time they enter a public health care centre. And give them the comfort and dignity of being treated by one of their own, in whom they can confide, a person whom they can trust. The herb and plant based medicines that they were being administered was also a safe medicine.

On another note, this was also an incredible democratisation of health care where more and more people understood what they were suffering from and which plant in their neighbourhood could offer the cure for it. Therefore, the need has arisen to institutionalise this work by creating a Healers Trust which is very close to completion. The Healers Trust will be composed of a group of highly caring, experienced and capable health care workers who will take on the management of all the health care work of the society including raising and taking care of community medicinal plantations.

Autonomous Community Media

The need for community controlled autonomous media lies in the context of globalisation, which has fashioned a frightening media situation. Under the unrelenting attack of the mainstream media (irrespective of their ownership), poorer and the less privileged people are on the verge of completely losing their media space. The media is unabashedly by the elite, for the elite and of the elite. It does not just report the elitisation of the DDS. It is ensuring that such an elitisation happens. Add to this the most dangerous the latest trend of taking over of production of media content by the producers of media technology. This pincer grip of media takes away all the control from the real people. It is this context, which makes initiatives like the Community Media Trust extremely relevant to the DDS communities.

The Community Media Trust (CMT)

The Community Media Trust came into existence on October 15, 2001 in fulfilment of the wishes of thousands of women from DDS Sanghams who demanded that their unrecognised voices are heard and acknowledged by the world outside. The Trust is mandated to metaphorically hand over microphones and cameras to marginalised rural women so that they can produce their own images and voices and contribute an authenticity to the Media scene which is otherwise dominated by commercial and political interests whose agendas work in direct conflict with the interests of marginalised communities. The DDS Community Media Trust has been striving to take the images and voices of rural women to the larger world outside and create an alternative Media ethos. This alternative ethos will evolve a media which can be accessed and controlled by the local communities, especially those that suffer continued exclusion. Twenty women, 17 of who are working with video and three with radio, constitute the DDS-CMT. The video group operates with Mini DV cameras, portable edit recorders, G-4 computer edit facility to make their films. They have set up their own edit suite and dubbing facility.

The Functioning of the CMT

The women film-makers of the DDS-CMT, who together have made more than 100 short films on various issues of their concern, have brought in fresh perspectives into film-making. While the primary engagement of the CMT lies in a horizontal communication with their own communities, they have also produced dozens of films for other groups and agencies on issues of development with which they have shared concerns. These include films the future of food and farming, better harvest of genetically engineered agriculture, water, lives and livelihoods, women's control over media, environment and agrobiodiversity. Through their films they have engaged with their own communities in debates over food and seed sovereignty, establishment of autonomous communities, control over natural resources, market and media. They have done critical evaluation of state policies and programmes, established solidarity with local communities in the South Asia and other regions of world.

Community Radio

In 1996, the DDS started its own community FM radio centre with a recording studio, control room, two transmitters, one transmitting tower and all other related facilities to enable the full functioning of a radio station. The radio facility works for eight hours a day. Three women, General Narsamma, Algole Narsamma and Chukkamma manage the station on a daily basis. Since they began, six years they have canned over 500 hours of programmes. The programmes incorporate almost every format in radio barring news. Every day the studio is busy for a couple of hours recording programmes by the local people, mainly women, on issues of agriculture, gender, biodiversity, education, folk music etc. At the end of the week the three programmers get together and make an audio magazine by putting together various programmes that respond to the theme of the week.

Each magazine has a timely focus. If it is the ploughing season there would be a likely discussion between experiences of farmers on the merits and demerits of let us say, deep ploughing. With the onset of sowing season, there could be another discussion on the exact *karti* (the rain bearing star) in which to sow a particular crop. Each of these timely discussions, talks, interviews will be interspersed with folk and/or traditional songs that are related to the particular farming activity, some other issues related to social issues like gender, education, child care etc. These audio tapes are sent to each of the 75 villages where the DDS works. In each of these villages, the members of the DDS *sanghams* sit and listen to the programmes. The feedback from the villages reaches the programmers so that they can build in necessary corrections in their future productions. These have been the major accomplishments of the women's *sanghams* of the DDS over the last two decades.

Advocacy

As they went on crossing one milestone after another, the DDS *sanghams* have also seamlessly progressed from doing their own advocacy from a local level to national and international levels. A major achievement of the advocacy was the agrobiodiversity plan done by the DDS women for the massive National Biodiversity Strategy and Action Plan (NBSAP) for the Government of India. This massive plan, which was an obligation of the Government of India to the Convention of Biodiversity, strongly recommended the DDS model of biodiversity for the entire dryland belt of the country.

The annual mobile biodiversity festival (MBF) is another tool which the women of DDS use to propagate agrobiodiversity which is a concern close to their heart. Now internationally famous for the celebratory discourse which these festivals use as their form, they have dialogued with over 300,000 farmers in the region on the issues of ecological farming, traditional crops and the biodiversity. MBF was the main tool used by the women for the preparation of their NBSAP. DDS women have also been instrumental in a seminal Prajateerup, a farmer's jury on the food and farming futures of Andhra Pradesh. The process and the verdict of this jury have echoed all over the world among the development communities including the parliament and the media of UK.

Conclusions

At the end of this two-decade long journey, when one looks back at the leanings made from the *sanghams* of DDS women, the conclusions become obvious.

1. Listening and learning from rural women can be a highly rich experience and can shape the way development can be envisioned.
2. There is no need to educate rural women. The education can be a self-generated process.
3. What needs to be done is to build peoples' confidence in their own knowledge. This confidence can create its own dynamics and generate an enhanced pace of development.
4. Women are the holders of enormous knowledge. Therefore it becomes the duty of development actors to absorb this knowledge, package them into instruments of learning and hand it back not only to the communities but also to the policymakers for whom this can be an unlearning of their development theories and a new learning to see development from peoples' perspective.
5. Autonomy is the key to development. The more participatory and decentralised that development can become, the road to autonomy can be clearly seen as the best tool for peoples well-being.

12 Poverty Reduction through Community Based Organisations

A Case Study of Indira Kranthi Patham

K. Raju, T. Vijay Kumar and
C.P. Nagi Reddy

Andhra Pradesh Districts Poverty Initiatives Project

Introduction[1,2]

The Society for Elimination of Rural Poverty (SERP) is implementing Indira Kranthi Patham (IKP) project. This is a state-wide, community demand driven rural poverty alleviation project aiming to cover all rural poor households in the state, with a special focus on 30 lakh poorer households. The main objective is to enable the rural poor in the state, particularly the poorest of the poor, to improve their livelihoods and quality of life. The IKP focusses on rural poor families in all the 1,097 rural *mandals* in 22 rural districts of the state. The IKP evolved in two phases as two projects. The first phase and first project was Andhra Pradesh District Poverty Initiatives Project (APDPIP). The second phase project is Andhra Pradesh Rural Poverty Reduction Project (APRPRP). Presently it is the extension of APRPRP to all rural *mandals* in 22 districts i.e., IKP. Both are partly externally aided projects, with financial support from the World Bank.

---

1. This report borrows generously from the existing literature at World Bank and SERP, especially from Project Implementation Plans of APDPIP and APRPRP and other internal documents. All are gratefully acknowledged. Financial support from the World Bank and the handholding support by the Task Team for APRPRP under the leadership of Mr Parmesh Shah is acknowledged.

2. Comments on an earlier draft by Prof D. Narasimha Reddy have improved the contents of this paper significantly. This is gratefully acknowledged.

The APDPIP covering 316 *mandals* in six districts with an outlay of Rs 654 crore was launched on 14 June 2000. The project duration was up to December 2006 and covered about 9.3 lakh poor households. The APRPRP that commenced on 1 June 2002 with an outlay of Rs 1,486 crore covers 548 backward *mandals* in 16 districts of the state and is estimated to cover 20,00,000 families. APRPRP also covers 260 coastal fishermen villages in non-project *mandals*. In 2004, APRPRP was extended to all the 1,097 rural *mandals* of the 22 rural districts of the state.

APDPIP was formally launched in June 2000 at Utnoor, Adilabad district by the Chief Minister. The Project is contracted to SERP through a Memorandum of Understanding (MoU). The genesis of APDPIP dates back to 1994-95 when the early proposals were drafted by the Government of Andhra Pradesh (GoAP), for social and capacity assessment of the districts during 1997-1999. The experience of South Asia Poverty Alleviation Project (SAPAP) in Mahabubnagar, Anantapur and Kurnool culminated in a unique way forward for reducing the poverty during 1995-2000. Based on experience, a proposal for a project with a huge coverage was made in March 2000.

At the operational level, the main lessons incorporated into the project design are: (a) creation of a decentralised project management structure with full control over sub-project approval to expedite decisions and to minimise political interference, (b) development of streamlined procurement and disbursement rules and regulations to ensure speedy implementation, (c) inclusion of competitive employment conditions for project management staff to attract and retain competent and motivated individuals, (d) inclusion of detailed operational manuals, computerised Management Information System (MIS), standardised financial management procedures, regular and rigorous auditing, and quantitative and qualitative monitoring and evaluation and (e) incorporation of physical and financial sustainability conditions in the sub-project eligibility criteria to ensure a continued flow of benefits.

GoAP was persistent in its request for Bank assistance for a project focussed on poverty reduction and included all necessary budgetary resources in its plans. GoAP was seriously concerned about the high level of poverty, illiteracy and poor health and has widely promoted participatory approaches to address the needs of the rural poor. It has also given high priority to improving the status of women through innovative approaches. The government supported this commitment by establishing a dedicated team to prepare the project proposal. An autonomous society, SERP was registered to implement the project with the Chief Minister as the chairman. In addition, a number of actions have been taken to enhance institutional readiness for implementation, including selection of the

Table 12.1

Component-wise Project Outlay of APDPIP

(Rs crore)

Sl. No.	*Name of the Component*	*APDPIP*
1.	Strengthening institutional, social and human capital	125.51
2.	Support to sub-projects of the poor	360.34
3.	Support to eliminate child labour*	133.82
4.	Project management	34.32
	Total	654.00

Note: * This component is being implemented by Andhra Pradesh Social Welfare Residential Educational Institutions Society (APSWREIS).

Source: Society for Elimination of Rural Poverty, Government of Andhra Pradesh.

Table 12.2

Expected Project Outputs from APDPIP

Sl. No.	*Programme Details*	*APDPIP*
1.	Districts	6
2.	Coverage of *mandals*	316
3.	No. of families to be covered	9,30,000
4.	Self-reliant people's institutions	
	– DWCRA groups (SHGs)	66,000
	– Village organisations (VOs)	8,000
	– *Mandal samakhyas* (MSs)	316
5.	Trained community activists, book-keepers and paraprofessionals	40,000
6.	Child labour elimination	1,00,000
7.	Educational support for girl child labour	
	No. of residential schools	24
	Girl children mainstreamed	36,000

Source: Society for Elimination of Rural Poverty, Government of Andhra Pradesh.

project *mandals*, staffing arrangements for the state, district and *mandal* units, preparation of the financial management manual, development and testing of the computerised financial management system, finalisation of the operational manual and guidelines for appraisal of demand based sub-project proposals. Table 12.1 gives the project outlay in each of the above mentioned components of APDPIP while Table 12.2 throws light on the expected project outputs from APDPIP.

Objective of APDPIP

The main objective of the project is to improve opportunities for the rural poor to meet priority social and economic needs in the six poorest districts of Andhra Pradesh (AP). To achieve this, the project would:

(a) Help create self-managed grassroot institutions.

(b) Build the capacity of established local institutions, especially the *gram sabha/panchayats* and GoAP's line departments, to operate in a more inclusive manner in addressing the needs of the poor.

(c) Support investment in sub-projects proposed by grassroot institutions of the poor to accelerate their entry and expand their involvement in social and economic activities.

(d) Improve access to education for girls to reduce the incidence of child labour among the poor.

Key Components of APDPIP

Institutional and Human Capacity Building

(a) The focus of this component would be to develop self-reliant and self-managed community based organisations. Accordingly, majority of funds available under this component would be utilised in capacity building of new or existing groups in the project districts. In addition, the line departments and Panchayati Raj Institutions (PRIs), especially *gram panchayats*, would be sensitised/re-oriented through training, consultant services, workshops and exposure visits so that they operate in a more inclusive manner in responding to needs of the rural poor.

Community Investment Fund

The activities to be financed under this component would be demand-driven sub-projects to be proposed by Common Interest Groups (CIGs)/ SHGS either on their own or jointly with communities (*gram sabha/ panchayat*) during implementation. The participants would have freedom to prepare sub-project proposals based on their felt needs provided these conform to the agreed criteria.

Educational Support for Girl Child Labourers and School Dropouts

Under this component, provision would be made to finance: (a) regular campaigns to sensitise parents, especially mothers and other community members about the importance of education and its long-term implications for child welfare and poverty, (b) in project districts/*mandals* with the highest concentration of child labour and dropout rates, establishment of a maximum of 18 residential 'bridge' and 6 regular secondary residential schools for girls.

Project Management, Monitoring and Evaluation and Studies

Provision has been made to cover the costs of incremental staff, technical assistance/consultants, training, workshops and study tours, vehicles, office equipment supplies and other incremental operating costs. Provision would also be included for special studies and preparation of a follow-up project. This component would include funding for a comprehensive monitoring and evaluation (M&E) system. Given the innovative nature and decentralised management structure of the project, the design adopted allows flexibility to change based on implementation experience as an ongoing activity. Additional sources of learning would be the studies on economic, social, financial and institutional aspects of the project.

Andhra Pradesh Rural Poverty Reduction Project

Introduction

While the Andhra Pradesh District Poverty Initiatives Project was 18 months into operation, the idea of Andhra Pradesh Rural Poverty Reduction

Project (APRRP) was contemplated. As discussed earlier, the objective of the APDPIP project is improving the opportunities for the rural poor to meet priority social and economic needs in the six poorest districts of Andhra Pradesh. The project development objectives of APRPRP are that the poor and particularly the poorest of the poor in the remaining 16 rural districts sustain self-reliant, empowered organisations to take advantage of their new opportunities, in a risk-managed environment. They convert their secure asset base into an economically viable, improved and sustainable living. Higher level of educational achievement, particularly among girl children of the poorest of the poor is the main focus. The map showing APDPIP and APRPRP *mandals* as envisaged is Figure 12.1.

Figure 12.1

APDPIP`and APRPRP Districts and Mandals

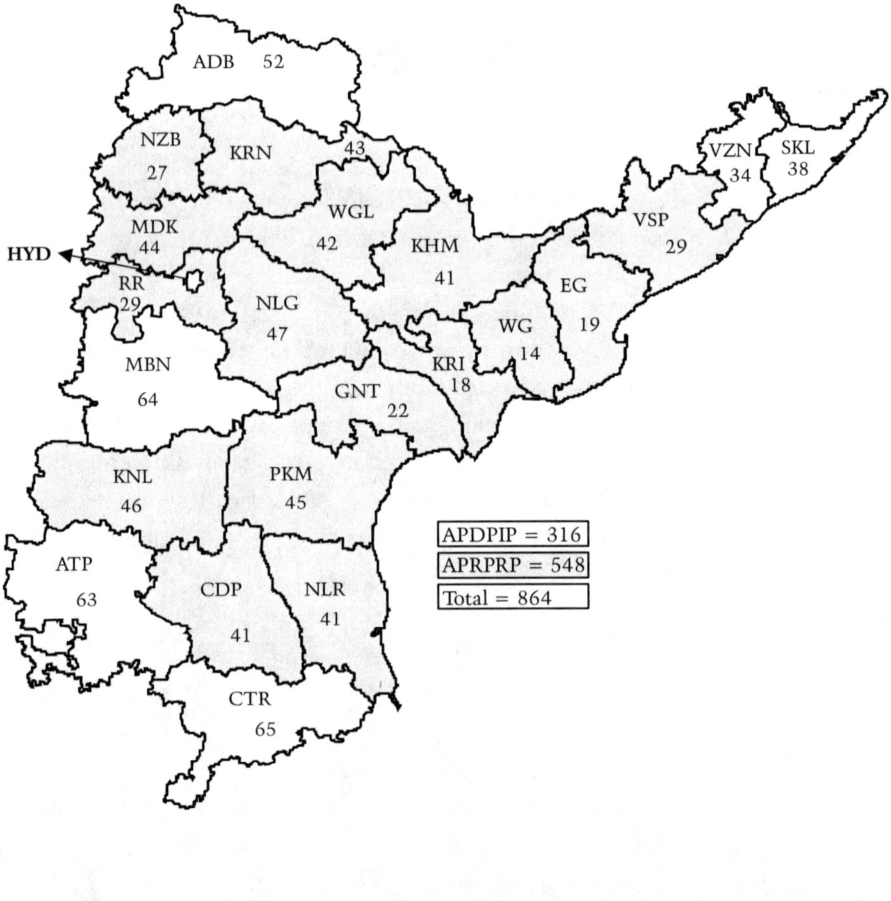

Rationale of APRPRP

The design adopted for APRPRP is similar to that of APDPIP but is a combination of the PRI model and the conventional social fund. While the APRPRP model focusses on self-managed organisation of the target groups and their organisations as the key players, it emphasises development of working partnerships with existing institutions, civil society actors, public sector organisations, line departments of the state government and PRIs. It is hoped that the participatory approaches and demand based investment decisions would bring about improvements in operation of the public institutions and the PRIs. At the same time, establishment of strong linkages with institution/programmes at the local level would contribute to the transfer of experience and learning as well as add to sustainability. Such linkages would ensure that APRPRP-financed interventions complement and supplement other poverty reduction schemes. The goal of the overall long-term rural poverty reduction programme is to help enable the poor to overcome poverty through a holistic approach of facilitating and promoting empowerment, creating opportunities, providing mechanism for social security, and working for equity.

Key Performance Indicators

The project would integrate bottom-up participatory development of the target groups with well-coordinated, transparent delivery of public services at the local level (*mandal* level primarily). The strengthening/ formation of self-managed organisations of the target groups and their federations at different levels, hinged onto common interest(s) (primarily individual and communal relationships of trust and mutual support) are two core outcomes of the project. Such organisations and their federations would lead to enhanced social and human asset formation at different levels, especially at the habitation and village levels and empower the poor to seek their entitlements. The improvements in good governance and organisational capacity of local governments (both elected officials and line department staff) at the sub-district levels and integration of different public sector interventions at the *mandal* level are other core outcomes of the project. These have been, on one hand, major barriers for public services to respond to the needs of the target groups, and on the other, for these groups to access their entitlements of public services. Redefining and restructuring more healthy and sustained interfaces (or linkages) between grassroot groups and local institutions.

The large segments of the rural population suffer from multiple poverty syndromes. They are not only income poor, but are also capability poor, the latter contributing to their isolation and alienation from the mainstream of development. Multiple disadvantage syndrome suffered by the poor, requires an integrated multi-pronged poverty alleviation programme. But despite best of intentions, a holistic approach, with horizontal integration of different poverty alleviation interventions, which can provide an integrated multi-pronged poverty alleviation programme, has not been fostered and nurtured in the past.

Geographical Focus

The project will strategically focus on targeting assistance to 548 most backward *mandals* in 16 districts of Andhra Pradesh, using nine criteria ranging from literacy to economic activity, for identification of backward *mandals*. These *mandals* fall in districts where APDPIP project is not currently underway.

Target Group

Within these identified 548 backward *mandals* in the 16 districts under reference, the target group will be of the poor who will include the poor scheduled castes (SCs), scheduled tribes (STs) and backward castes (BCs), people without control over and access to productive resources. Amongst these people, the development interventions will always begin for the 'poorest of the poor' i.e., for those who lie at the bottom of the poverty ladder.

Key Issues

Within the livelihoods approach the key issues that will be addressed in the project are:

- Protecting, maintaining and building the critical social, natural resources, financial and human capitals of the target groups.

- Empowering the target groups so that they can use these capitals productively with less restrictions.
- Providing the poor with more and better opportunities for using the capitals.

All of which resonate well with the Bank's three strategies for attacking poverty, namely, enhancing security, facilitating empowerment and promoting opportunities.

Project Components

Institution and Human Capital Building

The objective of this component is to facilitate promotion of self-managed and financially sustainable community based institutions of the poor and development of social capital for securing sustainable livelihoods and better quality of life for the poor.

Community Investment Fund (CIF)

The objective of CIF is to help strengthen and diversify the livelihoods of the poor and their quality of life. The CIF component is expected to promote the income and employment levels of the poor, decrease unproductive expenditure and help mitigate risks. The broad strategy is to enable the poor to undertake analysis of the major livelihoods, identify opportunities and constraints. The evolution of CIF sub-projects (CIFSPs) is expected to take place through the process of Livelihood Enhancement Action Plans (LEAPs) within the broad context of the livelihoods framework of the project. Certain sub-projects could also emerge outside the LEAP framework. The implementing bodies like Sub-Project Implementing Agencies (SPIAs) for the CIFSPs would be CBOs of the poor i.e., village organisations (VOs) at the *gram panchayat* level and *mandal samakhyas* (MSs) at the *mandal* level.

Support to Pilot Programmes

With the overall objective of taking up pro-poor experiments, demonstrations and trials, the project would support pilot programmes in these major areas:

Strengthening the Role of PRIs

The central objective of this programme is to support the GoAP's strategy of decentralised approach to poverty reduction. This is being done by strengthening the PRIs in 40 pilot *mandals*. Improving the capacities of the PRIs to respond to the needs of the rural poor, linking the PRIs with the rural poor and the community based organisations (CBOs) and promotion of downward accountability of the PRIs.

Social Risk Management (SRM)

The objective of this sub-component is to apply the SRM framework to address the downside risks faced by the poor. It is planned to do this by developing and strengthening community-driven processes for risk reduction, mitigation and coping. The CBO members would be facilitated to access a comprehensive insurance package. Different models of community managed insurance services to the poor would be tested in 15 *mandals* covering 450 VOs, 6,000 SHGs and 30,000 households.

Comprehensive Basic Health Package

The project would be piloted to demonstrate the ability of the community to enhance access to basic health services to the poor and to ensure that the health service providers are responsive and accountable to them. The central objective of the package is to improve the health status of the poor.

Support to Elimination of Child Labour

The fourth part of the project will be investment in weaning girl children away from work. It will provide for campaigns, social mobilisation and residential schools etc. One of the major focus areas of APRPRP is the elimination of child labour through a process of intensive mobilisation against child labour, sensitisation of the parents, the community, the employers and other necessary initiatives for mainstreaming of child labour. A social norm has been established against all forms of child labour and in favour of ensuring that every child in the 5-14 years age group is not only enrolled into the schools but also retained until the child completes class 10. This norm is based on a non-negotiable principle that no child must work and every child must attend full time formal day school.

Support to People with Disabilities

The fifth part of the proposed project will provide investments for meeting the special needs of the people with disabilities, mostly in software, capacity building, integration of people with disabilities into the mainstream, changing social mindset, developing community based rehabilitation (CBR) programmes, developing cadres of CBR workers etc. It will also include making investments in providing options to destitute widows and women.

The long-term objective of this component is to help disabled persons and their caregivers to improve their livelihood opportunities and quality of life. The project proposes to cover disabled persons in 80 *mandals*, with appropriate interventions during the project period.

Project Management

The semi-autonomous status of the SERP and decentralised institutional arrangement, allowing operational autonomy at the district level, allows decision-makers to come closer to the participating communities and allows rapid decisions on proposal submitted by the participating communities.

Evolution and Progress of Indira Kranthi Patham

Introduction

In 2004, the APRPRP was extended to all the rural *mandals* of the state in 22 districts and the programme is rechristened as Indira Kranthi Patham (IKP). IKP builds on the decade long, statewide rural women's self-help movement. The focus is on deepening the process, providing an institutional structure and developing a framework for sustaining it for comprehensive poverty eradication. The current APRPRP is a combination of erstwhile APDPIP in six districts and APRPRP in 16 districts. Table 12.3 gives the district and the number of mandals initially covered as well as all the mandals presently covered under APDPIP and APRPRP:

Table 12.3

District-wise Number of Mandals in APDPIP and APRPRP

Sl. No.	*District*	*Total Mandals*	*Mandals Initially Covered*	*Mandals Covered*
	APDPIP			
1	Adilabad	52	52	52
2	Anantapur	63	62	63
3	Chittoor	66	65	65
4	Mahabubnagar	64	64	64
5	Srikakulam	38	38	38
6	Vizianagaram	34	34	34
	DPIP Total	317	315	316
	APRPRP			
1	East Godavari	58	19	58
2	Guntur	57	22	57
3	Kadapa	51	41	50
4	Karimnagar	57	43	57
5	Khammam	46	41	46
6	Krishna	50	18	49
7	Kurnool	54	46	53
8	Medak	46	44	46
9	Nalgonda	59	47	59
10	Nellore	46	41	46
11	Nizamabad	36	27	36
12	Prakasam	56	45	56
13	Rangareddy	37	29	33
14	Visakhapatnam	53	29	39
15	Warangal	51	42	50
16	West Godavari	46	14	46
	RPRP Total	803	548	781
	Grand Total	1120	863	1097

Source: *ap.gov.in*

The original project outlay in APDPIP and APRPRP in each of the components and expected outcomes are given in Table 12.4 and Table 12.5

Figure 12.2

Number of Current Mandals in APRPRP

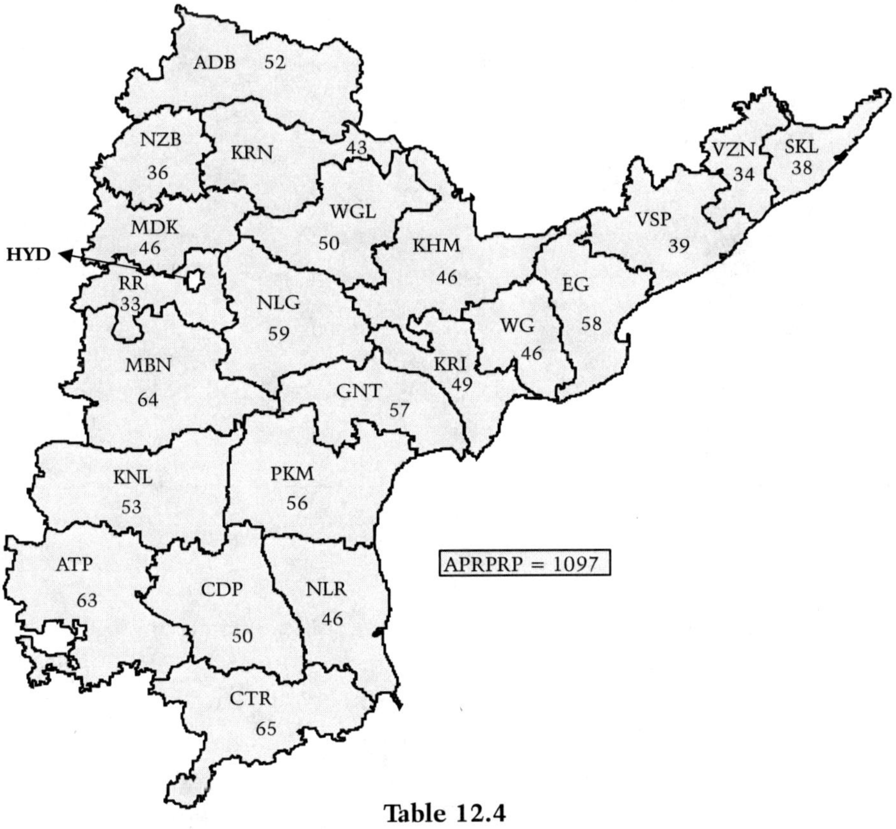

Table 12.4

Total Project Outlay of APDPIP and APRPRP

(Rs crore)

Sl.No.	*Name of the Component*	*APDPIP*	*APRPRP*	*Total*
1.	Strengthening institutional, social and human capital	125.51	135.10	260.61
2.	Support to sub-projects of the poor	360.34	845.40	1205.74
3.	Support to pilot programmes	0	40.04	40.04
4.	Support to eliminate child labour*	133.82	309.47	443.29
5.	Support for persons with disabilities	0	60.64	60.64
6.	Project management	34.32	95.38	129.70
	Total	654.00	1486.03	2140.03

Note: * This component is being implemented by APSWREIS.

Source: Society for Elimination of Rural Poverty, Government of Andhra Pradesh.

Table 12.5

Expected Project Outputs for APDPIP and APRPRP

Sl.No	*Program Details*	*DPIP*	*RPRP*	*Total*
1.	Districts	6	16	22
2.	Coverage of *mandals*	316	548	864
3.	No. of families to be covered	9,30,000	2,000,000	2,930,000
4.	Self-reliant people's institutions ,			
	– DWCRA groups (SHGs)	66,000	1,87,500	2,53,500
	– Village organisations (VOs)	8,000	15,000	23,000
	– *Mandal samakhyas* (MSs)	316	548	864
5.	Trained community activists, book-keepers and paraprofessionals	40,000	1,00,000	1,40,000
6.	Child labour elimination	1,00,000	3,00,000	4,00,000
7.	Educational support for girl child labour			
	No. of residential schools	24	64	88
	Girl children mainstreamed	36,000	90,000	1,26,000

Source: Society for Elimination of Rural Poverty, Government of Andhra Pradesh.

IKP Management

Society for Elimination of Rural Poverty (SERP) is managing IKP. SERP is an autonomous Society registered under Public Societies Act to undertake poverty alleviation programmes through effective involvement of CBOs. The management of the society is vested in seven-member Executive Council (EC). The Honourable Chief Minister is the president of the General Body of the society and the Honourable Minister for Rural Development is the vice-president of the General Body and the president of the Executive Council. The ex-officio members of the EC are principal secretary (Department of Rural Development), commissioner (Rural Development), commissioner (Tribal Welfare) and chief executive officer (CEO) of the society. The IKP is being implemented by the SERP through innovative project management structure. At the state level, there is a state project management unit (SPMU), consisting of CEO and additional CEO assisted by regional project directors (RPDs) and other functional specialists in institution building, training, gender, microfinance, communications, livelihoods promotion, marketing, monitoring and learning. At the district level, there is a district project management unit (DPMU), headed by a PD assisted by functional specialists. The activities of District Rural

Development Agency (DRDA) and IKP were integrated through a Government order. The PD of IKP is also the PD of DRDA. Specialists at both SPMU and DPMUs are drawn from government, NGOs and open market. At the sub-district level, there is one area coordinator for 4 to 6 *mandals* to concentrate on institution and capacity building of the poor, microfinance and livelihoods support. At the grassroot level, the CBOs—MSs and VOs implement various project components. The VO, which is a federation of all SHGs in a village is registered as a cooperative society under the Mutually Aided Cooperative Societies (MACTS) Act and the *Mandal Samakhya* is registered as a federation of cooperatives.

Progress of Indira Kranthi Patham

The achievements of the IKP are many. A careful examination of them shows that these achievements deal with at least 15 important activities which are discussed in detail here.

Social Mobilisation and Institution Building

The institution and human capacity building facilitates formation and strengthening of self-managed institutions of the poor and helps in building social and human capital. Actual social mobilisation was initiated in 2001 in 70 *mandals*. Emphasis was on the role of community coordinators (CCs) and this staff would go to South Asia Poverty Alleviation Programme (SAPAP) *mandals* for training. Over a period of time, the system of community resource persons (CRP) was introduced and this enabled the SHGs to emerge as strong groups. Slowly, but steadily, the programme expanded to all the rural *mandals* in Andhra Pradesh. This resulted in enrolling 101.82 lakh members into 8.51 lakh SHGs as at the end of March 2009. The historical development of SHGs and its members over the last several years is given below.

As a result of this massive social mobilisation, there are 10,182,181 SHG members in 8,50,671 SHGs organised into 35,525 VOs and 1,098 Mandal Samakhyas. In addition, there are 126 *Mandal Vikalangula Sangams*, 17 *Chenchu Mandal Samakhyas* and 15 Fishermen *mandal samakhyas* in the state. District *Samakhyas* (DS) have come into existence in all the 22 districts. More than 90 per cent of the poorest of poor and the poor SC and ST families in Andhra Pradesh are organised into SHGs.

Table 12.6

Number of Groups and Members

Year	*Groups Formed*	*No. of Members*
Upto 2000	284774	3957591
2000-01	95871	1332349
2001-02	42721	355069
2002-03	27882	410272
2003-04	59834	700820
2004-05	72667	818229
2005-06	44758	402911
2006-07	59746	646522
2007-08	20062	209065
2008-09	142356	1349353
Total	850671	10182181

Source: *Indira Kranthi Patham Report*, SERP, Government of Andhra Pradesh.

Bank Linkages

Interface with the banking system was intensified in 2005. Special efforts were made to ensure that the SHG members were able to access bank loans. The concept of giving loans to the SHG members based on the level of savings was basically done away with and the concept of good book-keeping and prompt repayment was considered for the sanction of loans. This brought a sea change in the attitude of the bankers in sanctioning the loans to the SHG members. Bank loans which totalled Rs 130 crore upto 2000 increased to Rs 7203.53 crore (42 per cent of loans to SHGs in India) in 2008-09 alone. The year-wise bank loans and the number of SHGs receiving bank loans are given in Table 12.7.

The SHGs in Andhra Pradesh were able to secure bank loans of around Rs 1,64,840 per SHG in 2008-09 which is around 3.4 times higher than the average for the rest of India figure that stands at Rs 48,000. Due to the strong support given by the state government, the banks have agreed to finance all genuine financial needs of the poor women enrolled in SHGs. This has led to the total financial inclusion (TFI) concept in the year 2006-2007 wherein the banks financed SHGs for all their needs including retiring high cost debts, income generation and social needs. Each SHG depending on their requirements was provided financial support up to Rs 5 lakh. This is very successful and in 2008-09 around 4,000 villages are covered under TFI. In the next three years, all villages will be covered under TFI.

Table 12.7

State Level SHG-Bank Linkages

Year	*No. of Groups*	*Rs Crore*
Upto 2000	55838	130.53
2000-01	103606	173.38
2001-02	88575	197.7
2002-03	165429	454.1
2003-04	231336	752.9
2004-05	261254	1017.7
2005-06	288711	2001.4
2006-07	366489	3063.87
2007-08	431515	5882.79
2008-09	437003	7203.53
Total	2429756	20877.90

Source: *Indira Kranthi Patham Report*, SERP, Government of Andhra Pradesh.

Community based recovery mechanism (CBRM) to recover 100 per cent of the bank loans was introduced in 2006. The phenomenal growth both in number of SHGs and in quantum of finance accessed by these SHGs requires a special focus to be given on recovery of loans under this programme. The timely repayment of loans should become part of the culture of these institutions of the poor and it is only possible through the CBRM.

Interest Subsidy/Pavala Vaddi

The SHGs in Andhra Pradesh have accessed bank loans to a tune of Rs 7,203 crore in 2008–09 alone. The poor women, through their disciplined utilisation of funds and prompt repayment, have achieved a very high repayment rate (more than 98 per cent). To encourage the women's groups further and also to motivate them to achieve 100 per cent repayment and to reduce their interest burden, the state government has introduced the *Pavala Vaddi* scheme from 2004-05. Under this scheme, the Government ensures that the interest burden to the SHG members on the loans taken from the banks does not exceed 3 per cent per annum. This has been a tremendous success among the women. It has succeeded in reducing their dependence on private moneylenders and also the private microfinance institutions who charge very high rates of interest. The amount of interest returned to the SHG members since 2004-05 is given in Table 12.8.

Table 12.8

Pavala Vaddi Incentive

Year	*No. of Groups*	*Rs Crore*
2004-05	200822	10
2005-06	274342	42.67
2006-07	290825	50.02
2007-08	554359	112.30
2008-09	714930	195.31
Total	2035278	410.30

Source: *www.ap.gov.in*

Because of magnitude of the loan amounts to our SHG members in rural areas and a very high rate of loan recoveries, the rural branches of banks involved in SHG lending have reported improved situation with regard to their non-performing assets. Thus, this new initiative of *Pavala Vaddi* has many beneficiary effects on SHG members and the bank involved in lending to SHGs members.

Community Investment Fund

The Community Investment Fund (CIF) provides resources to the poor communities for use as means to improve their livelihoods. This component supports the poor in prioritising livelihood needs by investments in sub-projects proposed and implemented by the CBOs. The cumulative CIF expenditure up to March 2009 is Rs 892.68 crore and the total number of beneficiaries is 2,365,606. Most of the CIF in the project is disbursed to the *mandal samakhyas* for onward rotation to the SHG members. The recovery rate of CIF is also very high at more than 90 per cent. The CIF component is a fixed amount in the project and all this budgeted CIF is expended. The following table gives the year-wise details of CIF and the number of CIF beneficiary families.

Table 12.9

CIF Expenditure and IGA Beneficiary Families

Year	*CIF (Rs crore)*	*IGA Beneficiaries*
2001-02	4.01	13367
2002-03	47.73	127280
2003-04	180.75	286752
2004-05	217.78	948428
2005-06	177.91	472864
2006-07	142.00	161106
2007-08	40.12	108384
2008-09	82.68	247415
Total	892.98	2365596

Note: IGA - Income generating activity.

Source: *Indira Kranthi Patham Report*, Society for Elimination of Rural Poverty, Government of Andhra Pradesh.

Although the budgeted CIF expenditure is given to MS as a grant, the MSs lend this amount to VOs who in turn lend to SHGs for ultimate lending to SHG members on the basis of Microcredit Plan (MCP) prepared by the SHG members themselves. The CIF borrowed by SHG members is paid ultimately to MSs who will rotate this CIF around VOs, SHGs and SHG members again and again. Thus, the CIF will get recycled among SHG members to improve their livelihoods. In the process of rotation of CIF among the SHG members, the CBOs at different levels (SHGs, VOs and MSs) get capitalised as these CBOs retain a certain proportion of interest paid by the SHG members. In general, the SHG member pays an interest of 12 per cent per annum to the SHG on the CIF. The SHG retains 3 per cent rate of interest and remits the remaining 9 per cent to the VO. The VO, in turn, retains 3 per cent interest and remits 6 per cent to the MS. This 6 per cent interest on CIF is one of the sources of income to the MS, as CIF is grant to the MS. The estimated number of families benefitted through CIF as on March 2009 is more than 23 lakh. However, in addition to CIF, the bank loans to SHG members also result in ever increasing improvements in the livelihoods of the SHG members.

Land Initiative

Under this component, productive and ready to use fertile land with assured irrigation facility is being given to the poorest of the poor households in the rural areas. As on March 2009, an extent of 4539.24 acres of land was purchased and handed over to 5,303 poor families. The year-wise details of the number of acres of land given to the poor households and the number of households are given below:

Table 12.10

Land Purchase

Year	*No. of Beneficiaries*	*No. of Acres*
2004-05	745	624.12
2005-06	2524	2177.22
2006-07	1355	1263.24
2007-08	399	409.35
2008-09	280	65.31
Total	5303	4539.24

Source: *www.ap.gov.in*

Another important initiative of IKP is the resolution of land disputes pertaining to the poor, especially the SC and ST households and to restore the ownership of land to the original owners. IKP has resolved more than 1.83 cases of land disputes and has restored 1.79 cases of land ownership to the original landowners.

Jobs for Rural Youth

As part of public-private partnership (PPP), IKP has forged a partnership with a corporate foundation, Livelihood Advancement Business School (LABS), Hyderabad for improving the employability and skills of vulnerable youth like girl widows, single mothers and children of landless labourers in rural areas and linking them to service sector jobs like hotels, banks and rural business process outsourcing (BPOs). Total number of jobs created up to 2008-09 is 1,79,751 (Table 12.11).

Dairy Initiative

The dairy activity is a major livelihood opportunity for the rural poor. Milk procurement centres established on pilot basis in Mahabubnagar and

Nizamabad districts, helped the milk producers to get better price for milk and promoted transparency in milk procurement, which triggered milk productivity in the villages. Based on the success evidenced in the pilots, the same model is replicated in 14 more districts in the state. The model consisted of establishing bulk milk cooling units (BMCUs) with a capacity of 2,000-5,000 litres capacity to collect and chill milk to the the desired temperature of 4^0 C, were established in 85 *mandals* in the state. In collaboration with the Andhra Pradesh Dairy Development Cooperative Fund (APDDCF) Limited, the SHGs and their federations have taken over 158 BMCUs covering 2,806 village milk procurement centres with 1.39 lakh milk producers and contributed 2.57 lakh litres of milk per day in peak season and 0.80 lakh litres of milk per day in lean season.

Table 12.11

Number of Jobs Created

Year	*No. of Jobs*
2002-03	540
2003-04	1460
2004-05	5000
2005-06	15000
2006-07	20300
2007-08	70135
2008-09	69316
Total	181751

Source: *www.ap.gov.in*

Food Security

Food security is one of the most important initiatives of IKP. In the lean agricultural season, many of the rural poor have barely one square meal a day. Food security intervention addresses this hunger gap in rural communities. Through this scheme, the VOs ensure that the SHG members draw their full public distribution system (PDS) quota and ensure that the members utilise this opportunity. For the balance, the VOs estimate the bulk requirement of all SHG members for rice and other essential commodities, negotiate and buy better quality commodities from the open market and supply to their members at a price lower than the retail outlets. This is recovered from the members in two to three installments. This scheme is being implemented in various forms at present to suit the local conditions of the poor. Some of the districts follow one month cycle while some others follow six month cycles to coincide with the harvest times. Moreover, many of the essential commodities such as cereals, oils, tamarind, chillies, salt etc., are added to the food security system in many districts. The number of families benefitted through food security over a period of time is given in Table 12.12.

Table 12.12

Number of Beneficiary Families of Food Security

Year	*No. of Beneficiary Families*
2003-04	82249
2004-05	501593
2005-06	990742
2006-07	1392287
2007-08	2110401
2008-09	2363735

Source: *Indira Kranthi Patham Report*, Society for Elimination of Rural Poverty, Government of Andhra Pradesh.

Through this intervention, the CBOs have developed institutional norms, financial management and supply logistics skills and capacity to handle complex functions with a high degree of self-management. The bond between the members and the CBOs becomes stronger. The members gain in several ways—most important, they are able to eat well and feed their children on time. They have other equally important gains—cost reduction, food assurance for one to three months, easy payment plan and good quality food. The cost reduction is very significant—they save Rs 80-Rs 120 per month, whereas their savings in the group is Rs 30-Rs 50 per month. Due to these impacts, the programme is rapidly spreading and in the next three years all the eight million poor households will be covered.

Collective Marketing

The SHG federations have enhanced returns to their poor producer members in selling their agriculture; horticulture and forest produce at the village level by opening a procurement centre and with quality control and marketing tie-ups. This collective marketing activity has been undertaken by more than 3,000 VOs in the state and has benefitted more than three lakh members. They have handled 81 different commodities. Based on their marketing capabilities, the state government has entrusted the operation of minimum support price (MSP) intervention for maize at village level in seven Telangana districts. This has been a great success and both the farmers and the women's federations have gained from this intervention. This proved that: (a) our CBOs can handle large procurement activities, (b) our collective marketing was supported by all in the villages and (c) this activity proved to be beneficial to the farmers. The quantum of collective marketing and the value of the produce procured through collective marketing over the last few years is given below.

Table 12.13

Collective Marketing Activity

Year	*Quintals*	*Rs Crore*
2001-02	6227	0.74
2002-03	31738	2.54
2003-04	73526	6.54
2004-05	180036	16.00
2005-06	2494160	141.90
2006-07	1824803	126.38
2007-08	4711000	320.15
2008-09	5930000	492.16
Total	15251490	1106.41

Source: Society for Elimination of Rural Poverty, Government of Andhra Pradesh.

Various marketing initiatives were adopted in 2008-09. Paddy procurement was taken up by our CBOs in many districts. The achievement for 2008-09, a procurement of 59.3 lakh quintals of an estimated value of Rs 492.16 crore.

Community Managed Sustainable Agriculture (CMSA)

The main objective of the Community Managed Sustainable Agriculture (CMSA) is to sustain agriculture based livelihoods, increasing net incomes by reducing cost of cultivation with adoption of practices involving low or no expenditure with special focus on small and marginal farmers in general and women farmers in particular. It promotes the technologies based on local natural resources and promotes local knowledge and innovations. Outreach of CMSA is gaining momentum. This programme began in the year 2005-06 in 450 villages in 25,000 acres and it spread to 18 districts, 3,171 villages and in 13.24 lakh acres and 3.18 lakh farmers by 2009. CMSA is a first step towards moving to organic farming, with community certification and to bring 50 lakh acres under organic farming in 5,000 villages. This has been approved by Government of India, under Rashtriya Krishi Vikas Yojana (RKVY), in Eleventh Plan (2007-2012) with an outlay of Rs 162.88 crore. The major impact of CMSA is visible in net savings of the farmers, ranging from Rs 6,000 per acre in case of chillies to Rs 1,200 per acre in case of groundnut.

Insurance

One of the most beneficial and innovative initiatives introduced by IKP is insurance protection to the SHG members, their families, assets, health, loans etc. The number of insurance beneficiaries is given below:

Table 12.14

Number of Beneficiaries of Community Based Insurance

Year	*No. of Families*
2005-06	887110
2006-07	2500262
2007-08	3882878
2008-09	8127020

Source: Society for Elimination of Rural Poverty, Government of Andhra Pradesh.

Rural families are concerned for death and disability under Aam Admi Bima Yojana (AABY), Janashree Bima Yojana (JBY) and other general insurance (IGI). Efforts are being made to introduce insurance on loans taken by the SHG members from the banks.

Education

The year 2007 saw the entry into education sector to ensure that no child of SHG member goes without education for want of money. Under this initiative, 201 community governed pre-primary schools are

Table 12.15

APDPIP and APRPRP: Year-wise, Component-wise Expenditure up to 2007-08

(Rs. crore)

Sl. No.	*Component*	*2000-01*	*2001-02*	*2002-03*	*2003-04*	*2004-05*	*2005-06*	*2006-07*	*2007-08*	*2008-09*	*Total Expenditure*
1.	Institution and human capacity building	2.00	8.35	21.18	57.12	77.01	84.17	125.57	98.10	94.82	568.32
2.	Community investment fund	0.00	4.01	47.73	180.45	217.78	177.91	142.00	40.12	82.68	892.68
3.	Project management	2.32	4.86	11.17	21.32	22.96	23.03	25.23	22.19	27.14	160.22
4.	Support to pilot projects	0.00	0.00	0.00	0.31	0.12	0.15	0.12	0.08	0.00	0.78
5.	Support to persons with disability	0.00	0.00	0.02	0.22	0.74	3.19	6.42	5.96	2.33	18.88
	SERP total	4.32	17.22	80.10	259.42	318.61	288.45	299.34	166.45	206.97	1640.88
	APSWERIES (School component)	0.04	1.71	35.44	93.04	89.70	52.80	57.00	36.49		366.22
	Grand Total	4.36	18.93	115.54	352.46	408.31	341.25	356.34	202.94	206.97	2007.10

Source: *Indira Kranthi Patham Report*, Society for Elimination of Rural Poverty, Government of Andhra Pradesh.

functioning with 4,000 children in 3-5 years of age group in Adilabad, Visakhapatnam, Vijayanagaram, Warangal and East Godavari districts. In addition, 7,786 meritorious poor students are admitted into private corporate colleges.

Gender

Under this component, 516 *mandel* level social action committees were formed and some of them have established 238 family counselling centres. These centres/committees resolved 10,971 cases of domestic violence. Alternative livelihoods are provided for vulnerable groups such as Basivinis, Yanadi, Chenchu, and single women/young widows. The women (80,812) are actively mobilised into VO social action committees to stand up for their rights and to help each other. Women's understanding of justice has changed radically. *Mandal samakhyas* sent around 400 children to schools and hostels. Children of sex workers were sent to a private residential school and children of young widows were sent to hostels and schools. Village level volunteers (140,000) were identified and provided training on HIV awareness under direct leadership of Mandal Samakhyas and Zilla Samakhyas. Women also have stopped many child marriages very boldly and created alternative opportunity of education for girls.

Disability

The objective of disability component is to help disabled persons and their caregivers to improve their livelihood opportunities and quality of life. Intensive activities are carried out in 78 *mandals*. However, activities are also under taken in the other programme *mandals*. Persons with disabilities (213,197) are organised into SHGs including 23,069 exclusive SHGs of PWDs. There are also 126 Mandal Vikalangula Sangams in the state. A total of 72,685 PWDs are given an assistance of Rs 55.40 crore through CIF, bank loans and revolving fund for enhancing their livelihood. Medical camps (416) were organised for PWDs and 1,42,951 certificates were issued to PWDs at no cost to them. Further, 5,317 surgical corrections were carried out and 64,187 PWDs were issued assistive devices at no cost to them.

Health and Nutrition

In order to strengthen the capability of the poor to handle their health issues, the health and nutrition initiative at IKP project has initiated interventions like health risk fund, community health activists, nutrition centres for pregnant and lactating mothers, medical care cover for their members by tying up with private medical colleges and hospitals, life insurance run by Zilla Samakhya, etc. The nutrition centres for pregnant women and lactating mothers is a unique intervention in our country where low birth rates are very common. The extensive health and nutrition strategies being adopted across 63 *mandals* include fixed schedule for regular capacity building of stakeholders at *mandal* and district levels, institutionalisation of the fixed nutrition and health days (N&H days) in convergence with line departments and regular health savings as safety nets for health emergencies. The intensive health and nutrition strategies focus on intensive health community resource person (CRP) strategy. Best practitioners (800) from the pilot *mandals* had been identified as health CRPs. Since January 2007, the health CRPs strategy has been implemented in 680 VOs and established 600 nutrition-cum-day care centres. The impact of prenatal and neonatal outcomes among the members attended and show 98 per cent safe deliveries, 88 per cent normal deliveries, no low birth weight baby born. No maternal, infant and neonatal deaths happened. A total of 2,100 deliveries occurred among the members enrolled at 600 nutrition centres.

Expenditure of IKP

Cumulatively, the total expenditure of IKP up to March 2009 including APSWREIS is Rs 2007.10 crore. The overall performance of IKP up to March 2009 is given in Table 12.16.

The Way Ahead for Poverty Eradication

The experience of IKP shows that there is a need for strong and sensitive support structures to foster women SHGs, federations of these SHGs into CBOs and continuous nurturing and handholding of these organisations over a period of 6 to 8 years for elimination of poverty in rural areas. In addition, a minimum investment of Rs 1,00,000 per family by way of numerous 'small' and 'big' loans over a period of time is necessary for a family to come out of poverty. The role of financial institutions like commercial and regional rural banks is also very crucial for providing low cost bank loans to SHG members. Convergence with all key line departments is also a prerequisite for elimination of poverty from rural areas.

Table 12.16

Overall Performance of IKP upto March 2009

Sl. No.	*Indicator*	*Grand Total*
1.	No. of *mandals* covered	1099
2.	Total No. of SHGs—women	850671
3.	No. of DAP SHGs	23069
4.	Total savings of the SHGs (Rs crore)	1962.5
5.	Total corpus of the SHGs (Rs crore)	4025.55
6.	Total number of members in SHGs—women	10182181
7.	Total No. of DAP members	213197
8.	No. of village organisaions formed	35525
9.	Normal *mandal samakhyas* formed	1098
10.	No. of MRPs/CRPs/CFs/CAs/book-keepers/PPs working	114535
11.	Total CIF expenditure under the project (Rs crore)	892.68
12.	Total No. of beneficiaries of IGA-SP	2365606
13.	No. of VOs covered under food security	15989
14.	No. of SHGs participating in food security	206241
15.	No. of households benefitting from food security	2363735
16.	No. of VOs with procurement centres**	1662
17.	Value of turnover under marketing (Rs crore)**	492.16
18.	No. of acres of land purchased	4539.24
19.	No. of beneficiaries of land purchase	5303
20.	No. of issues resolved under land access programme	183000
21.	Number of households covered under insurance**	8127020
22.	No. of persons placed for jobs**	69316
23.	No. of SHGs linked to banks**	437003
24.	Amount of bank linkages (Rs crore)**	7203.53

Note: ** Yearly in 2008-09.

APDPIP is closed as on 31-12-2006. However, APRPRP is extended to all the 22 rural districts of AP with effect from 1-1-2007. Achievements under APRPRP, as given above, include achievements up to December 2006 in the erstwhile six APDPIP districts.

Source: Indira Kranthi Patham Report, Society for Elimination of Rural Poverty, Government of Andhra Pradesh.

The AP model of poverty eradication is a low cost model and self-replicative in nature. The total investment in building institutions of poor women including the expected expenditure up to 2,014 works out to less than Rs 3,000 per family on the basis of membership of more than one crore SHG members in the project. The key outcome of the project by 2014 would be:

- More than one crore women in SHGs.
- Strong and self-sustainable institutions of the poor.
- All ultra-poor families supported.
- Rs one lakh per family provided towards credit support.
- Comprehensive food security.
- Risk to life, health, death, disability, assets and loans provided to all the one crore families.
- Jobs with reasonable pay for around six lakh rural youth.
- Low cost sustainable agricultural development in over 50 lakh acres.
- Access by the poor to all the anti-poverty programmes.

The perspective of the poor has changed from 'next day' survival to long-term planning with regard to livelihoods, health, education, food security, shelter, risks and belief in the government machinery. To conclude, the institutions of poor are well geared up to play a crucial role in enabling the state of Andhra Pradesh to plan to achieve the Millennium Development Goals (MDGs) relating to hunger and poverty eradication, women empowerment and gender equality, maternal health and reduction of child mortality by 2015.